Simulation for Policy Inquiry

Anand Desai

Editor

Simulation for Policy Inquiry

 Springer

Editor
Anand Desai
John Glenn School of Public Affairs
Ohio State University
Columbus, OH, USA

ISBN 978-1-4614-1664-7   e-ISBN 978-1-4614-1665-4
DOI 10.1007/978-1-4614-1665-4
Springer New York Dordrecht Heidelberg London

Library of Congress Control Number: 2012937212

Printed on acid-free paper

Springer is part of Springer Science+Business Media (www.springer.com)

Preface

The hope underlying successful policy inquiry has been that it would yield a useful approach to achieving desired goals by selecting the best means from a set of well thought out options. Much of such hope relies upon our ability to make sense of data. Despite increasing sophistication in the methods employed to identify patterns as well as to analyze, to synthesize, and to interpret data, this hope has yet to materialize. There are multiple reasons for this failure. First, there is the perennial problem of data quality and availability. Second, there is the difficulty of matching methods to data in order to capture their inherent complexities and interdependencies. Third, even if perfect data were available, they could only describe the past and would not necessarily tell us much about the future unless we assume that the future will be a repetition of the past. Even though some data patterns are robust and persist into the future, when human affairs are concerned, history rarely repeats itself.

Human affairs, and therefore policy inquiry, tend to be messy and unpredictable. The common thread that ties this collection of papers together is the belief that by simulating possible worlds and studying how these artificial worlds function, we might attain useful insight into how the real world works.

Through the use of examples drawn from public policy contexts, the papers in this book discuss how to develop simulations, illustrate model construction, analyze multiple scenarios, and discuss how simulations can offer research insights. Each of the chapters discusses an application of simulation modeling in a policy context. For our purposes, simulation is a tool for systematically capturing the contextual and temporal complexity of policy concerns for the purposes of informing decisions and action. Our hope for this collection is that it will serve as a primer to illustrate how, when, where, and to what end simulations can be gainfully used in policy inquiry.

In this collection, we present three of the variety of available simulation tools: Monte Carlo simulations, system dynamics, and agent-based models. Although our objective is to illustrate policy modeling and simulation use, not to proselytize, our agnosticism does not preclude the belief that simulation approaches are often better suited to addressing certain problems and can yield more useful insights than other approaches. In this respect, the view of simulation espoused in this collection is that it is an art form with a scientific and practical purpose. It is an art form in that the simulation is a representation of how the modeler views the object of study and includes in that representation the biases and experience deemed relevant to informing judgment and practice. It serves a scientific purpose in providing an exploratory environment for policy inquiry. However, the ultimate objective of any approach to policy inquiry is a practical one: to inform decisions and practice.

The basic premise underlying this collection is that an inquiry can be assisted and enhanced by computational methods of simulation. Thus, simulation-assisted thinking is likely to enable an inquirer or a community of inquirers to better capture and comprehend the complexity of the world of policy inquiry. If this complexity can be even partially captured in representations of the real or imagined world that simulations generate, then the hope is that manipulating the representations will yield insights into ways to address the complex issues with which policy makers, managers, and researchers grapple. To that end, this set of papers seeks to illuminate how a subset of available computational tools assists the process of policy inquiry.

This collection has three parts and an introductory chapter. The introductory chapter paints a picture in which the world of policy inquiry is emergent and complex. It suggests that certain characteristics of simulation models make them ideally suited for the pursuit of policy inquiry.

The point of departure for the simulations in Part I Chaps. 2 and 3 and Part II, Chap. 4 is statistical analysis, the general linear model, in particular. In Part I, Chaps. 2 and 3, Monte Carlo simulations are used to generate data when none are available.

In Chap. 2, Seligman describes a Monte Carlo simulation to explore worker investment patterns and timing and how their interaction influences potential returns from a defined contribution retirement savings program. Because of the novelty of such programs, the data series that exist are not long enough to study investment behavior and returns from those investments upon retirement. He constructs synthetic data to "travel out of the sample" to create hypothetical, but feasible situations to explore the wealth outcomes.

In Chap. 3, Heidelberg and Richardson report on a case study of the Nurse-Family Partnership Program in Louisiana. Here the problem that the authors address is also one of how to take the data out of sample, not across time but to a different context. In building a Monte Carlo simulation they make explicit the decisions and assumptions made regarding data from one context being used in another and in doing so, discuss the problems of drawing lessons from one context and applying them to another. Acknowledging the uncertainty of not knowing what is transferable, they choose to build scenarios to explore what might happen under different sets of circumstances.

In Part II, the focus of producing policy relevant information shifts from studying relationships among variables to studying interactions among entities or agents. This shift requires an adjustment in how one thinks about a problem. In focusing on entities—people, buildings, neighborhoods, households, policies—the problem formulation takes us away from measures and the relationships among them and instead toward thinking about interactions among heterogeneous entities and their individual behavioral patterns over time and space. These interactions result in emergent behavior that cannot be obtained through an averaging or aggregation process, for example, our current state of knowledge is such that even a detailed understanding of how individual birds fly cannot help us fathom the V-formation of a flock of geese in flight.

In Chap. 4 , Rice focuses on food deserts, their creation, and their effects on health outcomes. This first chapter of Part II is different from the two chapters in Part I in that it does not discuss an implementation of a simulation, but instead it presents a comparison of a multilevel linear model with an agent-based simulation model. Starting with a common conceptual model she discusses how asking similar questions using two different model implementations provides different insights.

In Chap. 5, Eckerd and Reames help us sort through the dynamics of urban change. Their objective is to understand the gentrification process and to determine the circumstances under which displacement occurs during gentrification. By developing an agent-based model of this process they wish to identify economic development policies that would bring about positive change while helping those most in need.

In Chap. 6, Eckerd, Lufkin, Mattimore, Miller, and Desai explore the life cycle costs of facilities. Using data on the costs of maintaining a US National Laboratory infrastructure, they develop an agent-based model that incorporates risk of failure and the effect of that risk on nearby facilities. The model serves as a decision support tool for facility managers as they grapple with the question of how to best allocate scarce resources.

In Chap. 7, Kim models the incidence of fraud in the Women, Infants and Children program. She builds a spatial model of participant–vendor interactions to study contact patterns. She compares model results with data to assess fidelity of such methods to observed reality.

In Chap. 8, Heidelberg studies the assumptions underlying home ownership and models housing policy to explore whether home ownership affects the quality of a neighborhood. In so doing, he puts to test the long held belief that home ownership leads to improved neighborhood quality.

In Part III, the modeling tool of choice is system dynamics where differential and integral equations form the basis of these models. General solutions to such equations were developed in the 1860s, decades before the invention of many of the statistical tools commonly used in the social sciences. The core concept underlying a system dynamics model is a stock. Associated concepts are flows and rates of flow into and out of this stock. Changes in this stock due to the inflows and outflows capture the dynamics of the system.

For most of us, the dynamics of stocks and flows are not obvious. From the knowledge of floods, we know that a river crests long after the maximum rainfall has ceased. In fact, the river crests and begins to ebb when the outflow of water equals and eventually exceeds the inflow. Yet, this specific understanding of floods does not usually translate into a general understanding of the relationships among rates of flow, feedback, and stocks. Until such understanding becomes a common feature of our thinking processes, system dynamics modeling offers a powerful formal tool for comprehending systemic behaviors that at first seem counterintuitive.

In Chap. 9, Lufkin, Hightower, Landsbergen, and Desai offer a different modeling perspective on facilities management from the one discussed by Eckerd and his colleagues in Chap. 6. Their purpose in this chapter is to develop a tool that facility managers can use to help them identify decision points and explore the consequences of decisions regarding funding maintenance and repair of facilities. They also discuss measures to capture the multiple facets of facility condition.

In Chap. 10, Zhong, Lant, Jeng, and Kim take the classic model of the dynamics of the spread and decline of infectious diseases and modify it to study risk communication and avoidance behavior of individuals during an influenza outbreak. Their simulation results suggest that communicating with the public regarding the underlying risks can be an effective strategy for slowing the spread of the disease.

In Chap. 11, Hightower suggests that policy narratives are the basis for simulations across modeling paradigms. Storytelling in general, and iterative storytelling more specifically, is the method by which policy intentions and options are translated into formal representations in computational models. Storytelling is an active process that engages the practitioner and the modeler in cocreation and development of simulations.

Simulation is not a spectator sport. People have to engage with it if they are to get full advantage of the learning that simulation offers. In this collection the authors make their assumptions explicit and offer rationales for the decision to use one characterization rather than another. In some instances, the authors themselves are unaware of their choices. Their decisions reflect habits of mind rather than considered deliberation over the choices available to them at each decision juncture in the process of creating the simulations.

We welcome you to a collection of essays devoted to investigating the method and merit of simulations in the context of public policy inquiry. We invite you to reflect on the authors' assumptions and question their choices. We challenge you to speculate about how you would select your options, describe your assumptions, and construct your own abstractions and representations of the problems you encounter.

Columbus, OH, USA   Anand Desai

Acknowledgments

Over the past half dozen years, a number of collaborations at the John Glenn School of Public Affairs at The Ohio State University have led to the use of simulations in public policy inquiry. Many of the chapter authors have been supported by funds not only from the School but also from the National Science Foundation, the National Institutes of Health and the Ohio Department of Job and Family Services. Lawrence Livermore National Laboratory and Whitestone Research have established a fellowship that has supported graduate students. We are indebted to them for this support, however, we should also mention that the views expressed in this volume are those of the authors and do not necessarily reflect the opinions of the funders.

There are a number of young scholars whose critical reading and commentary have helped improve the contents of this volume. In particular, the contributions of James Comeaux, Lisa Frazier, Lisa Gajary, Kristin Harlow, Hyungjo Hur, Stephen Roll, Nicole Thomas, and Tyler Winslow are gratefully acknowledged. Thanks also go to Yushim Kim who helped bring order during the final stages of putting this volume together. We are grateful to Jon Gurstelle at Springer US for his patience and support of this project.

Contents

Contributors

Anand Desai is a professor in the John Glenn School of Public Affairs at The Ohio State University. His interests include creation, dissemination, and use of models and modeling tools to inform public policy decisions and actions. He received his doctorate from the University of Pennsylvania.

Adam Eckerd is an Assistant Professor of Public Administration at Virginia Polytechnic Institute and State University where he conducts research on the interaction between policy decision making and the interests of and outcomes for urban residential populations. His primary interests lie in the remediation of environmental hazards and related issues of environmental justice, in addition to considering the role of nonprofit organizations in the provision of public services. Adam holds a PhD from Ohio State and an MA from Johns Hopkins.

Roy L. Heidelberg is a doctoral candidate at the John Glenn School of Public Affairs at The Ohio State University and a Visiting Scholar at Louisiana State University. He holds an MPA from Louisiana State University and a BA from the Louisiana Scholars' College at Northwestern State University. His research agenda includes work in housing, economic and community development, and interpretive research strategies.

Rudy Hightower II Lieutenant Commander (US Navy—retired), is a doctoral candidate at the John Glenn School of Public Affairs at The Ohio State University and project associate in the school's Ukraine Parliamentary Development Project. He holds an MA from the Naval Postgraduate School and a BS from Southern Illinois University. He is a former US Navy Intelligence, Reconnaissance, and Surveillance Manager, and his current research interests include military modernization policy and reconstruction and stabilization operations.

Megan Jehn is an Assistant Professor at the School of Human Evolution and Social Change and a Senior Sustainability Scholar at the Global Institute of Sustainability at Arizona State University. Her research interests include the application of quantitative research methods and technological innovations to improve emergency preparedness.

Yushim Kim is an Assistant Professor at the School of Public Affairs, a founding faculty of the Center for Policy Informatics, and a Senior Sustainability Scholar at the Global Institute of Sustainability at Arizona State University. Her research program examines how crises, emergencies, or undesirable events occur and progress in social and policy systems, as well as how these systems can recover. She received her doctorate from The Ohio State University.

David Landsbergen is an Associate Professor in the John Glenn School of Public Affairs at The Ohio State University. His research interests include the use of information systems in the public sector including examining how models and simulation improve decision making on complex problems. He earned his doctorate at the Maxwell School, Syracuse University.

Tim Lant builds mathematical and system dynamic models for the Decision Theater for a variety of topical areas including public health, water, and innovation systems. He builds models for use as scenario analysis tools and for policy and planning exercises. Previously, Tim was a doctoral fellow in long-term policy analysis at the RAND Corporation, a financial analyst in the Healthcare and Biotechnology Investment Banking Division of CIBC and an actuary for Actuarial Management Corporation.

Peter Lufkin is a principal and senior analyst at Whitestone Research. His current responsibilities include the development of an international model of life cycle facility costs. As an analyst, he specialized in economic impact analysis with Science Applications International Corporation, in warranty cost modeling for American Honda, and in health care cost analysis for Systemetrics/McGraw-Hill. He received an MA from the University of California, Santa Barbara.

Bernard G. Mattimore served as the Deputy Associate Director for Plant Services before retiring from Lawrence Livermore National Laboratory (LLNL). Previous to that position, he was Department Head of Plant Engineering. With over 45 years of experience as a senior manager in all areas of facilities, his innovative leadership has thrived on large-scale operations that support national security missions. In previous Plant Engineering positions, before coming to LLNL, he was responsible for developing innovative and cost-effective concepts for facilities maintenance management for the entire Naval Facilities Complex. Bernie has a degree in engineering and applied physics from Harvard University.

Jon Miller is Director of Operations at Whitestone Research Corporation, an employee-owned company with principals in economics, computer science, and operations research. He directs the technical work for many federal and private sector projects, and contributes to the designs of the MARS Facility Cost Forecast

System and CostLab, Whitestone's commercial software products. He is a coauthor of the annual Whitestone Building Maintenance and Repair Cost Reference and Facility Operations Cost References. Jon has a bachelor of science degree from Bates College.

Tony Reames is a Public Administration doctoral student at the University of Kansas. His research interest in urban governance includes topics, such as climate change, environmental sustainability, and infrastructure policy. Tony is a NSF-IGERT fellow in the Climate Change, Humans and Nature in the Global Environment Program. Tony holds a MEM from Kansas State and a BS from NC A&T State.

Ketra Rice is a doctoral candidate at the John Glenn School of Public Affairs at The Ohio State University and a Visiting Scholar/Instructor at Georgia State University. She holds an MS in Agricultural Economics from The Ohio State University and a BS in Marketing and MBA from Alabama A&M University. Her research agenda includes work in dietary health, food security, food deserts, rural development, and areas of social and economic policy.

James A. Richardson is John Rhea Alumni Professor of Economics and Director of the Public Administration Institute in the E.J. Ourso College of Business Administration at Louisiana State University in Baton Rouge, Louisiana. Dr. Richardson has served from 1987 through the present as the private economist on the Louisiana Revenue Estimating Conference, the panel with the constitutional authority and responsibility to provide official revenue estimates for the state. Dr. Richardson received his bachelors of art degree in economics from St. Mary's University of San Antonio, Texas, and his Master's degree in economics and the doctorate in economics from The University of Michigan.

Jason S. Seligman is Assistant Professor at the John Glenn School of Public Affairs, The Ohio State University. His work in public economics focuses on both finance (taxation and revenue management) and expenditures—especially in the context of social insurance programs. He has held positions at the University of Georgia, at United States Treasury's Office of Economic Policy, and with the President's Council of Economic Advisers. He has also served as an advisor to the Government Accountability Office, the Center for State and Local Government Excellence and the states of California, Georgia, and Ohio. He is a fellow of the TIAA-CREF Institute and the Center for Financial Security at the University of Wisconsin, Madison. He received his doctorate from the University of California at Berkeley.

Wei Zhong is an Assistant Professor at School of Public Affairs, Renmin University of China. Her research interests include public policy analysis, policy informatics and public emergency management. She received her doctorate from Arizona State University.

Chapter 1
Public Policy Inquiry and Simulations

Anand Desai

Abstract The methods we use to study policy issues must be able to apprehend the complexity inherent in these issues. This chapter describes some of the characteristics of policy issues that make them complex. Simulations are proposed as a class of readily available computational tools that can capture some of that complexity and can provide insights to inform policy decisions and actions.

1.1 Introduction

When we daydream about possible futures or wonder about "what-might-have-been" had the circumstances been different, we are imagining possible worlds—we are effectually simulating complex scenarios. By running these simulations, we are implicitly manipulating various contingencies to explore potential outcomes.

However, even though we mentally run various complex scenarios, our ability to think through complexity is unfortunately limited. As Norman (1993) put it,

> The power of the unaided mind is highly overrated. Without external aids, memory, thought, and reasoning are all constrained. But human intelligence is highly flexible and adaptive, superb at inventing objects and procedures to overcome its own limits. The real powers come from inventing external aids that enhance cognitive abilities. How have we increased memory, thought, and reasoning? By the invention of external aids: It is things that make us smart (p. 43).

As an example of how things "make us smart," consider the simple task of multiplying two 2-digit numbers. Multiplying them with and without the aid of paper and pencil can quickly show how much faster and easier it is with paper and pencil than it is to rely simply on one's mental arithmetic abilities (Card et al. 1999).

A. Desai (✉)
John Glenn School of Public Affairs, The Ohio State University,
Page Hall, 1810 College Road, Columbus, OH 43210, USA
e-mail: desai.1@osu.edu

A. Desai (ed.), *Simulation for Policy Inquiry*, DOI 10.1007/978-1-4614-1665-4_1,
© Springer Science+Business Media, LLC 2012

Compared to paper and pencil, computational models and simulations are sophisticated aids that enable us to create and manipulate elaborate imagined worlds.

Simulations mimic relationships and interactions among concepts, constructs, and data and, in so doing, provide working representations of the world. Among philosophers of science, however, simulations do not seem to have the same standing as models, frameworks, or theories, which are seen as the products of logical thinking and tightly reasoned arguments (Morrison and Morgan 1999). Because simulations appear to be more dependent upon the personal views and perceptions of the researchers who design them, they are subsequently considered ad hoc and lacking in theoretical rigor (Duhem 1954).

Simulations offer multiple and varied representations of the same complex system. These representations, in their profusion, can lead to more questions than answers. But this profusion of representations is not necessarily a drawback and might indeed be an asset. Some of these representations to which we simultaneously subscribe might imply conflicting worldviews: "Conceptual systems are pluralistic not monolithic. Typically abstract concepts are defined by multiple conceptual metaphors, which are often inconsistent with each other" (Lakoff and Johnson 1999, p. 78). However, through the resolution of these conflicts emerges a better understanding and appreciation of the complexities inherent in these systems.

Underlying every simulation are systems. For modelers, these systems exist as mental constructs that reflect their understanding of those systems. In research contexts, it is the mental constructs that are being simulated. Thus, there can be as many simulations of the same entity as there are mental constructs that define the entity as construed by the researcher. A simulation can be usefully compared to a cartoon, in that each represents simplifications of complex situations (Holland 1995). A cartoon, by definition, is a partial representation that leaves out many of the details while highlighting those details that are considered important in capturing the essence of the entity being represented. Similarly, simulations for policy inquiry are abstractions that aspire to incorporate what is relevant and assume away what is irrelevant or outside the scope of the current inquiry.

"A model focuses on a particular set of features that are important with respect to a *particular task or purpose*. Therefore, there can be *multiple* models for a given situation or thing, as different perspectives or purposes will highlight and ignore different features" (Murray 2006, p. 267, emphasis in the original). For instance, the term *chair* usually conjures up an image of an object with four legs, a flat horizontal surface that serves as a seat and a vertical, perhaps slightly slanted, surface that serves as back support. A quick walk though a furniture store is sufficient to dispel the notion that this imagined idealized form is an accurate representation of a chair. However, this idealized form matches sufficiently with our experience that it might be a conceptually adequate — indeed, practical — starting point for an exploration of what the term implies and to learn about its design and function. Similarly, simulations may begin as stylized idealizations but can grow into representations that allow us to describe, understand, and perhaps explain the systems being simulated.

For the purposes of this chapter, simulations are tools to aid systematic thinking about complex issues and entities. They come in various forms, ranging from the simple to the sophisticated. An example of a simple simulation model is Schelling's (1971) original model of segregation in communities. This simulation had no data and only two types of individuals, living in a checkerboard world, following simple decision rules. A more sophisticated simulation was conducted in advance of the attack on Osama bin Laden's compound. The attack simulations were not academic exercises implemented on a computer. They were elaborate in design, meticulously planned, and reflected the best expert opinion and practice informed by vast amounts of uncertain information (Schmidle 2011). Both of these examples, the simple and the sophisticated, are excellent, albeit fundamentally different, instances of the usefulness and use of simulation to inform policy decisions and actions.

As research tools, both simulations and reductionist methods have been successful in helping make sense of the world. However, reductionist approaches have not had the same level of success in the social and policy sciences as they have had in the natural and physical sciences. As a consequence, there has been a call for holistic approaches to capture the complexity and interdependence among interacting parts that make up the whole (Fisher 2003; Morçöl 2002). Unfortunately, developing holistic methods is not an easy task. Our mental capacities are limited and, as discussed above, enhanced by external aids of our own creation. But even these aids are limited, most notably by the limitations of our modern computers.

In a public policy context, a truly holistic effort can quickly become an unmanageable jumble of interacting entities, structures, and processes. Realizing that all the details of the entities under study cannot be captured, the first task in building a simulation to assist in policy inquiry is to determine what is to be within the scope of the simulation and what is not. Boundaries are thus established to circumscribe the complexity of the policy issues being modeled.

In public policy inquiry, we also aspire to help practitioners make decisions regarding practical matters. In addition to enhancing our judgment and understanding and advancing technical knowledge, we often ask of such research to offer practical wisdom to inform decision making and action (Raadschelders 2011). As a source of practical wisdom, simulations serve another important function in bringing communities of practice (Wenger 1998) and communities of inquiry (Shields 2003) to a common understanding of the research issues.

In this chapter, we discuss some of the issues that make public policy concerns particularly difficult to address and suggest that simulations offer a systematic approach to addressing some of these issues. So what are these characteristics of public policy concerns that we must address in our inquiry?

1.2 Characteristics of Public Policy Concerns

Public policy concerns are complex, intractable, and messy (Ackoff 1974, 2004; Rittel and Webber 1973). The issues domain of public policy inquiry is perhaps limitless, but the issues share a number of common characteristics. We describe five characteristics, in no particular order, that deserve consideration when attempting to study policy systems. This list of a handful of characteristics is by no means exhaustive and is culled from a longer list of characteristics, some of which are alluded to in the following discussion.

1.2.1 Dynamic

One only needs to observe how a policy issue such as health care rises to the top of a policy agenda to conclude that policy issues are dynamic: time and timing play important roles. Consequently, policy inquiry has to consider the irreversibility of time. In any policy or managerial context, once an action is taken or a decision made, it enables some and constrains other future options. The implication for policy modeling is that in the face of uncertainty, models must incorporate updating mechanisms so that new relevant facts may influence future opinions, behaviors, and actions. For instance, a policy intervention, such as a public health program, changes the affected system. Medicaid as a public policy intervention in the US health-care system is a system in itself, which over time has developed its own unique set of structures and processes. The implementation of the Medicaid program as a solution to the problems of health care for the poor has given rise to various consequences not only for the poor but also for the health-care system as a whole. These short- and long-term consequences include increased demand, congestion, and a shortage of trained staff in the overall health-care system. More generally, the consequences of the initial intervention feed forward into associated interlocking systems leading to other consequences, which must be addressed by future interventions.

This type of circularity from problem to solution to problem, often characterizes policy systems and policy interventions. Policy inquiry methods must help researchers model how interventions designed to address problems result in different problems of their own that require new policy interventions. Such methods should capture these dynamics and feedback to generate insights that can provide direction for future interventions to tackle the problems created in addressing the original issues.

1.2.2 Adaptive

Another aspect regarding the dynamic nature of policy issues is that the underlying systems are adaptive. The entities and phenomena we study exist in states of uncertainty. Sometimes, the uncertainty is due to a lack of knowledge, while at other times, it is simply due to random events. Most often, though, this uncertainty is due to lack of knowledge as well as random shocks. For instance, we know that random lightning strikes cause forest fires although the science underlying damage to habitats and their recovery from forest fires is poorly understood. Both the consequences of and recovery from forest fires is uncertain. However, we also know that forests are resilient living organisms that survive and thrive under various diverse conditions. What allows the forests to survive such random shocks is their adaptability.

An adaptive entity is one that has the ability to sense its contextual environment and respond to it (Haeckel 1999). Policy interventions that recognize the adaptability of these systems and are designed to allow for such adaptive responses are more likely to be successful. Gentrification, for example, leads to changes in the nature of a community. However, the precise nature of the change is uncertain. In some communities, the original residents continue to live in the gentrified areas and enjoy a better quality of life. In other instances, gentrification drives the original residents away, perhaps to a less desirable but less expensive community (Eckerd 2011). In either case, the eventual outcome will depend upon how residents make sense of their environment and adaptively respond to a new reality.

1.2.3 *Emergent*

The literature on complex systems is replete with discussions of emergence (Bedau and Humphreys 2008; Clayton 2004; Coveney and Highfield 1995; Holland 1995; Kauffman 1995). A view of emergence within the complexity sciences is that what emerges, particularly in nature, is an unfolding over time of what was previously enfolded. From this perspective, the emergence of, say, an oak tree is simply an unfolding of the information enfolded in the acorn. Another view perceives emergence as patterns produced spontaneously through interactions among the components of complex or simple systems (Bedau and Humphreys 2008). In this chapter, the second perspective is adopted. So, by emergence, we mean the apparently novel, and sometimes complex, outcomes of simple or complex interactions among simple or complex entities (Graves 2007).

Hurricanes and the flocking behavior of birds are examples of emergent behavior in nature (Waldrop 1992). Hurricanes form out of the interaction and feedback among wind, humidity, temperature, ocean currents, and the Coriolis effect. Patterns in flocks of birds in flight are formed from the seemingly intelligent cooperative behavior of birds that are in fact simply trying to stay close without colliding. Examples of emergence in simple contexts abound in human societies. For instance, a traffic jam is an emergent property of traffic flows, standing ovations or unruly mobs emerge from interacting individual actions, and cities emerge from the mundane actions and decisions of people who work, play, and live in close proximity.

Human societies are complex, as are the policy concerns that arise in the underlying political, social, economic, and demographic systems. Extreme forms such as communism and fascism, famines and wars, economic busts and booms, and population explosions and collapses are all emergent properties of human interactions within these complex systems. Comprehending these emergent problems requires an understanding of the interactions among and between the underlying systems. The resolution of the problems is to be found at the emergent level and not at the level of the interactions from which the problems emerged.

1.2.4 Purposeful

Public policy researchers study systems that are purposeful. Public institutions and programs are designed and implemented with specific purposes in mind. The intentionality underlying these entities does, and must, affect how we study them; furthermore, contexts change with the passage of time and often, so do the underlying values. Without values, we cannot talk about purpose: values precede purpose and values help define purpose. The values underlying purpose yield criteria for judging different states of policy. The research methods must therefore be able to incorporate these values and criteria in order to evaluate policies and outcomes that result in desired and desirable outcomes.

The explicit incorporation of values and their consequences in research raises a host of ancillary issues, in particular those regarding objectivity of the researcher and the research. A detailed discussion of objectivity is beyond the scope of this chapter; however, to the extent that the alignment of values and purpose can lead to different policy interventions, policy inquiry should be able to explore how adherence to different value systems might or might not yield differences in outcomes.

1.2.5 Reflexive

Reflexivity plays an important role in public policy inquiry because as soon as a policy is formulated, people tend to ignore it or look for ways to circumvent it or to take advantage of it. The researcher is not a disinterested observer but is an affected party who is studying the consequences of policy intervention while reflecting upon his or her own reaction to it. The researcher is attempting to interpret actions, processes, and structures that have already been interpreted by the actors that affect and are affected by the policies (Argyris and Schön 1974; Giddens 2000).

Economic policy making often has to take into consideration not only the intended consequences of a policy but also the potential reaction of economic actors to that policy. Shiller (2000) writes about the extreme reaction of the stock markets, which fell 3% in Tokyo and Hong Kong and by 4% in London and Frankfurt immediately after Alan Greenspan, Chairman of the Federal Reserve Board of the United States, made what seemed to be innocuous remarks about "irrational exuberance" in a 1996 speech (Greenspan 2007, p. 176). The role of expectations—rational or irrational—cannot be underestimated as in the case of Greenspan's speech where the reaction was not to a policy but rather to the utterances of a policy maker.

Not only does policy inquiry have to address circularity between cause and effect but, the inquiry itself is often a reflexive process. In many instances, the objects of policy inquiry are self-fulfilling prophecies where self-awareness and reflection upon the consequences of policy interventions not only influence the reactions to those interventions but also alter the researcher's interpretations of what is observed.

1.3   Why Simulations?

To update, to our present context, Ashby's (1956) maxim on requisite variety: the complexity of the objects of inquiry must be matched by the complexity of the approaches used to tackle them. The methods we use must adequately address the nonlinearities, feedback, dynamic interactions, and interdependencies that are the norm in public policy contexts. The homogenizing assumptions required by commonly used statistical techniques are not always appropriate because they assume away diversity in the populations, policies, and outcomes inherent in the domains of policy inquiry (Ragin 2000).

The purpose of the tools we use for inquiry is to inform both research and practice. Tools should highlight how we might manage, model, and interpret evidence as we address intractable issues. The attributes of simulation as a tool appropriate for that context have been discussed at length elsewhere (Epstein 2007; Gilbert and Conte 1995; Gilbert and Troitzsch 1999; Selia et al. 2003; Taber and Timpone 1996; Zacharias et al. 2008). We discuss some of them here.

1.3.1   Imitation

Tools that focus on estimating summary characteristics and typical behavior cannot capture the diversity that motivates policy. The processes that lead to emergence of traffic jams might not be fully understood, but simulations can be built mimicking individual behaviors of cars to explore what types of collective behaviors, such as traffic jams, emerge. Thus, simulations offer the possibility of exploring systemic behavior to identify the group dynamics at play when one outcome emerges from the set of all possibilities (Gladwell 2000). For instance, although we cannot always predict when traffic jams or smooth-flowing traffic might emerge, we can begin to explore the conditions that seem to be associated with traffic jams and free-flowing traffic.

The primary purpose of simulation as a tool for inquiry is to create a representation of the reality that we wish to explore. In the absence of a proper understanding of the underlying phenomena, we want rules that manifest a recognizable world, however synthetically. These caricatures of the underlying constructs, processes, and structures allow for a holistic examination of the policy world.

The ability to imitate and create observed conditions is particularly useful in the absence of theory. To be able to understand the phenomena under study, one must create simulations that go beyond a simple caricature of reality. Epstein (2007) has argued that the ability to construct social structures exhibiting the emergent behavior in which we are interested demonstrates that we have a possible explanation for that emergent behavior. That is, if we can recreate traffic jams in a computer simulation, we are on the way to developing a possible explanation for the formation and perhaps dissolution of traffic jams.

1.3.2 Confidence

Ideally, a simulation would be grounded in a sound conceptual framework and satisfy the practical needs of the users. The strength of any particular simulation lies in its acceptance by the users as an adequate representation of their reality. Although a basis in sound theory is an important consideration, the details of what is included in a simulation are often driven by its intended use.

In policy inquiry, the researcher is rarely a disinterested observer. Objectivity that was once considered a hallmark of science is no longer considered feasible, especially in the social and policy sciences (Kuhn 1962; Latour 1987). However, simulations can approach a level of agreement among developers and users about its representation of reality that is akin to objectivity.

According to Wittgenstein, all knowledge is socially and culturally situated (Toulmin 1995, p. xii). To obtain that collective understanding, simulation developers and users must understand the values underlying the purposeful system being simulated. They must also agree upon the purpose for which the simulation is to be used, and the users must understand the assumptions that were made in developing that imitation of reality. This intersubjective understanding of the capabilities and limitations of the simulation as a representation of reality is an important aspect of establishing confidence in the results of the simulation.

Simulations are often described as being a black box, opaque to all but the developers. However, that description is not accurate. On the contrary, simulations, especially those that are implemented on computers, make every underlying assumption explicit in order to program them. All steps in the simulation are detailed in the lines of code. Hence, it is possible to trace through each step and understand how the simulation was constructed and the results obtained, although the effort required for understanding complex models can be quite substantial

As advanced thinking, the simulation building process leads to practical wisdom through an iterative structure (Carwright et al. 1995). David Andersen and George Richardson at the State University of New York in Albany, with their colleagues in the UK, have worked with decision makers to identify mental models and to create mind maps (Ackerman et al. 2010; Horn 1998). These maps have then been used to create computer simulations. In order to reach an intersubjective understanding of the nature and scope of the simulations, the developers of the simulations present the simulations and their outcomes to the decision makers to determine whether they reflect their mental models and, if so, whether the outcomes were what they expected. If not, either the mental models or the simulations have to be revised until there is convergence between the mental models and the simulations. This iterative process of going back and forth between decision makers, modelers, and the outcomes of the simulations assures that all the involved parties understand what is being simulated and how the outcomes are obtained. Transparency in the development of the simulations goes a long way in assuring both the modelers and the users that they have simulated a reasonable representation of reality as they understand it.

Although the validity of simulations cannot be readily established, this intersubjective transparent process makes it possible to increase confidence in the simulations among both the developers and the users. This confidence is based on the collective belief that the simulations successfully imitate salient features of the reality under study.

1.3.3 Flexibility

The back-and-forth process just described boosts developer and user confidence in the simulation. However, a different type of iterative capability is necessary if the research tools are to be useful in policy inquiry. A fundamental aspect of policy inquiry is that it entails the study of complex contexts and, oftentimes, changes in these contexts. Because all the complexities of the context cannot be fully appreciated at the outset, new concerns arise as progress is made in understanding and addressing the issues. These concerns require a reevaluation of the way in which they are being studied, which requires that the research methods have the flexibility to adapt to changing analytical needs (Rittel and Webber 1973). For instance, expanding Medicaid eligibility does not necessarily imply that all the newly eligible individuals will have access to health-care. To be able to fully capture the effects of the policy change, one would not only have to estimate the number of newly eligible clients but also model their behaviors given the capacity of the local health-care system and other considerations such as availability of transportation and the ease of access to that system.

   In order to capture the effect of such policy changes, the research methods should not only be able to alter the boundaries of what is within and outside the scope of the analysis but should also be able to incorporate multiple units of analysis and dynamic and adaptive interactions among the systems, phenomena, and entities (Lindblom 1959; Balint et al. 2011). Although the early promise of artificial intelligence has not been fully realized, advances in computational modeling have led to the development of simulations that can adapt and learn (Holland 1995). Such modeling tools overcome the restrictions imposed by having to define, in advance, the nature and parametric form of the relationships among model components. The freedom afforded by such modeling flexibility can be used to design policy interventions and to explore their effectiveness in different contexts (Kim and Xiao 2008).

1.3.4 Multilevel

In order to study emergence, the simulation must have at least two levels where interactions at one level yield the emergent phenomena at the second. It is important to recognize that the two levels are logically different. The level at which the interactions occur is a different logical type from the one that exhibits the emergent properties (Whitehead and Russell 1910–13; Wilensky and Resnick 1999).

   Consider, once again, the traffic jam that emerges from the interaction of cars. The traffic jam is an emergent property of the traffic flow. The units of analysis—cars and traffic jams—are not only different at the two levels but they are also logically different in that the properties of one cannot be obtained by aggregating the properties of the other. Although cars make up the traffic jam, the jam is not a car and the properties of the traffic jam cannot be obtained by aggregating the properties of the cars. The relationship between cars and a traffic jam is analogous to the relationship between the members of a set and the set. The properties of the set are not necessarily some aggregate function of the properties of the members of the set. The failure to recognize that distinction between a group and the members of that group can lead to various paradoxes (Bateson 1972). For instance, a paradox ensues in attempting to determine whether the set-of-all-sets is a member of itself, or whether the prover-bial barber shaves himself in a village where the barber shaves all men who do not shave themselves. In both these instances, one part of the statement is about the group and the other is about a member of that group. Attempting to discuss the properties of the two logical types—group and individual—at the same level results in the paradox.

The ability to have research tools that allow the exploration of interactions among entities at one level and to study their emergent properties at another is vital for policy research where emergence is commonplace. Although multilevel statistical models exist, the information flow between levels does not allow for emergence. These statistical models distinguish between levels where the unit of analysis at the higher level is an aggregation of the units of analysis at the lower level. They do not, however, distinguish between the logical types as one moves from one logical level to another. Simulations, on the other hand, can readily accommodate different logical levels.

1.4   Conclusion

Inquiry has three primary characteristics: (a) it is emergent because the consequent learning is more complex that the process inputs; (b) it is reflexive because when learning, an inquirer must reflect upon that learning and its consequences; and (c) it is adaptive because as one learns and reflects, new issues arise that require adjustment to the inquiry process. Public policy research is a multifaceted process of problem identification and formulation, seeking incremental approaches to addressing concerns and monitoring and evaluating implementation so as to learn and to adapt to new contexts (Cigler 1999; Gray 1989). As a component of such research activity, simu-lation construction is a collective enterprise born out of agreement among develop-ers and users regarding the purpose, objective, nature, and scope of the project. For a simulation to be used, potential users have to find that it reflects their understand-ing of the issues. Other researchers and practitioners must have confidence that in using the simulation they will gain insights that will inform decisions and provide direction for action.

Simulations blend the art of the soluble with the art of the possible to generate not only systematic research but also offer practical recommendations that decision makers might implement. Even in the presence of complete and perfect data, all we know about is the past. Assuming that the future will be like the past is not particularly insightful because we know in advance that there will be change. We know that the future will be different, and it is the researcher's task to propose what some of these possible futures might be.

In public policy, there are no prime causes. The assassination of Archduke Franz Ferdinand is often cited as the event that sparked the conflagration that bloodied Europe and damaged a generation of young men. However, in spite of excellent historical records and information, historians continue to argue about the reasons and the events that led up to the First World War. Even when a triggering event can be attributed to having started off a sequence of consequences, conditions have to exist that assure that the momentum created by that event can be sustained—what those necessary sustaining conditions might be remains a mystery (Becker 1955). Identifying such events in advance is unlikely and projecting out what might follow is difficult. But, simulations, particularly those informed by sound experience and data can be used to create and explore possible future worlds. Simulations do not predict but, through the generation of multiple environments, they can create possible worlds where various outcomes and their likelihood can be explored to inform policy decisions and action.

Acknowledgment Comments from Jos Raadschelders, on an earlier draft of this chapter, are gratefully acknowledged.

References

Ackerman F, Andersen DF, Eden C, Richardson GP. 2010. "Using a group decision support system to add value to group model building." *System Dynamics Review,* 26, no. 4: 335–346.

Ackoff, R. 1974. *Redesigning the Future: Systems Approach to Societal Problems* New York, NY: John S. Wiley & Sons.

_____. 2004. Transforming the systems movement. Available at http://www.acasa.upenn.edu/ RLAConfPaper.pdf accessed on October 29, 2011.

Argyris, C. and D. Schön. 1974. *Theory in practice: increasing professional effectiveness.* San Francisco, CA: Jossey-Bass.

Ashby, W.R. 1956. *An Introduction to Cybernetics,* London: Chapman & Hall.

Balint, P., R. Stewart, A. Desai and L.C. Walters. 2011. *Wicked Environmental Problems: Managing Uncertainty and Conflict.* Washington DC: Island Press.

Bateson, G. 1972. *Steps to an Ecology of Mind: Collected Essays in Anthropology, Psychiatry, Evolution, and Epistemology.* Chicago, IL: University Of Chicago Press.

Becker, C.L. 1955. What are Historical Facts? *The Western Political Quarterly,* 8, no. 3: 327–340.

Bedau, M.A. and P. Humphreys. 2008. *Emergence: Contemporary readings in philosophy and science.* Cambridge, MA: MIT Press.

Card, S.K., J.D. Mackinlay and B. Schniderman. 1999. *Readings in information visualization: Using vision to think.* San Francisco, CA: Morgan Kauffman.

Carwright, N., T. Shomar and M. Suarez. 1995. The tool box of science. In: Novack L (ed.) *Poznan Studies in the philosophy of science.* Amsterdam: Rodopi

Cigler, B.A. 1999. Pre-conditions for the emergence of multicommunity collaborative organizations. *Review of Policy Research* 16, no. 1: 86–102.

Clayton, P. 2004. *Mind & Emergence: From Quantum to Consciousness*. Oxford, UK: Oxford University Press.

Coveney, P.V. and R.R. Highfield. 1995. *Frontiers of Complexity*. New York: Fawcett.

Duhem, P. 1954. *The Aim and Structure of Physical Theory*. Princeton, NJ: Princeton University Press.

Eckerd, A. 2011. Cleaning Up Without Clearing Out? A Spatial Assessment of Environmental Gentrification. *Urban Affairs Review* Vol. 47, no. 1: 31–59.

Epstein, J.M. 2007. *Generative Social Science: Studies in Agent-Based Computational Modeling.* Princeton, NJ: Princeton University Press.

Fisher, F. 2003. *Reframing Public Policy: Discursive Politics and Deliberative Practices*. New York, NY: Oxford University Press.

Giddens, A. 2000. *The Third Way and Its Critics*. Cambridge, UK: Polity.

Gilbert, N. and R. Conte. (eds.) 1995. *Artificial Societies: The Computer Simulation of Social Life*. London UK: University College Press.

Gilbert, N. and K.G Troitzsch 1999. *Simulation for the Social Scientist*. Buckingham, UK: Open University Press.

Gladwell, M. 2000. *The Tipping Point: How little things can make a big difference*. New York, NY: Little, Brown and Company.

Graves, M. 2007. Peircean approaches to emergent systems in cognitive science and religion. *Zygon*. Vol. 42, no. 1: 241–248.

Gray, B. 1989. *Collaborating: Finding common ground for multiparty problems*. San Francisco: Jossey–Bass.

Greenspan, A. 2007. *The Age of Turbulence: Adventures in a New World*. New York: Penguin.

Haeckel, S.H. 1999. *Adaptive enterprise: Creating and leading sense-and-respond organizations*. Boston, MA: Harvard Business School Press.

Holland, J.H. 1995. *Hidden Order: How Adaptation Builds Complexity*. Cambridge, MA: Perseus Books.

Horn, R.E. 1998. *Mapping Great Debates: Can Computers Think?* Bainbridge Island, WA: MacroVU, Inc.

Kauffman, Stuart A. 1995. *At Home in the Universe: The Search for Laws of Self-organization and Complexity*. New York: Oxford University Press.

Kim, Y., Xiao, N. 2008. FraudSim: Simulating fraud in a public delivery program. In: Liu L, Eck J. (eds.). *Artificial Crime Analysis Systems: Using Computer Simulations and Geographic Information Systems* (pp. 319–338). Hershey, PA: IGI Global.

Kuhn, T. 1962. *The structure of scientific revolutions*. Chicago, IL: University of Chicago Press.

Lakoff, G. and M. Johnson. 1999. *Philosophy in the flesh*. New York, NY: Basic Books.

Latour, B. 1987. *Science in action*. Cambridge, MA: Harvard University Press.

Lindblom, CE. 1959. The Science of "Muddling Through". *Public Administration Review*. Vol. 19, no. 2: 79–88.

Morçöl, G. 2002. *A new mind for policy analysis: Toward a post-Newtonian and postpositivist epistemology and methodology*. Westport, CT: Praeger.

Morrison, M. and M.S. Morgan. 1999. Introduction in M.S. Morgan and M. Morrison (eds.) *Models as Mediators*. Cambridge, UK: Cambridge University Press.

Murray, T. 2006. Collaborative Knowledge Building and Integral Theory: On Perspectives, Uncertainty, and Mutual Regard. *Integral Review*. Vol. 2: 210–268.

Norman, D.A. 1993. *Things that make us smart: Defending human attributes in the age of the machine*. Reading, MA: Addison-Wesley.

Ragin, C.C. 2000. *Fuzzy-Set Social Science*. Chicago, IL: University of Chicago Press.

Raadschelders, J.C.N. 2011. *Public Administration: The Interdisciplinary Study of Government*. Oxford: Oxford University Press.

Rittel, H. W. J., and M. M. Webber. 1973. Dilemmas in a general theory of planning. *Policy Sciences*. Vol. 4: 155–169.

Schelling, T. C. 1971. Dynamic Models of Segregation. *Journal of Mathematical Sociology*. Vol. 1: 143–186.

Schmidle, N. 2011. Getting bin Laden: What happened that night in Abbottabad. *The New Yorker*, August 8, 2011, pp. 34–45.

Selia, A.F., V. Ceric and P. Tadikamalla. 2003. *Applied Simulation Modeling*. Belmont, CA: Brooks/Cole Thomson Learning.

Shields, P. 2003. The Community of Inquiry: Classical Pragmatism and Public Administration. *Administration & Society*. Vol. 35, no. 5: 510–538.

Shiller, R. 2000. *Irrational Exuberance*. Princeton, NJ: Princeton University Press.

Taber C.E. and R.J. Timpone. 1996. *Computational Modeling*. Thousand Oaks, CA: Sage.

Toulmin, S. 1995. Foreword in R.F. Goodman and W.R. Fisher (eds.) *Rethinking Knowledge* Albany, NY: SUNY Press.

Waldrop, M.M. 1992. *Complexity: The emerging science at the edge of order and chaos*. New York, NY: Simon and Schuster.

Wenger, E. 1998. *Communities of practice: Learning, Meaning and Identity*. New York, NY: Cambridge University Press.

Whitehead A.N. and B. Russell. 1910–13. *Principia Mathematica* 3 vols. Cambridge, UK: Cambridge University Press.

Wilensky, U and M. Resnick, 1999. Thinking in Levels: A Dynamic Systems Approach to Making Sense of the World. *Journal of Science Education and Technology*. Vol. 8, no. 1.

Zacharias, G.L., J. MacMillan and S.B. Van Hemel (eds.) 2008. *Behavioral Modeling and Simulation*. Washington DC: National Academy Press.

Part I
Monte Carlo Simulation

Chapter 2
Simulation Design for Policy Audiences: Informing Decision in the Face of Uncertainty

Jason S. Seligman

Abstract Often a researcher or policy maker confronts a situation in which all possible decisions, including the decision to postpone choosing, carry risk. In such situations, one must attempt to reconcile a choice with information available today. Using two examples, this chapter highlights the generic benefits of simulation for projecting impacts of policies. Emphasis is placed on the basics of simulation design. In particular, the construction of alternate states of nature to accommodate contingencies, the vetting of designs, the determination of more and less important assumptions, the identification of stopping points for simulation and concerns regarding false precision are addressed.

2.1 Introduction

When Congress debates how to reduce Social Security's long-term underfunding of currently promised benefits, it relies on the Congressional Budget Office and others to build simulation models, parameterized to assumptions stated and agreed upon—like how labor productivity is likely to evolve or whether it should even be assumed to do so. Often a researcher or policy maker confronts a situation in which all possible decisions, including the decision to postpone choosing, carry risk. In such situations, one must attempt to reconcile a choice with information available today; gathering better information sometime in the future is not a costless option. Policy research tools tend to be purpose-built, but there is a great deal of basic technique regarding their construction researchers can familiarize themselves with. This chapter provides background and examples for the reader to learn from.

J.S. Seligman (✉)
John Glenn School of Public Affairs, The Ohio State University,
110 Page Hall, 1810 College Road, Columbus, OH 43210, USA
e-mail: seligman.10@osu.edu

A. Desai (ed.), *Simulation for Policy Inquiry*, DOI 10.1007/978-1-4614-1665-4_2,
© Springer Science+Business Media, LLC 2012

Consider the fundamental challenge that we simply do not have as much data on the outcomes of policy choices as we would like. We will have to make up for this lack of data as best we can, in this case, by making some! Making up data is simple enough to state, but how should that be done? Can we roll dice, draw cards, pull numbers from a book or computer at random, and expect to draw meaningful insights from these exercises? No, though there will be a random or near-random component within most synthetic data construction exercises, stopping there is akin to naively stating "anything might happen" (Efron 1982).

To make resonant data, we will have to consider what factors are likely to influence future outcomes. These factors can generally come from two places: either via evidence from the past or via knowledge and conjecture regarding future relations. Evidence from the past includes reported covariates from regressions, event histories, or anything that helps us to shape a relationship between policies and resulting outcomes. Knowledge and conjecture regarding the future may take the form of information about contemporaneous changes in law, global affairs, or resources, as I will now illustrate via historical example.

2.2   A Forecasting Example

For example, a researcher trying to forecast German emigration to the USA for the year 1920 in the middle of 1914 may rely on historic emigration trends to forecast a rate of growth and any tendencies toward acceleration or deceleration in that trend. The same researcher tasked with the same assignment 2 or 4 years later will have to grapple with the ongoing (1916) or just concluding (1918) impact of World War I. After building a simple model along the lines of the 1914 approach, the 1916 update might begin by setting the level of emigration to zero for war years, and then assuming that the level and rate of growth from before the war will simply resume. The designer may include three possible cases under which the war ends in 1917, 1918, or 1919. If the forecaster is politically savvy, he or she may try to anticipate the possibility of US involvement and any differential impact from German victory or defeat. To gain a better understanding of those dynamics, it may be beneficial to look at emigration patterns following wars in which two parties are neutral (as if the USA does not enter), warring (as if the USA opposes Germany), or allied (as if the USA supports Germany), and dependent upon the outcome (German victory or defeat)—six possible cases. All of these cases are synthetic. They are sometimes referred to as "hypothetical(s)," "what ifs," or "alternate possible worlds." Finally, the researcher may wish to consider whether factors are sufficiently similar or different enough to warrant the strict application, amplification, or damping of applied rates from those periods onto the current period in any scenario. The forecast will be contingent on assumptions such as the set of assumptions that the USA enters the war and Germany suffers defeat in 1918, for example. In this way, the forecast data on German emigration to the USA for the year 1920 are conditional. The individual making the 1918 forecast will know the outcome of the war for both nations, but he or she will still have to grapple with what the impact of that outcome will be for USA-pull and German-push factors motivating emigration as well as any lingering political or resource-based constraints on international travel across Europe and the Atlantic Ocean.

Notice that in retrospect, the relatively naive 1914 forecast was not bereft of a set of assumptions that map to the dimensions of war and commerce—the 1914 forecast was contingent on there being no such thing as World War I, and so no disruption via USA entry or German defeat—in short, an assumption of no sudden changes in either human motives or the structural capacity for emigration was present. As it turns out, the 1914 forecast relied on false assumptions, but a key point is not whether the assumptions turned out to be correct, but rather whether they were reasonable. In fact, it would not have been easy in June of 1914 to convince an audience that a 1920 forecast should include consideration of impacts for any sort of a "world war," much less one that lasted over 4 years and found the USA and Germany on opposing sides.[1] This example serves to point out that while we will depend on our assumptions to construct our data, we are not able to scrutinize their validity until after the data have been employed in our forecast. Ahead of time, all we can do is consider whether and to what extent the assumptions might be reasonable. If we find ourselves uncertain, then we might forecast for a finite number of contingencies (as with the 1916 case). If we find the number of contingencies to be large and each to be proximate to its nearest neighbor, then we may wish to consider not only each forecast outcome uniquely but also the distribution of forecasts across the dimensions of uncertainty. For example, in the 1916 case, allowing the war's duration to vary in monthly increments might give us a sense of the impact of the war's duration on the 1920 level of immigration.

2.3 Synthetic Data

The idea that we have to make assumptions may put us off to the notion of synthetic data creation, but the *data construction* assumptions in a Monte Carlo are counterpart to the *data relation* assumptions found in regression analysis, for example, that the data are independent and identically distributed and can be well characterized by their moments (Raychaudhuri 2008: 93–94). Ordinary Least Squares assumes a linear relationship among the variables as they enter the estimation model. We cannot escape assumptions in data analysis, and the same is true regarding synthetic data construction exercises. But assumptions can be more or less egregious in either

---

[1] Similarly, in June of 1929, it would have been difficult to convince an audience of the idea that forecasts for growth of the USA economy to 1935 should include a "great depression" of some sort, and in 2007, it would have been tough to convince an audience that a forecast of 2010 tax revenues should include consideration of impacts of the Great Recession.

setting, as well as being more or less important for outcomes. When they are important, the basic approach is to choose wisely or, when we cannot, to create outcomes for each potentially relevant case. When they are unimportant, then the selection process can be less deliberate without any loss of insight—much as for any nonbinding constraint in the context of an optimization. The main reason to construct synthetic data is that we do not otherwise possess them. The most popular justification for that is either the data do not yet exist, as in the case of forecasting, or they are hard to obtain, either due to time and expense, legal consideration, or some other constraint. What we do not possess and cannot purchase by necessity must be made. To this end, we can employ Monte Carlo simulations, a method by which we can make data through repeated random draws based on a given set of parameters (Vose 2008; Raychaudhuri 2008: 95–97).

One benefit of simulation is the ability to try out how hypothetical changes in policy or circumstance might impact outcomes, i.e., the ability to model different "worlds" or "counterfactuals." As in the case of forecasting, however, the accuracy of one's predictions tends to decrease as the hypothetical changes imposed on the data generation process increase relative to any current (baseline) scenario. We can think of confidence bands that explode into greater uncertainty, reducing the insights from any simulation over the multidimensional policy space as the change in any particular dimension increases. A natural stopping point for any simulation exercise occurs when uncertainty dominates all plausible outcomes. Intuitively, it follows that it will usually be easier to forecast the near future and more challenging to forecast distant periods because both the relevance of assumptions and relations among the data evolve over time. Thus, it would be easier to forecast 1920 emigration in 1919, and we would normally expect a 1914 forecast to be more reliable for 1915 than for 1920.

The previous example regarding a forecast of German emigration to the USA was chosen both because its context was relatively familiar to the audience and because it allowed us to contend with the challenges inherent in considering assumptions—be it tacitly (1914—assume no war) or formally (1916—assume war's end in {1917, 1918, 1919}). Next, we will consider a more involved case regarding expected individual returns from investing in the stock market using an employer-based retirement savings program.

Social Security, the investment of retirement savings, and private pensions are all natural landscapes for simulation analysis (e.g., Auerbach and Kotlikoff 1985; Burtless 2000; Samwick and Skinner 2004). They each contain all of the elements that normally make simulation a relatively appealing method: uncertainty, long timeframes, and compounding outcomes. What is more, the uncertainty and compounding take place in multiple dimensions simultaneously and feed into the determination of both lifetime income and the duration of final years of consumption (during retirement). In these sorts of problems, we care not only about lifetime income but also its distribution across the life cycle. Related to this, because accumulations of wealth are a function of savings patterns, we also have to care about how patterns of consumption coevolve.

2.4 Estimating Equity Returns in Employer-Sponsored Defined Contribution Programs

In 2004, Jeffrey Wenger and I set out to consider what rates of return workers should expect from stock investments if they did it though an employer-based "defined contribution" retirement savings program (Seligman and Wenger 2006). A key focal point of our inquiry was that we expected their rates of return would be lower than average because of the way labor and equity (stock) markets interact over the business cycle. Specifically, we believed that because the equity market tended to lead the business cycle and the labor market tended to thereby lag equities, persons would be most likely to be employed when equity prices were near peak values and least likely to be employed when these prices had fallen, following the onset of recessions.[2] This behavior suggested to us that employees would have a tendency to miss opportunities to buy stocks when they were relatively cheap. Figure 2.1 illustrates our central thesis.

This was a conjecture, or hypothesis, based on relative growth paths, as illustrated in Fig. 2.1. To test our hypothesis, we need to measure workers' labor market experiences relative to stock market valuations, net of other contemporaneous impacts. Did other factors overwhelm or diminish our insight so as to make it meaningless? To what extent was our conjecture important for workers to consider as they saved for retirement? To what extent should policy makers be concerned about related tendencies to undershoot savings goals in the population? A particular challenge for us in measuring workers' experiences was that they had not had many! To date, other authors had not tackled the issue directly.[3] Defined contribution systems are new enough that we could not simply survey persons to assess whether their savings at retirement met their goals and to see what they thought about their

---

[2]Generally, stock prices are linked to the economic value of firms. This is measured by way of firms' expected returns to shareholders over a number of years, for example, via (stock) price to (firm) earnings ratios (P-to-E). When earnings are growing, during the expansion phase of the business cycle, P-to-E falls, making stocks relatively cheap. This motivates purchases of the stock, and prices rise as a result, moving P-to-E back toward its long-term norm. Firms, facing robust demand for both finished goods and company stock, tend to expand, hiring workers and increasing production. At some point, demand is sated. As prospects for growth wane, P-to-E naturally increases as expected future earnings decline. This decreases demand for the firm's stock. As a result, the firm reduces investments in productive capital and labor. In this way, prospects for future demand impact current input markets. Generally, financial markets tend to move more rapidly toward the new P-to-E equilibrium, whereas the markets for labor and goods move more slowly. For more on the technical links between the values of stocks over the business cycle, see Silvapulle and Silvapulle 1999, and for more on unemployment, see Yellen (1984).

[3]A good example of the articles of that time is found in Samwick and Skinner (2004), which modeled career earnings synthetically assuming a random walk adjusted by a tuned age-earning factor. Those data are not simulated in a way that allows us to think about contemporaneous unemployment rates and equities prices.

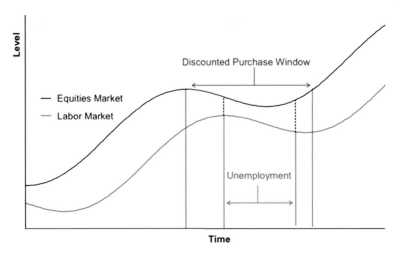

Fig. 2.1 Asynchronous equities and labor markets (stylized example)

experiences. Furthermore, we did not have access to a data set for testing whether equity returns in defined contribution accounts were different from returns outside of the accounts. With these limitations in mind, we turned to simulation a technique long-employed in pension and savings environments.

2.5   A Digression on Monte Carlo Simulation

As mentioned earlier, a Monte Carlo is nothing more than a method by which to make data, by way of repeated random draws conditioned by rules as to how these random draws are to be treated. Jeffrey Wenger and I therefore had to build some synthetic data via Monte Carlo simulation, evaluate our data as they were constructed and then employ the constructed data to consider whether unemployment and its timing observably impacted equity returns. As we considered the problem of unemployment, we focused on two substantial problems workers face: the occurrence and duration of unemployment. As a result, our simulation was built on two sequential random draws, or lotteries: one devoted to the probabilistic realization of unemployment and the other concerning its duration. But the *random* aspects of these draws are not all there is to them. We might argue either that all workers have some consistent probability of being let go or, alternatively, that better workers face lower probabilities of unemployment. In addition to and of particular importance for our conjecture, all workers might face higher probabilities of being let go following a stock market crash (Neftci 1984; Silvapulle and Silvapulle 1999).

2.5.1   Probability Distribution

The idea of a lottery is probably not new to the reader, but the idea of constructing the rules surrounding its outcome might seem daunting. One of the most important features of simulations involves the distribution from which a random draw occurs, and this distribution is shaped to a great extent by the rules by which draws are made.[4] How can we settle the debate as to whether workers face different probabilities of unemployment following a stock market crash, for example? To inform or "shape" our probabilities, we turned to data that we could observe. We gathered data from the Bureau of Labor Statistics (BLS) Current Population Survey and built a synthetic panel containing unemployment incidence and wages across worker types and ages following the method of Mandrian and Lefgren (2000).[5]

2.5.2   Time

Figure 2.1 highlights that our measures of unemployment and equity market returns had to be contemporaneous in order for us to determine whether, and to what extent, unemployment affected lifetime returns in workers' retirement savings accounts. Thus, time was important for us to consider carefully. The synthetic panel of wages and unemployment rates had to be matched to contemporaneous data on unemployment duration and equity market returns. For the latter two data series, we used unemployment duration data from the BLS and stock return data for the S&P500 index from the Center for Research in Security Prices. Overall, we were able to match data from 1980 to 2003 on a monthly basis producing an observation window of 287 periods.

---

[4]One classic rule that most students of probability are exposed to early on regards whether draws from a distribution remove those items from a distribution ahead of the next draw, or whether those items are replaced. In a lottery without replacement, the distributions from which draws occur evolve, whereas in lotteries with replacement, each new draw occurs over the same distribution of outcomes. Of course, the original set of items from which the first draw is made is important in either case. Broadly, Raychaudhuri (2008) gives a very nice set of rules based on the method of moments or sampling from continuous and discrete distributions in the context of Monte Carlo simulation.

[5]According to the Bureau of Labor Statistics: "The Current Population Survey (CPS) is a monthly survey of households conducted by the Bureau of Census for the Bureau of Labor Statistics. It provides a comprehensive body of data on the labor force, employment, unemployment, persons not in the labor force, hours of work, earnings, and other demographic and labor force characteristics." To learn more, visit: http://www.bls.gov/cps/.

2.5.3   Worker Quality and Gender

Distinguishing whether and to what extent better workers tended to face lower probabilities or lower durations of unemployment over all periods was something we wrestled with; we could not be sure that it was important for our work. Not only did we have to distinguish employment experiences, we also had to consider their experience with employer-sponsored savings offerings. Beginning with employment experiences, ignoring the idea that worker quality might affect our results would have failed to acknowledge the common observation that low-skill workers tend to have fewer employment prospects than high-skill workers—an observation supported by aggregate BLS data series on unemployment by level of education.[6] If unemployment spikes following equity market declines were only a fact for low-skill workers, any finding we might offer should be thus qualified (especially if these workers did not normally receive pension and savings benefits). If instead, negative impacts were experienced by all, then distinguishing among worker types would not affect our results, and that fact would be interesting as well. So we needed to segregate workers by quality, or a meaningful proxy thereof. In fact, while we could not observe the quality of workers via these data, we could observe their wages conditional on age, so we segregated our earnings observations into four groups based on earnings quartiles, positing that higher value workers might experience lower likelihoods of unemployment. Because the period of history we were studying was identified as one of evolving female participation and compensation in labor markets, we also distinguished women from men. In all then, we had eight study groups, representing each of four income quartiles by each of two genders. For the first lottery—the lottery for unemployment (job loss)—we estimated the underlying time-dependent hazard of unemployment for each of these eight groups. We found that low-wage workers, whether men or women, were more likely to become unemployed than workers earning higher wages over the full period of observation. Next, to learn more about retirement plan participation by worker type, we used data from the US Census Bureau's Survey of Income and Program Participation to determine that low-wage workers in the USA did tend to participate in employer pension and savings benefit plans.[7] In summary, we found all groups participated in employer-sponsored retirement plans, that retirement savings could be negatively impacted by labor market disturbances, and that it was important to distinguish among groups when assessing impacts.

---

[6] For more statistics on unemployment controlling for worker characteristics, see http://www.bls.gov/cps/lfcharacteristics.htm#unemp.

[7] The Survey of Income and Program Participation (SIPP) is focused on program participation, including employer-based retirement programs. It distinguishes between those for which employees receive pensions ("Defined Benefit" programs) and those in which workers receive contributions toward their savings for retirement ["Defined Contribution" programs—the kind we studied in Seligman and Wenger (2006)]. Appendix A of Seligman and Wenger (2006) documents pensions plan participation by earnings quartile and gender. For more on the SIPP, visit the US Census site: http://www.census.gov/sipp/intro.html.

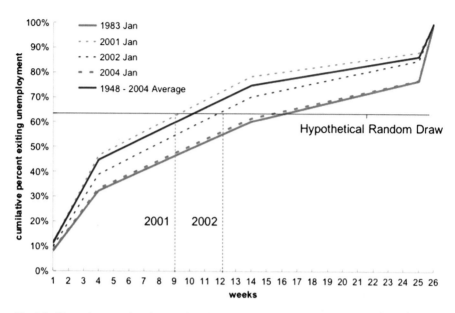

Fig. 2.2 Unemployment duration at selected times

2.5.4   Quasi-Randomization

One of the prominent features of a business cycle is that it is more difficult to find a job in a recession than otherwise.[8] As a result, we might expect that the duration of any unemployment spell would be greater in a recession—a time when equity prices are relatively depressed. But while this may be true on average, any one worker may still experience shorter or longer unemployment spells than another similar worker over the same period, if only by chance. Generally, a simulation requires a stochastic element as well—randomization contoured by the changing probabilistic evolution of, in this case, unemployment duration. With this in mind, we next engineered our lottery for duration. For each month between 1980 and 2003, we constructed a data-set that described the percentage of unemployed workers with duration of between 1 and 26 weeks (6 months). Because the BLS historically had not captured precise durations beyond 26 weeks (before the most recent recession, there were most often no unemployment benefits available to US workers after 6 months), we capped our duration and reapportioned the BLS 27+ week residual such that 100% of the sample had synthetic durations of 26 or fewer weeks. This embedded a specific simplifying assumption such that, in our constructed data, no single unemployment episode would ever be longer than 6 months. Figure 2.2 depicts how a single hypothetical draw yields two different duration outcomes for January 2001, compared to the following

---

[8] The classical arguments as to why involve the nonresponsiveness of wages to capital returns over the short run (Akerlof and Yellen 1985).

year. Notice that in either case, the probability of returning to the workforce in the 27th week is forced to converge to 100%.

Of course, there are other possible assumptions for treating the long-term unemployed, but they are inferior for two reasons. First, we did not have a reliable data source by which to describe the distribution of durations past 27 weeks. Second, curtailing longer duration unemployment periods actually worked against our ability to observe unemployment-derived losses in retirement savings. This is a very important rhetorical design consideration. In particular, it works against a rejection of the null hypothesis that our conjecture is unimportant. This is because curtailing observed unemployment durations works to diminish estimated impacts from long-term unemployment.

2.5.5   General Rules for Guiding Assumptions

All simulations require a series of assumptions, be they tacit or explicit. In general, we hope to make all assumptions explicit; to do so, however, would require full knowledge of future conditions and is therefore not realistic (recall our earlier 1914 emigration problem). Further, we hope for the opportunity to employ neutral assumptions—assumptions that inflict no predictable bias on results. However, this is not always possible. When we can predict bias, if there is an option between amplifying and attenuating the results of simulation procedures, it is intellectually more honest to choose conservative assumptions. Conservative assumptions are those that attenuate the chance of rejecting our null hypothesis. Being conservative reduces any tendency to sensationalize findings and thereby improves the credibility of the research.

There is at least one case is which the cautious approach may not be appropriate—the case where a researcher wishes to examine worst-case or generally more extreme scenarios. Even here, however, it is often still advantageous to leave many assumptions neutral or toward attenuating estimated impacts in a base case. Once established, this base case can be used to estimate marginal impacts of alternate assumptions, incrementally. For example, we might ask, "What would the impact of a 10% increase in the duration of unemployment spells be for retirement savings?" Notice in this example all other assumptions are left as they are; *only the assumption regarding duration is altered*. Notice too that results can now be described generically as follows: a 10% increase in the duration of unemployment spells is estimated to lead to an X percent decrease in lifetime savings. Further, because we have not in any way altered the equity market data, X might be estimated to be either greater than or less than 10% on average and might easily vary by group.

2.5.6   Implementation Issues

Guidelines for assumptions are useful, but some readers may still be daunted by the idea of implementing them. In most cases, implementation and the consideration of assumptions interact; we often consider each in turn several times. Beginning with a core set of assumptions assists in executing a simulation, and during that execution, we sometimes confront new decisions regarding assumptions that have to be refined or that have yet to be made.

Generally, executing the rest of the simulation was straightforward. Using median wages within each quartile, in each period, workers of each type drew from our two earlier described lotteries. If their first draw number was above the unemployment hazard threshold for their worker type, then they remained employed, drew the median wage for their group, and set aside a portion of their wages which were invested in equity markets at current market prices. In the following month, their account balance grew along with the S&P500, and of course they drew again from the lottery regarding possible unemployment. In any month, they became unemployed a second lottery number was drawn—for duration.

Duration was measured by comparing a second number to the duration chart, so that, for example, drawing in January of 1980 a "49" placed duration at 4 weeks (rounded to 1 month) and drawing an 85 placed a hypothetical duration at 19 weeks (rounded to 4 months). In periods of unemployment, workers accrued equity market gains or losses on account balances but made no purchases or sales. Notice the two embedded assumptions this entails—first that the worker does not withdraw balances during periods of unemployment and second that he or she does not make contributions to the retirement account by alternate means.

At the end of any unemployment spell, the worker once again entered the work place, drawing from the unemployment lottery. Assuming they were not immediately dismissed from their new position, the employment cycle began once more. Workers drew pay and again made contributions to their retirement accounts. This process went on for 287 periods for each of the eight worker types; thus, our simulation generated a single observation of career unemployment and savings for each of eight distinct worker types.

By "single observation," we mean that the random lottery draws representing the "state of nature" each period did not vary by worker quality or gender. In this sense, the single lottery draw suggests a consistent state of nature or a single macroeconomic environment. However, the implications of the random draw did vary by worker group based on unique, period-specific, worker-type thresholds. A draw of some lottery number might find all, some, or none of the work types dismissed. (That is how lotteries work—a single draw can create none, one, or more than one "winner.")

A single synthetic observation of how eight worker types are differentially impacted by a set of economic conditions is well and good, but the problem with having only a single Monte Carlo outcome observation is analogous to the problem with anecdotal evidence. Anecdotal evidence demonstrates the existence of a particular outcome, but it does not reveal how representative that outcome is. So, for example, if we find our highest-earnings quartile female worker has the least loss from unemployment, we still do not know whether to generalize that based on only one outcome. We cannot advise a household or a government agency to target human resource investments accordingly with any degree of assurance. But one of the greatest strengths of a well designed simulation is the relative ease with which it can be repeated: what can be done once can also be done 10, 100, or even 100,000 times by means of a programming loop.

So far, the mechanics of this procedure including all design and construction elements were the product of two researchers alone. It is often when results are presented to audiences that oversights on the part of a research team become clear. Important audiences include academic seminars, policy decision meetings, and reviewers at peer-reviewed journals. In fact, over the course of presenting and submitting our work, we got two questions which were both challenging to address and important for relevant audiences. The first question had to do with propensities for upward and downward mobility following unemployment. The second had to do with distilling how much of our observed unemployment impacts were due to simply being out of work versus the *timing* of spells. This helps to again illustrate the importance a researcher should attach to specifying assumptions as an aid to both their own understanding and external review. The results of any model are heavily reliant upon what the designers think is important. Others may or may not agree with the design emphasis. Simulation models begin with an individual set of assumptions, but it is primarily through iteration and the sharing the model with others that confidence is built to support the usefulness of results.

2.5.7 Developing Scenarios

The first question regarding earnings mobility did not initially strike us as important. We conjectured that if low-earnings quartile workers could move up and high-earnings quartile workers could move down the earnings distribution, then savings and loss patterns would converge somewhat. In other words, we did not expect the nature of our findings to change much. Still, when issues like this are brought up, it is incumbent on the researcher to address the question. Conjecture, however reasonable, is not usually a close substitute for information. To allow for labor market mobility (a historical hallmark of the US economy), we had to gather data on the likelihood of moving from one earnings quartile to another, which we derived from the Current Population Survey (CPS) over the years of 1994–2004 in 2-year increments. We then averaged all of these into a single generic long-term mobility matrix. This was prudent given the relative lack of observations on quartile mobility in the data. Alternatively, we could have considered mobility to depend on the month of reemployment via time-variation in our CPS data, but this would have driven large changes in our estimates based on relatively few observations on earnings quartile mobility. It would have been unclear whether changes in these data were representative of the changes in mobility over the fuller period or simply the result of idiosyncratic variation in the sample. Thus, there was the potential of introducing spurious variation into the data—generating a risk of false precision. False precision is a particular risk with simulation because small differences can be amplified or interacted in ways that reduce the generic resolution of results—the researcher thus takes on the risk of overstating his or her findings or of misinforming the readership.

Labor mobility was built into a dataset from which a third lottery was entered. At the end of each unemployment episode, the returning workers drew a random number that was compared to the probability of their landing a job in any quartile. Here, again we faced one final decision, whether hypothetical workers who begin "life" in our simulation in any quartile should, following any unemployment episode, read their draw conditional first on employment experience, or whether the draw should be conditioned on probabilities from their most recent earnings quartile, or some hybrid of the two (first; most recent), or some further career average.

Generally, if the available data will support it, a case can be made for any approach. Our own thinking was influenced by Farber (1999). Structurally, there are three considerations that should motivate the researcher—the first is based on the researcher's objective, the second is rhetorical, and the third is factual.

First, we should consider the researcher's objective in terms of the environment being modeled—in this case, we are trying to understand the likely impact of unemployment on employer-sponsored retirement savings invested in equities markets. If we were modeling a more rigid society, then we might be inclined to have unemployed workers draw conditional on their first job. If we were drawing from a fluid society, we would choose to make the draw conditional on the most recent wage, and if we felt we were somewhere in between, we might take an average of first and most recent wage or a weighted average of earnings over career-to-date. All else equal, if we had chosen one of the hybrids (based on the idea that our society was somewhere between the rigid and the fluid), we would have had to be careful about how the blending assumption impacted our results, and so we would likely have run one or both of the more straightforward assumptions (first, most-recent) to explore the level of variation as a result of our modeling assumption. Of course, hypothetically, should the choice of assumption be found to matter, then the researcher should select one more carefully or publish both sets of assumptions and results.

Second, in general, our audience will appreciate tractability and is likely to have a limited attention span, so if we can make the same points with a simpler design, we should. A straightforward approach is more rhetorically useful. The first design of our model had the worker be entirely immobile. Audiences of this work had asked what mobility might mean for our results, and so it was reasonable to try to give them the broadest sense of this, regardless of our initial take on the matter.

In fact, and this is the third point, the broad view regarding labor mobility was all that our data were capable of measuring anyway. We did not have longitudinal data that offered patterns of labor force participation. All we had were data that measured the probability of landing a job in any earnings quartile conditional on loss of a job from any particular quartile.

Because factually we were limited by what our data measured, rhetorically this modeling approach best addressed the audience's query, and the USA is often characterized as having relatively high labor mobility (Long and Ferrie 2003), we had a very easy time selecting a model where mobility was derived from only the last labor market experience. This approach allowed us to be agnostic about whether those who started in a particular earnings quartile should persist in the quartile over the whole of their lifetimes—we let the data speak for themselves. As an example of how this plays out in the final model, a draw of a number, say 0.16 for returning to work would imply that first quartile workers would stay put, while second third and fourth quartile workers would shift down an earnings quartile when taking their next job. By contrast, a higher draw, say 0.72, would move a previous first or second quartile worker up one earnings quartile, while a third or fourth quartile worker would stay put. At the extremes, a draw of 1.0 would land any worker a new job in the highest earnings quartile, and a 0.0 would move any worker to the lowest earnings quartile for their next job. There we have it: synthetic labor mobility as our audience requested.

Our second question concerned how much of our measured impact of unemployment on savings was due to simply being out of work and how much could be attributed to the *timing* of spells. Notice that it was the timing aspect that sparked interest in the research design from the beginning, and yet we had managed to build a simulation that actually stopped short of answering the question. We were so taken with our progress that we fell short of our goal! To put the problem in perspective, recall President John F. Kennedy's goal of for the United States to land a man on the moon and return him safely to Earth (Kennedy 1961). It would have been difficult for NASA to live down missing the second part of that objective because the events transpired in physical space, but in a simulation, there is little in the way of physical evidence to remind the researcher of whether they the objective has been achieved. Building the model was (and in my experience usually is) enjoyable and as such it can be somewhat mesmerizing. Peer review helped us to fix this oversight, but not all projects have the same level of scrutiny available to them. The key point here is that part of the design team's work must be to review whether the simulation in fact addresses the research question being asked.

If the point is to inform policy, and the policy maker is not familiar with the process undertaken by the researcher/analyst, then the risk of misinforming the audience is unfortunately quite high. Thus, reviewing the work and asking whether it addresses the question the research claims it does should explicitly be made a part of the original protocol for simulation in the context of policy analysis.

As for how we addressed the problem of measuring the timing impact as distinguished from the general unemployment impact, we randomized a key model process to serve as a counterfactual. We harvested the precise number of simulated unemployment periods as observed for each worker type and case and redistributed them randomly across the life cycle earnings history. Doing this was fairly straightforward. We simply tracked the percentage of time that all cases spent unemployed in the primary run, say "x" percent, and then built a new matched case for every one we had generated. In the matched case, all else but the distribution of the unemployment periods was kept the same. Specifically, in each period, the matched case was assigned a lottery number (287 of them—one for each monthly period from January 1980 forward), the lowest "x" percent of these random numbers were tagged as unemployment periods, and in these periods, no wages or related contributions were credited to the second, matched, case. Then we compared the results between the primary run's probabilistic pattern of unemployment and the subsequent run's random pattern of otherwise equal unemployment—the difference in the two retirement balances measured the timing impact. While previously, earnings quartile jumps tracked the completion of unemployment spells in our primary case, changing the placement of these spells required some thought as to how unemployment timing and earnings mobility were interacting. After some work considering a number of options, we opted not to vary the timing of earning quartile changes; doing so would have made it more difficult to attribute the difference in timing alone—and we needed to address just the timing issue.

Of course, our decision here benefitted from review. Having implemented these changes, we sought out new audiences for external review. When presented to subsequent audiences, both the quartile-switching method and the timing impact estimation method were found to be in line with research objectives.

2.5.8   Stopping Rules

The final question was when to stop generating Monte Carlo data and proceed to writing up results. Determining a stopping rule is not a trivial issue. Stopping too soon reduces confidence in the results, but running the machine longer is wasteful and delays interpretation of the results. Delays at this (or any) stage should be kept to a minimum because delays limit the opportunity to afford decision makers a longer timeframe with which to make decisions. In the case we are working on, however, there was no explicit decision timeframe, and so we could address the question without any deadline-type constraint. That said, recall from the very first sentence of this chapter that the decision to postpone choosing a policy can carry its own salient risk. In general, the number of Monte Carlo iterations required is a function of the complexity of the process generating the data; building a method by which to collect and analyze results of small numbers of runs can be part of this process as well. Our initial simulation ran 25 cases for each of the eight worker types and their randomized unemployment-spell counterparts as well. Gathering 25×16 (400) data points required each of our 25×8 (200) hypothetical workers to engage in 287×4 lotteries or roughly 229,600 random numbers (the first three for unemployment, duration, and reemployment wage quartile, the fourth for randomizing the unemployment patters ex post to generate the 200 counterpart timing impact analogues). Running this sequence and recording a summary of the life cycle data generated by the process took about 3 seconds (s), and every great once in a while, the computer would freeze and crash before preserving results. Gathering 1,000 data points on our 16 workers required us to run 40 batches of 25, a procedure which took about 3 minutes (min). (Notice the nonlinearity. This is a little longer than we might expect since 40 times 3 yields 120 s or 2 min.) As we ran 3-min batches, we would copy and paste summary stats on the maximum, minimum, median, average, interquartile range, and standard deviation for measures of interest (the percent loss, dollar loss, percent of periods unemployed, and average market return over periods of unemployment). We could look at how different these batches were to see whether our distributions were stable; when we found they were not stable, we knew we needed to run the process longer

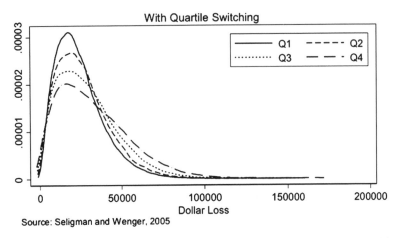

Source: Seligman and Wenger, 2005

Fig. 2.3 Simulated distribution of Dollar losses, men. *Source*: Seligman and Wenger (2006)

and create bigger batches of results. We next scaled the procedure up by a factor of 10 and began running batches of 10,000. Computationally, we noticed that these batches took longer than 30 min—they tended to take about 2 hours. (Gathering 10 times the data appeared to take more than 40 times as long.) What's more, the probability of a computer crash mid-run was important to consider. Further, we noticed that our summary statistics could still vary significantly via standard statistical tests (*t*-tests), so we scaled up the procedure by another factor of 10. We did this not by simply adding a zero to our do-loop; we did it by building off of the 10,000 batch model. This was preferable because it reduced the risk of loss from a computer crash and because we could distribute the runs across a couple of machines. In fact, we tasked two machines to each run 50,000 cases in 5(×2) batches of 10,000 and compared results—they were found to be statistically equivalent. To choose the final Monte Carlo sample we worked with for reporting results, we engaged all of our 50,000 case samples for a total sample size of 100,000 runs. Having a big data set like this allowed us to go beyond simply reporting summary statistics for our data. We could reference plots of full distributions to observe impacts. Figure 2.3 is a picture of the probability density function depicting estimated dollar losses stemming from unemployment (total effects, timing, and otherwise).

We can see from the graph that workers who begin their careers in the first quartile experience much more concentrated (certain) dollar losses (the solid Q1 line), whereas workers who begin their career in the fourth quartile (the highest paid) experience much more variable losses (the dash–dot–dash Q4 line).

When we considered losses as a proportion of lifetime savings, we found impacts sometimes as large as 20%, but that it appeared much more common to lose 10% or less—a level small enough for a wise worker to build into his or her savings plan. Finally, regarding timing, we noted average timing impacts on average accounted for 6–8% of the total losses, but that, from case to case, timing impacts could be negative, positive, or neutral (Seligman and Wenger 2006).

2.6 So What

This chapter has addressed a simple question—how the creation of possible worlds can help us understand and explore policy issues. Our "worlds" (really, partial environments) are synthetic, but they let us travel out of sample to the future and to any hypothetical counterfactual we might imagine for policy. Policy makers can use simulation data like those generated and discussed in this chapter to consider what the changes from private employer pensions to retirement savings might imply for transferred equity investment risks toward workers. This transfer may affect the design of Social Security minimum benefits legislation or motivate regulation stipulating that workers hold some small proportion of their accounts in cash or low-risk liquid securities, like US Treasury Bonds, which can be sold with proceeds to be invested in equities during periods of unemployment to counter-timing effects. Policy makers can also decide that based on the results of the work, none of these actions is warranted. In this latter case, the simulation will still have been important to undertake for two reasons: first, the inaction is conscious and informed, and second, if conditions change, new data on equities and unemployment patterns can be fed into the model so that new results are now quite a bit easier to generate.

In using simulation models, it is important to remember that assumptions drive results, and that there are many tacit assumptions we make by way of omission as well as by way of inclusion. In most cases, the omission of considering a single factor is very straightforward; it simply assumes that the future will be like the present. But just as in the example on German emigration to the USA following World War I, for Social Security, the number of elderly has grown over time—so omitting consideration of this population's future growth patterns is problematic. Policy advice based on such a model would not predict future outcomes where people continue to live longer lives and could have disastrous fiscal implications for the society the program is meant to serve.

Generally, there are two motives for omission. First, the factor may not be very important for the analysis; second, people may not have the requisite knowledge about how to include it. Over time, as society's policies have become more complex, more and more factors have become important. While our facility for inclusion has improved, it has done so in ways that are discontinuous, and that makes for one of the biggest challenges any simulation faces—false precision. Consideration of the problem of false precision here makes for but one anecdote, but false precision is an immense challenge because often the policy audience (be they the other members of a household, a business firm, or the US Congress) as consumers of the information are not in a place to appreciate or critique the producer of that information. This inability to assess could be because the audience lacks the technical skill and because it is not common for the designers and users of these models to spend a lot of effort explaining technical details to policy audiences. False precision arises for a number of reasons, but fundamentally, it is due to improper consideration of factors in order of importance. Does this hazard suggest that we not proceed with synthetic constructionist analysis? On the contrary, it suggests that people take time with what they build, and that they share their methods and intermediate results with audiences of fellow simulation designers and take time to audit the work. There is no substitute for thinking about one's work critically before presenting it to less technically capable audiences.

Acknowledgments The author would like to acknowledge the editorial assistance of Stephen Roll. Additionally, the author gratefully acknowledges the collaborative work of Jeffrey Wenger, coauthor of the simulation the article is based on. Others made meaningful contributions to that work as well, in particular seminar participants at the RAND Corporation, University of Georgia, UC Santa Cruz, and UC Berkeley, Alan Auerbach, Carlos Dobkin, Michael Hurd, Nicole Maestas, Jim Poterba, Karl Scholz, James Smith, all made beneficial comments on the work at various stages. Ben Zipperer assisted with the analysis of the SIPP data, and the W. E. Upjohn Institute for Employment Research granted funding in support of the research this article is based on.

References

Akerlof, G. A. and J. L. Yellen 1985. A Near-Rational Model of the Business Cycle, With Wage and Price Inertia. *The Quarterly Journal of Economics*, 100 (s) 823–838.

Auerbach, A.J. and L.J. Kotlikoff. 1985. ""Simulating Alternative Social Security Responses to the Demographic Transition" *National Tax Journal*, 38(2) 153–168.

Burtless, G. 2000. How Would Financial Risk Affect Retirement Income under Individual Accounts?, *Briefs*, 5(1), Center for Retirement Research.

Efron, B. 1982. *The Jackknife, the Bootstrap and Other Resampling Plans*. Philadelphia, PA: Society for Industrial and Applied Mathematics.

Farber, H. S. 1999. Mobility and stability: The dynamics of job change in labor markets. In Ashenfelter, O. C. and Card, D. (eds), *Handbook of Labor Economics,* Vol. 3, Part 2. Elsevier Science, pp. 2439–2483.

Kennedy, J. F. 1961. Special Message to the Congress on Urgent National Needs. *Congressional Record* 107 (May 25, 1961).

Long, J. and J. Ferrie. 2003. Labor Mobility. In Joel Mokyr (ed.), *The Oxford Encyclopedia of Economic History*. Oxford, UK: Oxford University Press.

Madrian, B. C. and L. J. Lefgren. 2000. An Approach to Longitudinally Matching the Current Population Survey. *Journal of Economic and Social Measurement* 26: 31–62.

Neftci, S. N. 1984. Are economic time-series asymmetric over the business-cycle. *Journal of Political Economy*, 92: 307–328.

Raychaudhuri, S. 2008. Introduction to Monte Carlo Simulation. *Proceedings of the 2008 Winter Simulation Conference* S. J. Mason, R. R. Hill, L. Mönch, O. Rose, T. Jefferson, J. W. Fowler eds. (accessible on-line via the INFORMS-SIM Web site ‹http://www.informs-sim.org›)

Samwick, A. A. and J. Skinner. 2004. How will 401(k) pension plans affect retirement income? *American Economic Review*, 94: 329–343.

Seligman, J. S. and J. B. Wenger. 2006. Asynchronous risk: retirement savings, equity markets, and unemployment. *Journal of Pension Economics and Finance*, 5(3) 237–255.

Silvapulle, P. and M. J. Silvapulle 1999. Business Cycle Asymmetry and the Stock Market. *Applied Financial Economics,* 9: 109–115.

Yellen, J. L. 1984. Efficiency wage models of unemployment. *American Economic Review*, 74: 200–205.

Vose, D. 2008. *Risk Analysis, A Quantitative Guide* (Third ed.). New York, NY: John Wiley & Sons.

Chapter 3
Using Simulation as a Scenario Builder for Decision Making: A Case Study Using the Nurse-Family Partnership Program in Louisiana

Roy L. Heidelberg and James A. Richardson

Abstract In this chapter, we discuss the use of Monte Carlo simulation to develop a cost–benefit analysis of the Nurse-Family Partnership (NFP) program in Louisiana. We discuss how we used information from studies conducted in other cities and times to inform our analysis of the program and detail the decisions made about the relevance of these empirical studies to a separate context altogether. The NFP program is an early childhood intervention program with long-term expected benefits, so we also discuss how to incorporate this information into the decision-making apparatus of public policy programs. Uncertainty is a feature we must deal with in public affairs, and this chapter attempts to illustrate how this can be done through a case study.

3.1 Introduction

Research in public affairs should always have a practical component. Applying our research, however, is not as simple as transporting ideas and findings in one context into another spatiotemporal setting. Contexts and conditions change, and often our research is not directly applicable to the situation in which we want to use it. Nevertheless, we are challenged frequently with the application of our knowledge, and these challenges result in decisions being made about the use of data and findings when the situation is in flux. In this chapter, we discuss the decisions made in a project in which we were asked to analyze a program in the present based on the studies that were initiated as long as two decades ago.

R.L. Heidelberg (✉)
The Ohio State University, 1810 College Rd., Columbus, OH 43210, USA
e-mail: royheidelberg@gmail.com

J.A. Richardson
Louisiana State University, 3200 Patrick Taylor Hall, Baton Rouge, LA 70803, USA
e-mail: parich@lsu.edu

A. Desai (ed.), *Simulation for Policy Inquiry*, DOI 10.1007/978-1-4614-1665-4_3,
© Springer Science+Business Media, LLC 2012

In 2010, we were asked to conduct an economic analysis of the Nurse-Family Partnership (NFP) program in Louisiana. The NFP program provides professional support to vulnerable first time mothers and their babies. It is designed to provide nurse-support visits to the homes of first time mothers-to-be beginning during pregnancy and continuing through the child's second birthday.[1] The purpose is to provide the mothers with the support necessary to have a healthy pregnancy and to consistently provide competent care to their children. The NFP program targets women who are with low income, unmarried, and teenagers.

The NFP program follows a model that is replicated in every state in which it is utilized. The nurses stress (1) positive health-related behavior including appropriate diets and reducing the use of cigarettes, alcohol, and illegal substances, (2) proper care by the mothers for their children, and (3) personal development, including family planning, educational choices and opportunities, and participation in the workforce. Dr. David Olds, Professor of Pediatrics, Psychiatry, and Preventive Medicine at the University of Colorado, Denver, started the program in the 1970s and has been instrumental in persuading the federal government and other states to invest in the program and to maintain the uniformity of the program in all states. With other colleagues, he conducted a series of controlled studies in Elmira, New York; Denver, Colorado; and Memphis, Tennessee over two decades. Randomized controlled samples of families participating in the NFP program and families who chose not to participate in the program were followed over periods of 3, 6, 9, 12, and 15 years. The results of these studies suggested that the program positively influenced the outcomes of both teenage mothers and their children in a cost-effective manner. Consequently, the program was implemented in select cities around the country in 1996, funded by the US Department of Justice, Office of Juvenile Justice and Delinquency Prevention. The program has now spread to 28 states as of October 2009. Louisiana has been participating in the program since 1999 and it now covers 52 parishes (counties) in the state.

This study was funded by a grant from the Pew Charitable Trusts and administered through Tulane University. We did not have the time nor resources to complete a study as had been done in Elmira, Denver, or Memphis. Consequently, our challenge was to adapt the empirical findings from these studies to the NFP program provided and funded in the state of Louisiana.

In designing our study, we had to determine how to observe indeterminate future decisions about the use of public assistance. We decided to utilize Monte Carlo simulation (MCS) in lieu of simply applying central tendency statistics to our analysis. A valuable use of simulation is that it serves as a complement to empirical studies in order to elaborate on the applicability of empirical findings in other contexts (Carlson 2011). This is especially applicable in economic and community development work, where benefit–cost analyses are utilized for deciding upon the appropriateness and

---

[1] Not all young mothers continue with the program for the full 30 months for which assistance is provided, but the program is designed to allow young mothers to have this much assistance if they want it.

strategic utility of certain policies. It is well known that benefit–cost analyses are inhibited by the difficulty of assigning prices and values to important considerations, such as human life and health or happiness and satisfaction. A less often discussed challenge to benefit–cost analyses is that it is very difficult to conduct when the consequences of the public policy extend for long periods of time and affect large, diverse populations. In our case, we had to determine how to observe a decision by an individual mother about the use of public assistance in the future. We used the MCS to introduce some controlled randomization into that observation recognizing that contexts differ and individual behavior is not constant over time.

In this case study, we are applying the MCS model to the NFP program in Louisiana. We believed that MCS was the appropriate technique because it permitted us to incorporate uncertainty into our analysis. This is important because of the difficulties inherent in monetizing desirable outcomes of social programs such as reduced teen pregnancy and crime prevention. It is also important because we cannot observe the multitude of factors that contribute to an individual's decisions to apply for or not to apply for public assistance programs. This is a very important factor in the analysis of social programs in which people elect to participate, and it is not often included in an analysis of public assistance programs. MCS allowed us to explore what might happen under multiple uncertain but potential circumstances by embedding the uncertainty about the decision to participate in welfare programs through the use of probabilistic functions.

Another quality of the Monte Carlo technique that is especially useful is that it enables the researcher to generate additional data from statistics provided in separate contexts. In this case, we used studies in the three cities mentioned above (Elmira, New York; Denver, Colorado; and Memphis, Tennessee) in order to provide information on a program intended to reduce dependency upon social programs and improve the quality of life and opportunities for teen mothers and their children in a different state (Louisiana). The use of studies conducted over many years presented challenges to our design because of variations in the reporting of statistics, which we will discuss in Sect. 3.2. Nevertheless, once we settled upon how to apply the statistics from the various studies, we were able to run three separate scenarios that randomize the unobserved characteristics that may influence the likelihood that an individual would use public assistance. The MCSs were used as scenario builders in order to provide information about the monetizable effects of the program and to identify factors that influence the potential outcomes of the benefits that might accrue.

We begin with a brief introduction of the scope of the work required for the study. Section 3.2 discusses the reports and studies that inform our analysis. Section 3.3 presents the savings calculated based on our models, and Sect. 3.4 briefly discusses the non-monetizable benefits that could be a part of the decision to fund the program and how we decided to address them in our reporting of results. Section 3.5 summarizes the discussion and reflects upon the use of MCS as a scenario builder.

3.2 Scope of Work for the NFP Project in Louisiana

The scope of work for the NFP project in Louisiana was straightforward: provide the best estimate of any savings for other public assistance programs that can be reasonably connected to the NFP program. The purpose of the request for the study is obvious since evidence-based policy has become a focus in public affairs as emphases shift to outcomes related to public spending. Benefit–cost analyses in particular are a common attempt to measure how good an "investment" certain spending programs are. Nevertheless, a straightforward task does not necessarily imply a straightforward method of finding the answer. In line with many other studies of this sort, our baseline approach was a benefit–cost analysis, but such an approach presents its own complex array of complex issues.

A 1998 study by the RAND Corporation estimated that the NFP program returns nearly four dollars in improved outcomes and reduced public assistance demands across both generations for every dollar invested (Karoly et al. 1998). This study extended the analysis to include various discount rates and savings to governments and overall benefits to society. A study focusing upon crime reduction by the Washington State Institute for Public Policy suggested a higher rate of return for the NFP program than for other comparable programs, including pre-kindergarten education, for children aged 3 and 4. These studies established very high expectations for the outcome of any study being conducted in which early childhood development programs, such as the NFP, are being analyzed.

Many of the other benefit–cost analyses are based on the findings from the controlled experiments conducted by Dr. Olds and his fellow researchers in communities in New York, Tennessee, and Colorado (Kitzman et al. 1997, 2000; Olds et al. 1994, 1997, 1998, 2002, 2004a, b, 2007, 2010). The experiments conducted in Elmira, New York focused primarily upon the child outcomes. These outcomes certainly are of interest to public policy, but they are a challenge from the standpoint of an economic analysis. A critical difficulty is establishing accurate and valid shadow prices for an outcome with such a long-term horizon as child behavioral and emotional outcomes.[2]

More immediate outcomes, in particular the use of other social assistance programs, can be quantified more reasonably. The studies in Memphis, Tennessee, and Denver, Colorado, provide insight into how the NFP program potentially influences the demand upon other social assistance programs that can be quantified and monetized and which are used extensively by many households in lower income categories.

In a 2008 RAND study entitled *Valuing Benefits in Benefit–Cost Studies of Social Programs*, Karoly (2008) divided social programs based on how frequently other studies monetized the outcomes. The division demonstrated how few outcomes actually have established monetization procedures while there remains a lack of consensus on monetizing many social outcomes. In Table 3.1, we provide a break-down based on this discussion in the report.

---

[2]A shadow price is a computed or estimated price as opposed to an actual price determined in the market place. The shadow price reflects the same concept of the opportunity cost of an activity to society. The purpose is to establish a dollar value for public outcomes that are not typically monetized.

Table 3.1   Social program and analytical monetization

Outcomes never or rarely monetized
- Child/youth behavioral/emotional outcomes (e.g., behavior problems, school suspensions/expulsions, mental health outcomes)
- Child/youth cognitive outcomes (e.g., IQ scores)
- K–12 grades, school attendance, school engagement
- General health status of children/youth
- Contraceptive use
- Adult parenting measures
- Marriage and divorce
- Adult mental health
- Adult reproductive health
- Employment
- Income and poverty status

Outcomes without clear consensus on monetization
- Achievement test scores
- High school graduation
- College attendance
- Teen pregnancy
- Tobacco use, alcohol abuse, illicit drug use
- Crime and delinquency
- Child abuse and neglect
- Earnings

Outcomes with more-established methodology for monetization
- Special education use
- Grade retention
- Transfer payments and other means-tested program

Adapted from Karoly 2008

The outcomes that are challenging to monetize are still important through indirect effects upon other public expenditures by influencing the behavior of the mother and/or child. These outcomes can arguably be even more important than, say, a reduction in expenditures on public assistance programs. As Karoly et al. (1998) noted:

> Cost-savings analysis is a useful tool because, when the results are positive, it provides strong support for the program worth. That is, it shows that only a portion of the benefits—those easily monetizable—outweigh the program's entire cost. However, because only some of the benefits are taken into account, a negative result does not indicate that a program shouldn't be funded. *Policymakers must then decide whether the nonmonetizable benefits—e.g., gains in IQ, in parent-child relations, in high school diplomas---are worth the net monetary cost to the government.* (emphasis added)

We confronted two major challenges as we attempted to project the benefits from the NFP program for the state of Louisiana. First, we recognized that there are non-monetizable factors that have a prominent role in the judgment about whether or not to support and fund a program with public dollars. Second, decisions are nevertheless often made on incomplete information, and sometimes this is a necessary condition for reaching a consensus. This uncertainty played a major factor in our analysis, and it was through the use of MCS that we were able to partially account for it in reporting our findings. Using the Monte Carlo technique did not enable us to quantify the unquantifiable aspects of the benefit–cost calculation, but it did permit us to consider another uncertain factor—how might individuals who utilize the program change their behavior with respect to other public programs? It was important to consider that we did not know, with certainty, under what conditions individuals who chose to participate in this program would actually use or bypass other public services.

Finally, the studies conducted on the NFP program focused upon public programs for the poor. We had to deal with the practical issue that public programs change over time. In the time since the Elmira, Denver, and Memphis studies were initiated, welfare reform dramatically transformed Assistance to Families with Dependent Children (AFDC) into Temporary Assistance to Needy Families (TANF), and Medicaid coverage expanded. This issue of changing public programs is a challenge to anyone dealing with longitudinal studies. Consequently, we made the practical decision to assume that information about AFDC could be applied to TANF, even though the two programs were structurally very different.

3.3   Tests and Results in Elmira, Denver, and Memphis Relating to NFP Program

We started our analysis of the economic outcomes of the NFP program in Louisiana focused primarily upon the studies conducted in Memphis and Denver, mainly because these were studies conducted in large cities and were done more recently than the studies in Elmira, New York.

Our central concern was to develop meaningful parameters from the results of the controlled tests in other cities in order to construct impact analyses of the program activities in Louisiana. Because the studies in New York, Colorado, and Tennessee developed over a long period of time, the statistical techniques used to determine the effect of the programs varied.[3] In some cases, the effect was discussed as a difference of the means between the control group (those mothers who did not receive any nurse treatment) and the treatment group, while in other cases the effect size was reported. Later in the report we will note how the studies varied from each other (see Table 3.7), but first we will explain how our interpretation of the parameters depended upon the statistical treatment of the program analysis.

Where possible, we used the effect sizes determined either by the authors of the studies or derived by us when the necessary data were available. For example, based on the Memphis program and focusing on the 6-year study, mothers who had

---

[3]Dr. Olds acknowledges that the reporting of the results evolved as the statistical techniques became more refined. This, however, is to be expected as studies are conducted over long periods of time.

Table 3.2 Variables measuring social assistance programs in research of Nurse-Family Partnership program

Observed social benefit variable	Study basis	Effect size	Confidence interval
Months on AFDC/TANF per year (0–9 years)	Memphis, 9	−0.14	−0.25 to −0.04
Months on food stamps per year (0–9 years)	Memphis, 9	−0.17	−0.28 to −0.07
Months of AFDC (54–72 months)	Memphis, 6	−0.22	–
Months of food stamps (54–72 months)	Memphis, 6	−0.24	–
Months of Medicaid (54–72 months)	Memphis, 6	−0.15	–
Months received AFDC (0–60)[a]	Memphis, 3	3.64	0.88 to 6.40
Months received food stamps (0–60)[a]	Memphis, 3	3.47	1.07 to 5.88

Note: The Denver 2- and 4-year studies did not find any significant difference between the NFP participants and the control group in either AFDC, Food Stamp, or Medicaid use
[a]The effect size was not calculated for the Memphis 3-year study, so the difference of means is given. In this case, the NFP group used less, so this calculation is the control group mean minus the NFP group mean

participated in the NFP program were likely to use the AFDC program 0.22 months per year less than mothers who had not participated in the visitation program.[4]

Otherwise, we depended upon the difference between the means of the two groups and the confidence interval at the 95% level. This provided a *range of possibilities* for outcomes in our analysis; for example, after 9 years, mothers in Memphis who had participated in the program were likely to participate in the AFDC program between 0.04 and 0.25 months per year fewer than mothers who did not participate in the NFP program. When we constructed the effect sizes, we did so using only the standard deviation of the treatment group (those mothers who did receive nurse assistance) in order to standardize the effect based on the variation in the outcomes. Table 3.2 provides a brief overview of the significant variables.

From Table 3.2, we use the confidence intervals to explore the range of variation around which an individual may or may not elect to use public assistance. The confidence intervals provide us with the high and low points of difference compared to the members of the population who do not have NFP but are in a similar socio-economic situation. For example, if we assumed that the program had a very large effect on the number of months an individual used AFDC/TANF, then we may, from the first row of Table 3.2, model each individual as using 0.25 months fewer of AFDC/TANF over 9 years. However, this approach is too rigid.

Instead, we impute some probability that an individual will use public assistance in a given month based on these observed differences. Factors other than enrollment in the NFP program can influence an individual's decision to use public assistance, but these factors are not observed. A key assumption in our cost–benefit analysis is that there are many factors other than enrolling in the NFP program that can influence a person's propensity to use public assistance programs. The randomization of the MCS enables us to introduce the possibility of exogenous, unobserved factors

---

[4]These studies were initiated prior to Personal Responsibility and Work Opportunity Act of 1996, commonly referred to as the Welfare Reform Act.

Table 3.3 Imputed probability of using public assistance in any given month

	Likelihood of using AFDC	Likelihood of using food stamps
Low-difference estimate	0.47	0.62
Mid-difference estimate	0.43	0.58
High difference estimate	0.40	0.55
Control average	0.49	0.65

into our analysis. Another simplifying assumption is that an individual makes an independent decision about the use of public assistance each month.[5] We want to isolate the program's effect without isolating the individual from other potential effects. So we compared multiple iterations of an individual with the same propensity to request public assistance influenced only by the suggested effect of the program on her inclination to request or her need to request. These imputed probabilities are listed in Table 3.2.

To determine the probability that an individual would use public assistance, we simply extracted the average number of months measured and calculated the ratio based on the total months observed. So, if the study was conducted over 10 years (120 months) and the average number of months in which assistance was used was 35.4 months, then the probability that an individual would request assistance in any given month was (35.4/120) or 0.295. We did this for all studies and used the most reasonable estimate based on the level of confidence, the number of individuals in the study, and the reported significance.

Table 3.3 provides a breakdown of how we operationally define our parameters based on the findings in Table 3.2. We considered our analysis based on the difference in the use of public assistance suggested by the studies on the program. Based on these studies, we considered three different levels of difference in the likelihood of using public assistance: high, mid, and low. Consequently, we have three different scenarios to compare—when the difference in the probability of using public assistance between the control group and the treatment group is low, mid, or high. We could not directly use the information in Table 3.2 because, in some cases, the studies showed variation between the outcomes of the same variable or, in some cases, it was necessary to aggregate the information in order to make it meaningful and interpretable. We generated our best estimates of the NFP program as a public investment by comparing how substantially the program reduced future use of public assistance. In this manner, we were able to construct a clear benefit–cost analysis because the program, a form of public assistance itself, was expected to reduce other utilizations of public assistance.

---

[5]It could be argued that individuals' use of public assistance in the prior month increases the likelihood that they will request such assistance in the present month. We acknowledge that this is the case, but for our purposes, and in order to minimize the complexity of the model, we assumed that each month is an independent decision based strictly on differences suggested by the effect of the program.

We based our operational definitions strictly on the Memphis studies for two reasons: the Memphis studies are more recent and Memphis is more similar demographically to large metropolitan areas of Louisiana. This is also meaningful because Memphis is similar demographically with many of the large metropolitan areas in Louisiana. It could be argued that there is no effect on social welfare programs (supported by the Denver studies), but we proceeded as though there was based on the Memphis studies. The reason that we assumed a difference is that, as noted, we had to make choices about the studies that we felt most completely fit the Louisiana economic and social environment. Given the similarities of Memphis and Louisiana, we felt that basing our analysis on the Memphis studies would provide a more reflective data set when using this information in a comparative context, and these studies did find an effect.

Our calculations included the impact of the program upon AFDC/TANF benefits and Food stamps. We excluded the Medicaid program because, according to our literature research, the NFP program has no discernible impact on Medicaid usage; the studies did not find a statistically significant difference between the two populations in their use of Medicaid. This is very important because other studies have included Medicaid as a program in which the use is discernibly reduced by the NFP program. This is highly problematic because the regression analyses do not suggest that the impact is any different from zero. Thus, we excluded Medicaid use from our model.

Additionally, we used the 10-year point as our maximum based on the 12-year Memphis studies, which did not find a statistically significant difference in the effect of the program on other public assistance programs after year 10. This suggests that the program has a lifecycle for every cohort who uses it, and the benefits expire after a time. Table 3.4 provides a breakdown of the findings in the Memphis studies regarding the social assistance variables. As is clear, the influence of the program on the use of Medicaid is never significant at the 5% level, meaning there is no statistical difference between the populations.

3.4   The Workings of the Monte Carlo Model

The model that we used is very simple and straightforward. We composed a matrix that consisted of 120 columns and 6,184 rows. The 120 columns represent months over 10 years, and the 6,184 rows represent the population of low-income families with children. The state of Louisiana served roughly 11,000 families through the Family Independence Temporary Assistance Program (FITAP)[6] in 2008, a component

---

[6]FITAP is the Louisiana cash grant assistance program for families suffering financial hardship. According to the Department of Social Services in Louisiana, the goal of FITAP is "to decrease the long-term dependency on welfare assistance by promoting job preparation and work." Like all TANF-related state support, it is not a lifetime assistance program and is intended to provide families an opportunity to recover from a "financial crisis." The average grant for a family in Louisiana is $200.

Table 3.4 Breakdown of findings in Memphis studies pertaining to public assistance programs

		Control	NFP participants	Mean difference	Confidence interval
3-year study[a]	Total months mother or child received AFDC	36.19	32.55	3.64	0.88–6.40
	Total months mother or child received food stamps	45.04	41.57	3.47	1.07–5.88
	Total months family received Medicaid	41.08	39.59	1.49	−0.88–3.86

				p value	Effect size
6-year study	Months of AFDC use (54–72 months)	8.96	7.21	0.01	−0.22
	Months of food stamps (54–72 months)	11.5	9.67	0.004	−0.24
	Months of Medicaid (54–72 months)	13.08	11.98	0.08	−0.15
9-year study	Annual average of months of AFDC use	5.92 (0.15)	5.21 (0.22)	0.008	−0.14
	Annual average of months of TANF use	4.01 (0.22)	3.39 (0.33)	0.117	−0.12
	Annual average of months of food stamps	7.80 (0.14)	6.98 (0.21)	0.001	−0.17
	Annual average of months of food stamps (ages 6–9)	5.92 (0.24)	4.89 (0.36)	0.017	−0.21
	Annual average of months of Medicaid	10.07 (0.13)	9.71 (0.19)	0.119	−0.09
	Annual average of months of Medicaid (ages 6–9)	8.74 (0.23)	8.79 (0.34)	0.889	0.01

[a]The effect size of the program was not calculated for the 3-year study, and the standard errors were not reported; so no effort was made to calculate for ourselves a standardized effect size. Instead, we used the raw difference in means, which provides less certainty because of the failure to standardize based on observed variation

of the federal TANF program. We chose the 6,184 number under the assumption that the NFP program could reasonably consider half of those families as *potential* clients, given the existing composition of this population in Louisiana and the feasibility of the program reported to us by the NFP program designers. The program will not serve all potential clients, so we assumed that it successfully enrolled 10% of the potential clientele. Practically speaking, the total number is not as important as the percentage that enroll in the NFP program; in this case, we assumed that the NFP program could serve 10% of potential clients.

Our focus in this study is on individuals who *qualify and may request* public financial assistance. Every cell was assigned a random number at each iteration. This random number was used to determine whether or not the cell used public assistance—either food stamps or TANF. The first 600 rows (10%) were considered clients of the NFP program. For each program (food stamps and AFDC/TANF), we ran simulations. The simulations were run based on the imputed probabilities in Table 3.3 and the three levels of difference in the use of assistance between NFP clients and the rest of the population—low, medium, and high. The 600 rows representing NFP clients were each assigned a threshold in accordance with the imputed probability. The remaining cells were assigned a threshold equal to the control value in Table 3.3. If the random number in the cell was *less than* the imputed probability, then that cell was counted as having used the assistance being considered (and assigned a one)

The model is able to produce two types of analysis. In one case, we can view the matrix as a cohort of 6,184 individuals viewed over 10 years, producing a savings rate for a total cohort. In another case, we can consider the matrix to be an analysis of the use of public assistance in any given month, thus producing a monthly savings generated from the program. This is achieved depending upon how the totals are summed: counting all of the ones in each row will provide data on how many months of public assistance are requested by the individuals in the cohort; counting the ones in the columns will show us how many individuals used public assistance in a given month. The model was run once for each scenario (low difference, medium difference, and high difference) and public assistance type (TANF or food stamps) combination.[7]

Tables 3.5 and 3.6 provide the descriptive statistics of the simulations. In Table 3.5, the descriptive statistics are collected 120 times for any given month (the totals of the columns). The untreated population is the baseline—if no individual enrolled in the NFP program and everyone had the same probability of using public assistance, then this is the distribution. In this case, at the median, 3,031 individuals elect to receive AFDC assistance and 4,004 elect to receive food stamps in any

---

[7] Another challenge with longitudinal studies of social programs is that the programs often change in response to external changes. In this case, we were required to use evidence constructed upon the basis of AFDC to analyze a completely different program (TANF) with a similar underlying objective, namely public assistance to families in financial need. There are very important structural differences between AFDC and the program that replaced it, TANF, most importantly the discretion left to the states to define their programs. AFDC was administered based on a federal definition of need, while TANF is a time-restricted program (families can only use the program for up to 5 years, unless otherwise restricted by states) where the demonstration of need is not sufficient for receiving assistance. This time restriction is certainly an important consideration in determining benefits from reduced use of public assistance, but all of the studies on the NFP were initiated under the policy of AFDC. Indeed, restricting how much an individual can use TANF actually undermines the potential benefits that the program brings through reducing public assistance demand, especially when a 10-year horizon is considered for the calculation of benefits. Consequently, our analysis was hampered by two considerations. First, the qualifications for TANF in Louisiana were not the same as qualifying for AFDC in New York, Tennessee, or Colorado. Second, our 10-year horizon must restrict the demand by putting a ceiling on the amount of assistance demanded. These factors, we determined, were not as important as gauging the relative difference generated from reducing public assistance demand, and so we considered our analysis as one that is structurally AFDC but based on the costs of TANF. This assumption would inevitably lead to an *overestimation* of the benefits wrought by the program.

Table 3.5 Descriptive statistics of Monte Carlo simulation by month

Untreated	Median	Mean	Standard deviation	Standard error	Kurtosis	Skewness	25th percentile	75th percentile	Min	Max
AFDC										
Estimate	3,031	3,029.933	283.675	3.151	0.543	−5.159	3,008	3,051.75	2,926	3,125
NFP										
Low	3,011.5	3,015.358	39.068	3.566	0.401	−4.785	2,991.5	3,041.25	2,894	3,113
Medium	2,991	2,991.733	44.250	4.039	0.561	−4.747	2,971	3,009	2,902	3,077
High	2,972	2,977.550	36.938	3.372	−0.313	−4.693	2,951	3,004.5	2,896	3,086
Food stamps										
Estimate	4,004.5	4,009.367	37.218	3.398	0.409	10.950	3,985	4,029.5	3,917	4,112
NFP										
Low	4,006	4,001.833	41.803	3.816	0.804	−4.970	3,979.75	4,027	3,871	4,117
Medium	3,978	3,975.917	40.058	3.657	−0.255	−4.943	3,946.75	4,004.25	3,875	4,073
High	3,957	3,954.142	36.818	3.361	−0.236	−4.878	3,927.75	3,981.25	3,852	4,041

These summary stats explore the simulation as a series of iterations in a given month. Thus, the numbers are the total number of individuals who would, given the imputed probabilities, request public assistance in that month, and the randomness is generated by the assumption that all other factors in their decision are equal. A way to interpret these numbers is to assume that the state is looking at this as a demographic of concern, and there is a total cost to the state in public assistance. The program (NFP) correlates with a reduced likelihood of requesting or utilizing public assistance, so the cost to the state is reduced. This reduction is the primary concern: we can compare the total cost to the state with and without the program and measure the savings based on the investment in the program

Table 3.6 Descriptive statistics of Monte Carlo simulation by individual

Untreated	Median	Mean	Standard deviation	Standard error	Kurtosis	Skewness	25th percentile	75th percentile	Min	Max
AFDC										
Estimate	60	59.195	6.455	0.589	−0.702	0.285	53	63	49	74
NFP										
Low	58	58.513	5.534	0.505	−0.154	−4.785	55	62	40	77
Medium	58	58.007	5.855	0.535	0.049	−4.747	54	62	36	77
High	58	57.779	6.404	0.585	0.279	−4.693	54	62	31	80
Food stamps										
Estimate	78	78.027	5.192	0.474	0.045	10.950	75	82	60	97
NFP										
Low	78	77.655	5.316	0.485	0.029	−4.970	74	81	60	97
Medium	77	77.152	5.800	0.529	0.083	−4.943	73	81	56	96
High	77	76.730	6.436	0.588	0.589	−4.878	73	81	48	95

These summary stats explore the simulation as a series of iterations of 6,184 individuals, 599 of whom enroll in the NFP program. Thus, the numbers are the average number of months that individuals can be expected to request or utilize public assistance based on general probability differences found in the research on the NFP program given month. The range (minimum and maximum) provides insight into the random nature of the simulation. We would expect that the mean and median would be very close together, and we also expect that the averages correspond to the probabilities assigned. In the case of AFDC assistance, the imputed probability is 0.49 and the percent of individuals who use the assistance in any given month is roughly 49.01%. The important thing to note, however, is that in any month the number of individuals who elect to use food stamps or AFDC ranges and is not constant across time, i.e., it is not consistently 49.01% of individuals who use TANF in a month. This variation is an important consideration when projecting costs and potential benefits.

With this important consideration in mind, the effect of the NFP is analyzed according to varying levels of effect. Two aspects from the descriptive statistics should be noted. First, we would expect that the minimum and the maximum would each decrease as the difference increases. However, in the case of AFDC, the minimum actually increases from "low" to "medium" and the maximum increases from "medium" to "high." This illustrates the nature of the randomization. Also, the standard error of AFDC-medium category is substantially higher than the other categories in AFDC. Again, this is a product of the randomization.

Table 3.6 provides the same information but under the assumption that 6,184 individuals are making binary decisions over 10 years (the totals of the rows). The numbers will be lower because this analysis takes the average demand at the individual level, whereas the previous analysis looks at the demand of all individuals in a given month. To interpret this table, consider the numbers to be the average of 6,184 individuals making a decision about whether or not to elect to receive public assistance. The row sum, then, represents the number of months in which individuals did receive public assistance.

Using these numbers from the MCS, we calculated both the expected costs of the TANF program and the food stamp program. We then compared the various scenarios in which the differences were presumed to be low, medium, or high and calculated the projected savings based on this randomization. With the savings calculated, we subtracted the cost of the program when roughly 10% of the population is involved in the NFP program. This provides the benefit–cost analysis based strictly on the reduced use of public assistance.

3.4.1 Costs

The Louisiana TANF plan primarily includes the FITAP and also includes programs such as the Kinship Care Subsidy Program. Unwed mothers qualifying for TANF assistance will receive the statewide FITAP grant, a flat amount of $188 per month (for a two-person household). This value was used to quantify the cost of TANF assistance.

The cost per capita of food stamps was derived from the Department of Social Services FY 08-09 report. The average payment per household was $287.36, and the average household size was 2.41 persons for a per person average of $119. This

Table 3.7 Costs used in computation of benefit–cost analysis

Food stamps (monthly per household)	
Low	210
Medium	240
High	270
FITAP (monthly per household)	
Flat grant	188
NFP	Total (per month)
Low	185,091
Medium	224,625
High	273,593
NFP	Total (per mother)
Low	7,416
Medium	9,000
High	10,962

value was used to impute the range of costs for the two-person families: low esti-mate = $210; medium estimate = $240; high estimate = $270 per month.

For a participating mother, the cost of the NFP program is carried through 2 years, after which that particular mother no longer receives any assistance through the pro-gram. As with any public program, there is a monthly cost. Consequently, we wanted to compute the savings using both scenarios: a participant in the program benefiting from the program over 10 years, and the savings in a given month given the cost of the program. Table 3.7 outlines the costs used in these computations. To serve 25 new mothers, the NFP program incrementally costs roughly $96,000 annually (more if a new supervisor is required).[8] We can presume that the program has a recurring cost each month for new enrollees, or we can measure the cost of a particular cohort. We also recognize that the program may have some variation in cost due to factors other than personnel costs. Consequently, we simulate based on three tiers of cost for the program (low, medium, and high). These calculations were based on the monthly cost of serving 600 individuals and the cost per individual (Table 3.7).

We also focused upon the calculation of cost and savings for a particular cohort, in this case all 600 individuals together. To do so, we included the possibility that there would be a range of costs, and thus based our calculations on the low, medium, and high estimates per individual. The cost of the program for this cohort equaled the total cost per individual (low = $7,416; medium = $9,000; high = $10,962) multi-plied by 600 individuals. This range of costs incorporates the estimate of an addi-tional $96,000 for another nurse for a cohort of 25 new participants. A discussion of these calculations is provided in more detail in Tables 3.13 and 3.14. In this case, we

---

[8]This information represents the cost of adding one new nurse to the program since the program specifically limits the number of cases that a nurse can handle. The cost of adding one new nurse came from the Louisiana Office of Public Health.

estimated that the program payments end after 2 years but the benefits (discussed below) continue to accrue through the tenth year.

3.4.2 Benefits (Savings)[9]

Calculating the savings from the program required us to compare how much would have been spent on the programs against how much would be spent if roughly 10% of qualified individuals enroll in the program. The cost of the TANF and food stamp programs was applied at each of the iterations of the simulation. The cost of the NFP program was applied to 600 of the observations that had a *reduced propensity to request public assistance*. Using the simulation we were able to compare the benefits with the costs for three separate scenarios. Scenario 1 focused upon the average individual. In this case, the mean values from Table 3.6 were used. The cost was calculated based on the values in Table 3.7. The total savings from the reduced probability of using TANF or food stamp assistance is shown in Table 3.8 at the individual level.

This same approach was used to compare the savings in a given month. Scenario 2 addressed the savings generated by the reduced demand for public assistance in an average month (based on the simulation of 6,184 individuals). This breakdown is provided in Table 3.9.

Finally, scenario 3 explored the full depth of the simulation. This calculation was actually sensitive to the size of the program, but it was also more responsive to randomness because it did not eliminate variation by using a calculation of central tendency. Essentially what we were looking at was a cohort of 6,184 individuals who all make a decision each month about the use of public assistance. Ten percent of this cohort has a lower propensity to use public assistance because of the NFP program, but the cost of this is the actual NFP program *for that cohort*. So, we compare the savings of these scenarios to the actual expenditures on only those 10% and do no presuppose recurring costs. This is an analysis of the investment in that particular cohort.

3.4.3 Savings–Cost Comparison

The NFP program estimates an incremental cost of roughly $96,000 to serve 25 new clients in a given year. If a new supervisor is required, the cost rises to $106,000; this suggests that the average person electing to participate in the NFP program will

---

[9]We use "mother" and "individual" interchangeably when discussing costs since the program focuses on pregnant women, but the ultimate benefits of the program (the reduction in other public assistance programs) will relate to the family once the child is born.

Table 3.8 Scenario 1—savings from NFP program on public assistance expenditures, TANF and food stamps, for the average individual

	Cost TANF	Difference	Food stamps (low)	Difference	Food stamps (med)	Difference	Food stamps (high)	Difference
Nonparticipants								
Baseline	$11,129		$16,386		$18,726		$21,067	
NFP participants								
Low	$11,000	$128	$16,308	$78	$18,637	$89	$20,967	$100
Medium	$10,905	$223	$16,202	$184	$18,517	$210	$20,831	$236
High	$10,862	$266	$16,113	$272	$18,415	$311	$20,717	$350

Table 3.9 Scenario 2—savings from NFP program on public assistance expenditures, TANF and food stamps, for the average month

	Cost TANF	Difference	Food stamps (low)	Difference	Food stamps (med)	Difference	Food stamps (high)	Difference
Nonparticipants								
Baseline	$569,627		$841,967		$962,248		$1,082,529	
NFP participants								
Low	$566,887	$2,740	$840,385	$1,582	$960,440	$1,808	$1,080,495	$2,034
Medium	$562,446	$7,182	$834,943	$7,025	$954,220	$8,028	$1,073,498	$9,032
High	$559,779	$9,848	$830,370	$11,597	$948,994	$13,254	$1,067,618	$14,911

increase costs by roughly $4,000 annually.[10] As mentioned above, the flat grant for TANF assistance is $188 per month (which is the cost we used for AFDC recognizing the differences in the two programs), and the cost of food stamps varies between roughly $210 and $270 dollars a month. If a household used these public assistance programs for each month of the year, the annual cost for TANF assistance would be $2,256 and the annual cost for food stamps would range from $2,520 to $3,240. These are costs that will be spent regardless of the NFP program, so in analyzing the impact of the program upon those social assistance program costs, it is important to consider that we are analyzing a system of individuals who are more or less likely to utilize this assistance that is already available. As noted previously, the NFP program does not compromise an individual's right to request assistance, but it does reduce the likelihood that she will.

With this in mind, we conducted three different analyses based on the simulation. The NFP program never pays for itself based solely on the savings generated from expected reductions in other public assistance programs. However, the NFP program does reduce the cost of other public assistance programs over time.

---

[10] We focused on the cost of adding a nurse and any variable costs, such as traveling. We assumed the nurse would be charged with overseeing up to 25 new clients and that the overhead costs would not increase. A new supervisor will be required if eight additional nurses are required, according to those who design the program.

Table 3.10 Net Savings of NFP program based on average individual projections

		NFP cost		
		Low	Medium	High
Low difference in probability				
Public	Low	−7,285	−8,869	−10,831
Assistance	Medium	−7,274	−8,858	−10,820
Cost	High	−7,262	−8,846	−10,808
Medium difference in probability				
Public	Low	−7,084	−8,668	−10,630
Assistance	Medium	−7,058	−8,642	−10,604
Cost	High	−7,032	−8,616	−10,578
High difference in probability				
Public	Low	−6,952	−8,536	−10,498
Assistance	Medium	−6,914	−8,498	−10,460
Cost	High	−6,875	−8,459	−10,421

Table 3.11 Net savings of NFP program based on average month projections

		NFP cost		
		Low	Medium	High
Low difference in probability				
Public	Low	−180,769	−220,303	−269,271
Assistance	Medium	−180,543	−220,077	−269,045
Cost	High	−180,317	−219,851	−268,819
Medium difference in probability				
Public	Low	−170,885	−210,419	−259,387
Assistance	Medium	−169,881	−209,415	−258,384
Cost	High	−168,878	−208,412	−257,380
High difference in probability				
Public	Low	−163,646	−203,180	−252,148
Assistance	Medium	−161,989	−201,523	−250,491
Cost	High	−160,332	−199,866	−248,834

First, for the average individual, the losses from the program range from a low of $6,875 (when the cost of the NFP program is low and the presumed difference in the probability of using other assistance is at its peak) to a high of $10,831 (when the presumed difference is lowest and the NFP program is presumed to be most costly). Table 3.10 provides a breakdown of the losses. As the NFP program more effectively reduces the likelihood that the individual will request other assistance, the savings to the state amount to roughly $4,000 more per person.

In Table 3.11, the average month is analyzed based on the simulation. In this case, the numbers appear higher because we are looking at the cost of the program not for a single individual over 10 years, but for a single month in which 6,184 individuals make a judgment about the use of public assistance, roughly 10% of whom are less inclined because of their participation in the NFP program. The NFP program in our simulated month costs between $160,000 and $269,000 more than the savings generated from reduced public assistance demand.

Arguably, our method of analyzing only the central tendencies fails to capture the nuances within the randomness of the simulation. To compensate for this, a third analysis was conducted in which all 6,184 individuals were analyzed across 10 years. As shown in Table 3.12, the projected savings from the program on TANF and food stamp usage is far greater when considered over this long-term horizon.

The total cost of the NFP program was calculated for 600 individuals fully completing the program to range between $4.4 and $6.5 million (see Table 3.13). Thus, in a scenario such as ours in which we have 738,480 person-months, the program must eliminate either at least 23,400 person-months of TANF assistance requests or 18,333 person-months of food stamp assistance requests (or some relative combination thereof). In fact, the program does not come close to this based on our operational definitions determined by the research: at most roughly 6,000 person-months of TANF assistance and 6,500 person-months of food stamp assistance were saved.[11] As Table 3.14 shows, the program does not sufficiently cover its cost through savings on public assistance programs when analyzed according to a cohort over 10 years. However, this analysis is confounded by the fact that TANF restricts the number of years that a family can receive assistance, something our model does not do. Consequently, one could argue that the savings are actually lower, or more negative.

The NFP program is unable to sustain itself based strictly on its impact on other public assistance programs. But this was never the primary intent of the program. As noted earlier, the program is intended to address individual well-being, maternal life course (improving the opportunities of young mothers), and childhood outcomes (such as educational attainment or reduced behavioral problems). It is very challenging to monetize such effects, but that does not mean we should neglect them in our consideration of policy. Improvements in these individual attributes may well reduce the use of other public assistance programs over time. The preceding section provides a benchmark for the program that it must meet in order to break even as a public investment. We used MCS in order to build a benefit–cost analysis that allowed for variation in the behavior of individuals deciding whether or not to utilize public assistance. But this model only allows us

---

[11]To calculate the person-months saved for TANF and food stamps, we used the presumption of a high difference in probability to use public assistance by NFP participants (relative to general population) and used the calculated savings from Table 3.12. We then divided by the monthly cost of the public assistance ($188 for TANF and $240 for food stamps) in order to generate the person-months saved.

Table 3.12 Scenario 3—savings from NFP program on public assistance expenditures, TANF and food stamps, for the cohort over 10 years

	Cost TANF	Difference	Food stamps (low)	Difference	Food stamps (med)	Difference	Food stamps (high)	Difference
Nonparticipants								
Baseline	$68,355,296		$101,034,570		$115,468,080		$129,901,590	
NFP participants								
Low	$68,026,484	$328,812	$100,846,200	$188,370	$115,252,800	$215,280	$129,659,400	$242,190
Medium	$67,438,608	$916,688	$100,193,100	$841,470	$114,506,400	$961,680	$128,819,700	$1,081,890
High	$67,173,528	$1,181,768	$99,642,690	$1,391,880	$113,877,360	$1,590,720	$128,112,030	$1,789,560

Table 3.13 Projected cost of NFP program for 600 individuals fully completing the program (one cohort)

Cost of NFP program			
Low	$7,416 per individual	600 individuals	$4,449,600
Medium	$9,000 per individual	600 individuals	$5,400,000
High	$10,962 per individual	600 individuals	$6,577,200

Table 3.14 Net savings of NFP program based on analysis of cohort

		NFP cost		
		Low	Medium	High
Low difference in probability				
Public	Low	−$3,932,418	−$4,882,818	−$6,060,018
Assistance	Medium	−$3,279,318	−$4,229,718	−$5,406,918
Cost	High	−$2,728,908	−$3,679,308	−$4,856,508
Medium difference in probability				
Public	Low	−$3,317,632	−$4,268,032	−$5,445,232
Assistance	Medium	−$2,571,232	−$3,521,632	−$4,698,832
Cost	High	−$1,942,192	−$2,892,592	−$4,069,792
High difference in probability				
Public	Low	−$3,025,642	−$3,976,042	−$5,153,242
Assistance	Medium	−$2,185,942	−$3,136,342	−$4,313,542
Cost	High	−$1,478,272	−$2,428,672	−$3,605,872

to set a benchmark for discussing the programs benefits and its potential for influencing individuals in a desirable manner. If society as a whole values the outcomes that are difficult to monetize at levels that would sustain the program, then the program is beneficial. This is a judgment that is not necessarily based solely on quantifiable criteria, such as dollars saved from other public assistance programs, since there is no consensus on how to assign value to the outcomes. We will discuss this aspect in the next section.

3.5   Non-Monetized Benefits

Public programs do not and should not function strictly on monetized benefits. Nevertheless, monetizing benefits, when possible, enables decision makers to judge the relative value inhered from those benefits that are less easily "valued." Undoubtedly, the public values programs that reduce crime, improve educational outcomes, and provide for better health outcomes. The NFP program explicitly states that the objective of the program is, among other things, to improve parental caregiving and maternal life course. Each of these components presumably has indirect effects upon children and the community.

The study done in Memphis at the 12-year point indicates that the long-term intent of the program is not strictly a reduction in spending on other public assistance programs, but rather on socioeconomic and behavioral outcomes. The outcomes of concern involve educational attainment as well as health/behavioral outcomes (such as cigarette use which has documented influences on children and long-term health issues). The Memphis study finds that the outcomes are influenced at the margins by the program. Indeed, the Memphis 12-year study suggested that after about 9 years, the benefits of the NFP program are related to behavioral improvements and not reduced spending by the public sector in other public assistance programs.

However, it should be discussed why these outcomes are difficult to monetize and therefore difficult to value from the public perspective. Two important effects of the program are reductions in criminal behavior and improved educational proficiency. Regarding the former, assume that the average cost of incarceration of teens is roughly $100,000. It would be fallacious to claim that preventing one individual from being incarcerated would lead to a savings of $100,000. The reason for this is that averages do not capture the marginal differences: an additional inmate can presumably use the same electricity and be supervised by the same corrections officers with only slight increases in the cost.[12] It is also true that most children do not get incarcerated, so only a small number of the children will be *expected* to be incarcerated; analytically, our concern is a counterfactual: how does the program succeed in preventing an individual who would have been imprisoned were it not for the intervention?. Claims based on counterfactuals are a daunting and problematic aspect of social science. Moreover, the cost of incarceration is measured based on the perspective of government, while the true benefits of a reduction in crime are enjoyed by individuals who are not victimized when they otherwise would be. The prevention of such a crime will have substantial benefits to society, but it is very difficult to monetize these benefits.

As for educational outcomes, the measurement of these differences matters very much when determining the value to the public. In the Memphis study, for example,

---

[12]The marginal cost of any operation will at some point exceed average cost. But ascertaining if marginal costs are less than or greater than average costs in assessing the value of an early childhood program is difficult. For example, the prison system is built; the number of guards needed is established; even the utilities associated with the facilities are defined. Preventing one person from going to jail does not save that many dollars; the marginal costs saved are most likely well below the average cost. At some point the prison system will not accommodate any additional prisoners, so the added costs of adding a new prisoner at this point will force additional costs at the prison. If these programs affect the long-term behavior of large groups of people, then we would not have to build as many prisons in the future, so the marginal costs saved from having more people in jail could be substantial and well above the average cost. In this case we are shifting the cost curves downward. The major point is that in making comparisons of possible savings from programs that ideally changes the behavior of young people must be carefully done.

the researchers determined that children whose parents participated in the NFP program scored three points higher, on average, than their counterparts on the Peabody Individual Assessment Test in reading and math. What this means for long-term outcomes is very uncertain. There may be correlative evidence that students who score higher on these tests have better opportunities, but the threshold is completely unknown, and it is not clear that three points, although statistically significant, is practically meaningful.

Another intended purpose of the program is to reduce subsequent pregnancies or prolong the time between pregnancies. This is a very challenging issue to discuss from an economic policy perspective. A reasonable case can be made that having children in close temporal proximity to each other can be beneficial to a working mother because, presuming she does not have any more children, her occupational path is less infringed. For example, a woman may have a child at 19 years of age and be forced to postpone her schooling. She could wait to have another child until after her schooling is complete, but then she will interrupt her career. This is especially pertinent to low-income mothers who are not as likely to have jobs that grant maternal leave. Alternatively, she could have her second child soon after her first, get additional use out of the materials used with her previous child, and perhaps postpone her commencement by one additional semester.

Ultimately, the findings based on monetized benefits are intended to give context to the considerations of this section. The easiest example would be to focus upon a single hypothetical cohort, as is done in Tables 3.13 and 3.14, despite the discrepancy between AFDC and TANF. In this case, we note that the program, in the most cost-effective scenario, costs around $1,500,000 more than the benefits generated in terms of the reduction in public assistance. The question that remains is whether the other benefits, in the form of behavioral, educational, health, and life-course outcomes for those 600 individuals, is valued at more than $1,500,000 for the public as a whole. Does the public benefit from the improvements to those individuals' lives? It absolutely does—when crime is reduced, neighborhoods become more livable and property values rise; when educational outcomes improve, the workforce improves and civic involvement rises. The question that is put forth to judgment is whether, in this hypothetical case, the marginal improvements to the outcomes for 10% of the potential clientele is worth more than the costs that remain unaccounted for by reduced public assistance costs.

3.6   Summary and Comments

In this study, we were interested in assessing the economic benefits and costs of the NFP program. To do so, we focused primarily on the monetized benefits that were determined to be significantly different in the trials conducted over the course of multiple studies. Based on the findings of these studies, we compared the savings of the program in terms of AFDC/TANF grants and food stamps.

To provide information, we used MCSs on three levels. The MCSs permit us to allow some level of randomization in the decision of whether or not to use public assistance rather than simply calculate a difference based on some abstract representation of the individual. We conducted simulations for the individual, for a random month, and for a cohort of NFP participants. The former two simply allowed us to see how the central tendencies of the program might behave. In this case, we were able to note what the savings would be to the state for a single average individual and in a single random month. The simulation of the cohort is more appropriate because it retains more of the random nature in the calculation. This simulation presumed that the state was "investing" in a collection of individuals who might, over time, require less assistance. This random cohort of individuals allowed us to assess the overall cost of the program for these individuals against the projected savings over 10 years. We found that the program has a negative return ranging from roughly $1.5 million to over $6.0 million.

Our findings suggest that the program will reduce expenditures on food stamps and TANF by between $500,000 and $3 million (based on the calculations made of a random cohort of over 10 years) although this does not fully offset the NFP program expenditures. The calculations generated from the MCSs are intended to complement the decision-making process in which other outcomes that are less easily monetized are assessed. In the case of the NFP program, such outcomes include reduced behavioral problems, improved educational outcomes, and better life-course outcomes for both child and mother. These benefits are very difficult to monetize because of their abstraction, but they are nonetheless essential considerations in public policy. Monetization enables decision makers to benchmark the analysis in order to know what value behavioral benefits must have to warrant the programs incipience or continuation.

As we completed the Monte Carlo analysis, we were impressed by the degree of complexity involved in analyzing the long-term impact of a program that focuses on early childhood development and in establishing an accurate rate of return on the public dollars invested in such a program. A few points are worth reiterating, one involving the technique used and three others that are important considerations in the analysis presented.

First, the Monte Carlo analysis as used in this chapter made use of other information acquired through controlled randomized experiment of a sample of families over a period of time. Given that the outcomes of any program directed at early childhood development are expected to materialize over a long period of time, it is important that the controlled randomized studies be conducted accordingly. However, the longer the time period, the more likely the public programs or public policies will change over time. This makes any calculation of a benefit/cost estimate for future years potentially wrong given that the amount of dollars to be allocated per person for public assistance programs may increase or decrease.

Second, public assistance programs such as TANF and Food stamps are relatively inexpensive programs compared to Medicaid. Consequently, it is important to the analysis of public spending if health care programs do not show up as being less expensive for the treatment group (affected by the program) that participated in the early childhood development program when compared to the control group that did not participate in the program. In this study, the information upon which we based our simulated analysis did not present evidence that Medicaid spending was reduced for the population that participated in the program. Moreover, because of the nature of the studies on the NFP program, we used data based on a now defunct program (AFDC) in order to inform decision makers about a related but substantially different program (TANF). As mentioned above, long-term studies of public programs frequently encounter issues of this kind. Some public programs will change over time. These changes present serious problems for comparisons in the analysis.

Third, the cost of any early childhood program should be focused on the marginal cost of extending the program to another group of people just like the expected benefits of the program should be focused on the marginal benefits that are projected to occur. To study these margins, however, requires that we consider the random and unpredictable aspects that may influence participation in and outcomes from the program. To simply base an analysis on central tendencies neglects the important nuances involved in private decisions that may not be easily observed in an analysis but are nonetheless very important.

Finally, the application of results from a previous study in a different time and place to a population requires a series of assumptions about how this new population will respond to options presented to them (in terms of job opportunities, public assistance programs, etc.), about the marginal costs of the program, about the projected marginal benefits of the programs, and other relevant information. The Monte Carlo model requires that we state specifically these assumptions as they apply to the new population when constructing the simulated environment; this contrasts with a baseline central tendency approach in which the means acquired from a previous analysis are used for a benefit–cost analysis. The Monte Carlo model, in our judgment, highlights the complexities of the quantification of benefits and costs of any public program that create a series of results over a long period of time even if it does not resolve them. We constructed a very simple model to function as a useful public policy instrument, but it can be increased in complexity by including many factors as probabilities in the model.

Acknowledgments The authors acknowledge and appreciate a grant from the Pew Charitable Trusts administered through Tulane University for support of this research. The analysis and any findings suggested in the study represent the work of the authors and do not necessarily reflect the opinions of the Pew Charitable Trusts or Tulane University.

References

Carlson, D. (2011). "Trends and Innovations in Public Policy Analysis." Policy Studies Journal **39**: 13–26.

Karoly, L. A. (2008). Valuing Benefits in Benefit-Cost Studies of Social Programs. Technical Report. Santa Monica, CA, RAND Corporation.

Karoly, L. A., P. W. Greenwood, et al. (1998). Investing in Our Children: What We Know and Don't Know About the Costs and Benefits of Early Childhood Interventions. Santa Monica, CA, RAND Corporation.

Kitzman, H., D. L. Olds, et al. (1997). "Effect of prenatal and infancy home visitation by nurses on pregnancy outcomes, childhood injuries, and repeated childbearing." JAMA: the journal of the American Medical Association 278(8): 644.

Kitzman, H., D. L. Olds, et al. (2000). "Enduring effects of nurse home visitation on maternal life course." JAMA: the journal of the American Medical Association 283(15): 1983.

Olds, D., C. R. Henderson, et al. (1998). "Long-term effects of nurse home visitation on children's criminal and antisocial behavior." JAMA: the journal of the American Medical Association 280(14): 1238.

Olds, D. L., J. Eckenrode, et al. (1997). "Long-term effects of home visitation on maternal life course and child abuse and neglect." JAMA: the journal of the American Medical Association 278(8): 637.

Olds, D. L., C. R. Henderson, et al. (1994). "Does prenatal and infancy nurse home visitation have enduring effects on qualities of parental caregiving and child health at 25 to 50 months of life?" Pediatrics 93(1): 89.

Olds, D. L., H. Kitzman, et al. (2004a). "Effects of nurse home-visiting on maternal life course and child development: age 6 follow-up results of a randomized trial." Pediatrics 114(6): 1550.

Olds, D. L., H. Kitzman, et al. (2007). "Effects of nurse home visiting on maternal and child functioning: age-9 follow-up of a randomized trial." Pediatrics 120(4): e832.

Olds, D. L., H. J. Kitzman, et al. (2010). "Enduring effects of prenatal and infancy home visiting by nurses on maternal life course and government spending: follow-up of a randomized trial among children at age 12 years." Archives of Pediatrics & Adolescent Medicine 164(5): 419-424.

Olds, D. L., J. A. Robinson, et al. (2002). "Home visiting by paraprofessionals and by nurses: a randomized, controlled trial." Pediatrics 110(3): 486.

Olds, D. L., J. A. Robinson, et al. (2004b). "Effects of home visits by paraprofessionals and by nurses: age 4 follow-up results of a randomized trial." Pediatrics 114(6): 1560.

Part II
Agent-Based Models

Chapter 4
The Utility of Multilevel Modeling vs. Agent-Based Modeling in Examining Spatial Disparities in Diet and Health: The Case of Food Deserts

Ketra Rice

Abstract From a policy perspective, the presence and persistence of food deserts and the subsequent diet and health effects on those living in such areas pose a modeling conundrum. Should the deserts be the focus of attention where the modeling effort is on identifying the interactions and interdependencies across space and time that contribute to their creation, or should one focus on the consequences of lack of access to food and attempt to explore the adverse nutrition and health outcomes that can be attributed to such deserts? Attempting to address these questions requires not only different conceptual models but also different data models. To that end, we offer to compare and contrast the utility of using multilevel regression modeling vs. agent-based modeling in examining spatial disparities in health, specifically looking at how each type of model can address these aforementioned questions. The primary purpose of this chapter is to give emphasis to the value of operational thinking in model design and encourage building conceptual and data models that are more useful to policymakers when proposing policy interventions.

4.1 Introduction

Exploring spatial disparities[1] in diet and health is an important topic for policy analysts as trends indicate that health disparities across geographic regions continue to persist (CDC 2011a). These trends raise concerns for policymakers as they attempt to strengthen current food distribution policies, food assistance programs, and address growing health disparities within the United States.

---

[1] Spatial disparities in diet and health are differences in diet and health outcomes and their determinants between different groups of people, defined by geographic location (Carter-Pokras and Baquet 2002).

K. Rice (✉)
Andrew Young School of Policy Studies, Georgia State University,
14 Marietta Street, NW Suite 524, Atlanta, GA 30303, USA
e-mail: krice@gsu.edu

A. Desai (ed.), *Simulation for Policy Inquiry*, DOI 10.1007/978-1-4614-1665-4_4,
© Springer Science+Business Media, LLC 2012

While the USA is deemed a rich nation, the attributes of our nation often blind us from some of the more intractable problems of our society, such as the inadequate distribution of healthful and nutritious food. As a nation, our per capita income is such that we spend less than 10% of our disposable income on food (USDA 2011). Yet, statistics for 2009 showed that nearly 15% of Americans lived in food-insecure households (USDA 2011). These are households with limited access, at all times, to enough food for an active, healthy life for all household members.

While food insecurity is largely driven by factors such as low wages, poorly structured safety-net programs, and limited opportunities for accumulating assets, within, and perhaps beyond, these dreadful conditions are communities that have come to be known as "food deserts." These communities, by definition, lack health-ful food sources, such as grocery stores, supermarkets, and other healthful food retail outlets.[2] This lack implies a spatial disparity in food access, which requires that researchers understand how access to nutritious foods affects health and well-being in specific communities. The concept of "space" is central to understanding food deserts as most of the spatial research examines differences in outcomes as they relate to social and economic well-being (Bourdieu 1984; Kearns and Joseph 1993; Lobao et al. 2007). Consumers who live in food deserts are at greater risk of poorer dietary health because the risk of not meeting recommended daily servings of fruits and vegetables is greater where fresh produce is rarely available. In addition, the majority of Americans acquire their food from retail sources, not by growing it themselves (Fulfrost and Howard 2006). As the American Heart Association reports, there is a direct link between low fruit and vegetable consumption and major health problems, such as diabetes, heart disease, and stroke (American Heart Association 2009). Thus, health vulnerability is exacerbated in a food desert. While an economic perspective may suggest that the decisions made by food retail firms are perfectly rational choices as firms seek to locate in more profitable areas, the social costs imposed on those forgotten communities, in terms of nutritional deficiencies from an inadequate supply of food, raise vital concerns for social scientists and applied economists in public policy.

From a policy research perspective, the presence and persistence of food deserts pose a modeling conundrum. Should the deserts be the focus of attention where the modeling effort is on identifying the interactions and interdependencies across space and time that contribute to their creation, or should one focus on the consequences of lack of access to food and attempt to explore the adverse nutrition and health outcomes that can be attributed to such deserts? Attempting to address these questions requires not only different conceptual models but also different data models. To that end, we offer to compare and contrast the utility of using multilevel regression modeling vs. agent-based modeling in examining spatial disparities in

---

[2] Healthful food retail outlets are establishments generally known as traditional food stores, such as supermarkets, grocery stores, and specialty food stores primarily engaged in retailing a general line of food, such as fresh fruits and vegetables, fresh and prepared meats, canned and frozen foods, dairy, and whole grain food products (USDA 2011).

health, specifically examining the dietary and health effects of consumers living within food deserts. These models serve different purposes. The statistical model seeks to determine whether the data support specific functional forms of the relationships among variables that are deemed relevant to the study of food deserts. Testing which patterns are best supported by the data yields insights regarding the efficacy of different policy interventions in influencing the outcomes being modeled. Simulation models, on the other hand, allow the exploration of policy interventions and assumptions underlying the models. Such exploration can lead to an enhanced understanding of the interdependencies among the modeled components potentially yielding insights regarding the consequences of implementing different policy interventions. In the next section, we will provide a background of food deserts, followed by a conceptualization of the policy problem. We then will provide conceptualizations of using both modeling methods, laying out the conceptual and methodological advantages and challenges of each method.

4.2   The Reality of Food Deserts

In 1996, the Low Income Project Team in the United Kingdom (UK) formally defined food deserts as "areas of relative exclusion where people experience physical and economic barriers to accessing healthy food" (Food Deserts.org 2006). In 2009, the United States Department of Agriculture (USDA) commissioned a comprehensive report on food deserts and defined food deserts as communities, particularly low-income areas, in which residents do not live in close proximity to affordable and healthy food retailers (USDA 2011). These definitions suggest that there exists some form of spatial inequality, where the distribution and the provision of healthful foods across certain communities are insufficient or inadequate.

USA studies on food deserts have shown that across all US regions, rural areas, as well as poor urban areas, are more likely to be food deserts (Blanchard and Lyson 2002, 2003; Gallagher 2006; Kauffman 1998; Morton et al. 2005; Rose et al. 2009; Sharkey and Horel 2009; Ver Ploeg et al. 2009). These communities are faced with limited choices for healthful food. In these areas, the presence of convenience stores, gas stations, and corner markets ensures that some type of food store is accessible to almost all consumers; however, the nutritional quality of food available in these types of stores is limited as compared to the nutritional quality of foods available in supermarkets.

Research has found that supermarkets carried twice the average number of heart-healthy foods compared to neighborhood grocers and four times the average number of heart-healthy foods compared to convenience stores (Morland et al. 2001). Heart-healthy foods are those foods defined by the American Heart Association, screened and proven to be low in saturated fat and cholesterol for healthy people over age two (American Heart Association 2009). These are typically fresh vegetables and fruits, whole grains, and lean sources of protein. Additionally, groceries sold in food deserts were found to cost an average of 10% more than groceries sold in non-food desert areas (USDA 2011). This means that in addition to inadequate access, consumers in food deserts must pay a premium for the food that is available.

Further research conducted by Blanchard and Lyson (2003) found that food desert residents were 23% less likely (on average) to consume at least five servings of fruits and vegetables per day than non-food desert residents of similar age, education, and income levels. This suggests that food deserts have a negative impact on the ability to secure a healthful diet. According to research by Godwin and Tegegne (2006), one of the key factors affecting consumption of fruits and vegetables is accessibility and proximity of consumers to supermarkets. Morland et al. (2001) found an association between fruit and vegetable consumption and the availability of supermarkets in a study linking the local food environment with residents' diets. Their research showed that the presence of at least one additional supermarket increased adult fruit and vegetable intake. The research on food deserts shows that a lack of food supply in these areas poses a major threat to the food security of the most vulnerable rural citizens, with the rural poor suffering the most when available food retail is relatively excluded from the immediate geographic areas in which they live.

In 2009, The USDA assessed the extent of the problem of limited access to food stores and the characteristics of those communities. They found that urban core areas with limited food access are characterized by higher levels of racial segregation and greater income inequality. Additionally, in small-town and rural areas with limited food access, the lack of transportation infrastructure was the most defining characteristic (Ver Ploeg et al. 2009). While some residents in food desert areas have the ability to adapt, many residents living in food deserts are more captive to their physical environments, such as the poor and elderly. They are most negatively affected by the under-provision of food in their communities because of lower levels of resources and greater constraints on mobility. Additionally, research has shown that simply providing financial means (in the form of food stamps) to the poor living in food deserts is insufficient, because the financial means are not enough when the access to food retail is simply not there (Rice 2010). Communities that have no or distant grocery stores, or have an imbalance of healthy food options, have increased premature death and chronic health conditions (Gallagher 2006). It is clear that food deserts pose serious health and wellness challenges to the residents who live within them.

4.3 Conceptualization of Policy Problem

The spatial patterning of diet and health evolves as individuals and their environments adapt and change over time (Auchincloss and Roux 2008). Retail food environments in the USA have evolved and changed over time, with a shift from a wide distribution of small-scale local grocers to a concentration of supermarkets in more highly populated geographic areas (Lyson and Raymer 2000; Blanchard and Lyson 2002).

Additionally, populations have evolved and changed over time, with more young people migrating away from smaller, rural cities and higher-income residents migrating away from some urban city centers (Domina 2006; Brooks and Redlin 2009). Within many rural towns and poor urban areas, there are simply fewer food stores for purchasing healthful foods as compared to higher-income urban and suburban areas (Auchincloss et al. 2011).

It is critical to understand the significance of diet for health. According to the Centers for Disease Control, five out of the top ten leading causes of death in the USA are related to an individual's lifestyle, including, but not limited to, diet. Several of these diseases include coronary heart disease, high blood pressure, stroke, diabetes, and some types of cancers (CDC 2011b). Because of their potential contribution to disparities in diet and health, food deserts have become a greatly discussed policy issue. As food deserts represent areas where distributional inequities in food provision exists, how can we examine the dietary and health effects of living in food deserts, in order to inform policy?

While food deserts are a factor, disparities in diet and health are a result of more than just the physical environment in which we live; there are also socioeconomic, demographic, and environmental factors that play a role in diet choices and health. In other words, diet and health are influenced by multiple factors, including who we are, who we associate with, where we live, and the conditions in which we live. Perceptions about diet and health oftentimes differ among the sexes, and health concerns and behaviors concerning personal health tend to change and alter with income, age, and education (Kuo and Lin 2000; Mancino et al. 2004). Another explanation for disparities in diet is that consumption simply reflects socioeconomic preferences, with higher-income consumers preferring healthier foods and choosing to live in areas with greater access to healthful food stores. However, individuals oftentimes choose where to live based on socioeconomic constraints or are sorted into neighborhoods based on discriminatory practices, and diet and health behaviors may in part be the result of similar people clustered within the environment (Auchincloss et al. 2011). Other explanations are that culture shapes food preferences and the social environment shapes food culture, with consumption behavior being both an expression of identity and a means of reproducing class distinctions in society (Bourdieu 1984).

It is unlikely that the physical environment, the social environment, or socioeconomic and demographic factors individually cause poor diet and health, but it seems clear that each of these factors are interrelated and associated with an individual's diet and health and thus contribute to the complexity of examining the effect of living in food deserts on diet and health. Table 4.1 provides detail of multiple factors and variables affecting differences in diet and health.

Figure 4.1 provides a conceptual model of differences in diet and health. The model illustrates the multiple feedback loops and interrelated nature of each of the factors and variables described in the table. The variables are operationalizations of the factors, and the factors are the constructs that are assumed to affect health. The model shows how individual characteristics as well as characteristics of the social and physical environment affect diet and health outcomes (Story et al. 2008).

Table 4.1 Factors affecting differences in diet and health

Factor	Variables	Description
Individual demographic and socioeconomic characteristics	Race Age Gender Income Education	Dietary choices and health behaviors tend to vary based on some demographic and socioeconomic characteristics. For example, as individuals age, income and education levels increase; their dietary choices and health behaviors tend to positively change (Kuo and Lin 2000; Mancino et al. 2004). However, factors such as race and gender have been historically associated with income and education opportunities (Neckerman 2004)
Social environment	Family Social networks Culture/food preferences	Diet choices and health behaviors are influenced by family, social networks, and culture. People adapt their dietary choices and health behaviors in response to the collective behaviors within their social environments (Kearns and Joseph 1993). For example, if the diet choices of people within your family or larger social network are unhealthy, you may also adapt the same unhealthy choices. The social environment can also reflect how customs and traditions have shaped food culture and led to variation in diet and health preferences
Physical environment	Natural landscape Built environment	Diet and health behaviors may be due to factors in the natural landscape, such as land terrain (mountains, plains, rivers, oceans, etc.), natural resources, and climate (Curtis and Jones 1998). The landscape also plays a role in shaping the built environment, which consists of the man-made structures that provide the setting for human interaction in the community. The built environment may include the availability of places for procuring healthful foods, as well as the availability of places for promoting an overall healthy lifestyle (Frank and Engelke 2001)

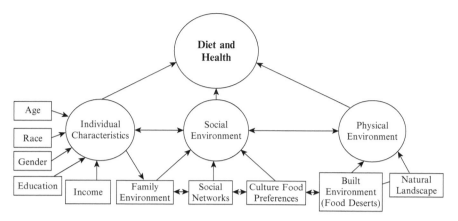

Fig. 4.1 Conceptual model of differences in diet and health

All factors affect diet and overall health; however, as shown, the relationship among these factors is not a one-way relationship. In the figure, the double arrows flowing between factors and variables denote an interrelated nature, meaning there is a reciprocal relationship with feedback mechanisms between those factors and variables. As shown, there is an interrelated nature among individual characteristics, the social environment, and the physical environment, with each contributing to each other, and hence contributing to diet and health. Moving from left to right, individual and household characteristics identified in the model consist of specific demographic and socioeconomic traits, with the sum of individual traits composing the overall family environment. The social environment identified in the model consists of the family environment, social networks, and culture and preferences, with each being interrelated with each other. The physical environment identified in the model consists of the natural landscape and built environment, with the landscape playing a role in shaping the built environment and the built environment being interrelated with variables in the social environment.

The variety of these factors highlights that dietary health inequalities likely occur within a complex system of interrelated processes. As individuals change and adapt, their social environments change and adapt, and their physical environments respond by adapting. For example, if individuals/households change their diet and health behaviors, more people in their social environment may change their dietary preferences to eat healthier. Collective behavior change may then result in the community revealing their preferences for healthier food retail, resulting in healthier food retail outlets potentially locating in the community, thus changing the physical environment. Conversely, if the physical environment changes, the social environment responds by changing, resulting in individuals within the environment changing. For example, if healthier food retail locates in a community, the availability of the store may promote healthier consumption and individuals may begin to change their dietary routines to eat healthier. Whether we are discussing the individual, the social environment, or the physical environment, each factor is continuously affecting the others.

In examining spatial inequalities, there has been little examination of the extent to which the built environment, specifically, food deserts, affects diet and health outcomes, and there has also been little examination of the interactions and interdependencies across space and time that contribute to their creation. In an effort to understand the utility of analytical methods for examining these issues, a comparison and contrast of multilevel regression and agent-based modeling will be conceptualized and explored.

4.4   Multilevel Modeling

Our conceptual model illustrates that individual-level outcomes (diet and health) are not solely explained by individual-level characteristics. The context of the social and physical environments also affects diet and health. We use a multilevel model because our policy problem is multilevel in nature and reflects both a micro-level of analysis (the individual) and macro levels of analysis (the social and physical environments). The multilevel model is a data model that can answer the question "What are the consequences of lack of access to food?" We can examine the data in the model to measure the effect of space on diet and health outcomes.

In our model, we establish three levels of analysis: the individual at the first level, the social environment at the second level, and the physical environment at the third level. Specifically, we have individuals nested in their social environments and the social environment nested in the physical environment. Multilevel models allow us to study diet and health outcomes that vary by each level of analysis. By using a multilevel model, we have the ability to identify the effect of each level of the environment on spatial inequalities in health. Figure 4.2 provides a diagram of our multilevel structure.

Multilevel models have been a major type of statistical model used to examine the effects of the environment on health because they allow the researcher to estimate the effects of macro related factors on micro-level factors while controlling for some factors that are conceived to be related to both the micro and the macro (Duncan et al. 1998; Roux 2000; Bingenheimer and Raudenbush 2004). In examining spatial inequalities in diet and health, multilevel regression is a desired model for testing assumptions about the environmental effects on diet and health, as an individual's diet and health may be determined by multiple factors and variables at different micro- and macro-levels (Luke 2004). It is a statistical model applied to data collected at more than one level of analysis in order to explain relationships at more than one level of analysis. The goal of a multilevel model is to predict values of a dependent variable based on a function of explanatory variables at both the micro- and macro-level. Specifically, the goal of our multilevel model is to identify the effect of food deserts as an influence on health, thereby giving us greater context of the effects of space.

To demonstrate a multilevel model for analyzing health inequalities in food deserts, let us consider an ordered logit multilevel model, in which we use an ordered

Fig. 4.2 Multilevel structure
of determinants of diet and
health

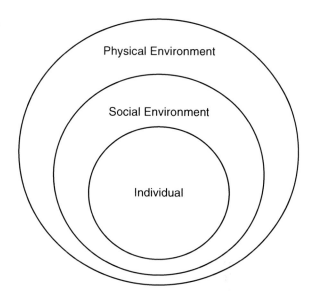

measure of health utility as the dependent variable. The variables in the health data set that we may use include a measure of health utility based on the individual's health status. The health utility scale ranks health as poor, fair, good, very good, or excellent. The explanatory variables in the analysis reflect the individual's socio-economic status as well as the social and physical environments. In this example, we will use income as an individual-level variable as research has shown that income is associated with health (Kuo and Lin 2000; Mancino et al. 2004). The social environment will be operationalized as the neighborhood in which the individual lives. We assume that the neighborhood reflects the immediate social environment and includes family, social networks, and elements of the individual's culture. The physical environment will be operationalized as the census tract in which the individual lives. It is assumed that the census tract reflects the immediate natural landscape and physically built environment affecting the individual. In addition, there is available census tract data from the USDA that identifies which census tracts are food deserts. Because individuals are nested in neighborhoods and neighborhoods are nested in census tracts, the multilevel structure of the model will be three levels, with the individual at level 1, neighborhood at level 2, and census tract at level 3. The proposed three-level model may be formally expressed in three sets of equations as follows:

$$\text{Individual environment:} \quad \eta_{ijk} = \log it(\gamma_{ijk}) = \pi_{0jk} + \pi_{ijk}(\text{Income})_{ijk}$$

where η_{ijk} is the health utility of the ith individual in the jth neighborhood in the kth census tract and ranges from 0 to 4, with 0 being poor, 1 being fair, 2 being good,

3 being very good, and 4 being excellent. π_0 and π_1 are the level one intercept and slope. Level 2 is defined as follows:

Neighborhood environment: $\pi_{0jk} = \beta_{00k} + \beta_{01k}(\text{Neighborhood})_{jk} + r_{0jk}$

$$\pi_{1jk} = \beta_{10k} + \beta_{11k}(\text{Neighborhood})_{jk} + r_{1jk}$$

In level 2, we see that the level one intercept and slope are now indirectly estimated through the level 2 β's. The r's are the error terms for the unmodeled variability in the level 2 units. This equation shows that we are allowing the level 1 intercept and slope to vary (random effects) across level 2. Random effects are additional sources of variability and are placed in multilevel models because of the potential variability in micro-level variables across macro levels of analysis. This is a key concept in multilevel modeling (Snijders 2005). Level 3 is as follows:

Physical environment: $\beta_{00k} = \gamma_{000} + \gamma_{001}(\text{CensusTract})_k + \mu_{00k}$

$$\beta_{01k} = \gamma_{010} + \mu_{01k}$$

$$\beta_{10k} = \gamma_{100} + \mu_{10k}$$

$$\beta_{11k} = \gamma_{110} + \mu_{11k}$$

In level 3, we see that the level 2 intercept is conceived to be affected by the level 3 predictor and is modeled as a random effect at level 3. These sets of equations can be reduced to the following single mixed-model equation:

$$\eta_{ijk} = \gamma_{000} + \gamma_{001}(\text{CensusTract})_k + \gamma_{010}(\text{Neighborhood})_{ik} + \gamma_{100}(\text{Income})_{ijk}$$

$$+ \gamma_{110}(\text{Income})(\text{Neighborhood})_{jk} + \mu_{00k} + \mu_{01k}(\text{Neighborhood})$$

$$+ \mu_{10k}(\text{Income}) + \mu_{11k}(\text{Income})(\text{Neighborhood}) + r_{0jk} + r_{1jk}(\text{Income})$$

where η_{ijk} is the health utility of the ith individual in the jth neighborhood in the kth census tract. The j and k subscripts tell us that a different level 1 model is being estimated for the levels 2 and 3 units. The γ's in the model are our slopes and intercept, and the μ's and r's in the model are our variance components (random effects). It is also clearer to see that there is a cross-level interaction of income and neighborhood in the model, as those variables directly influence each other.

With this conceptualization, observed health data can be used for our analysis. We can use data to explore if health status varies across neighborhoods and census tracts. Specifically, with our model, we may be able to determine the likelihood that health utility is poorer for individuals living in neighborhoods or census tracts, defined as food deserts. The analysis from our model can isolate independent affects and provide us with explanations of variability of health utility across each level of analysis. We may be able to answer the question, "What are the consequences of lack of access to food?" by analyzing the variation in health utility across food desert and non-food desert census tracts. Our model can tell us what has happened; however, it cannot tell us how it happened. The model cannot give us the full explanation of the interrelated relationships among each of our levels of analysis. As stated, the spatial patterning of diet and health evolves over time as individuals and their environments adapt and change. The challenge is that standard statistical approaches are incapable of incorporating multiple feedback and adaptive mechanisms between people and their environments over time. To further look at our policy problem, an examination of agent-based modeling will be explored as an alternative.

4.5 Agent-Based Modeling

Agent-based models and other simulation techniques have been used in health studies to examine income inequalities in diet in the context of residential segregation (Auchincloss et al. 2011), walking behavior in communities (Yang et al. 2011), and alcoholic drinking behavior (Gorman et al. 2006). Simulation models can overcome some of the challenges of traditional regression approaches, such as the inability of regression models to incorporate feedback between variables used in the model. Agent-based models are computer simulations in which we can simulate an environment composed of micro- and macro-level factors. These micro- and macro-level factors can be given characteristics and assigned behavioral rules, and placed in a defined spatial context, in which we can explore adaptations and changes occurring within our simulated environment. We also have the ability to introduce changes (i.e., policies) into the environment in order to explore how micro- and macro-level factors may change and adapt in response. In addressing our policy problem, the agent-based model can simulate the interactions and interdependencies across space and time that contribute to the creation of food deserts, provide for the analysis of diet and health outcomes that can be attributed to them, and allow for the exploration of policy interventions to address them.

To demonstrate the multidirectional relationships of our health model, let us consider a simulation of diet choices and health disparities in the context of food deserts. The purpose of the agent-based model is to explore the emergent food desert environment and the aggregate dietary choices and health outcomes of individuals living in food deserts and further explore if policies may reduce any diet and health disparities between residents living in food deserts and those living in non-food deserts. The model components will include elements of the physical food environment and social environment. Finally, several socioeconomic characteristics of individuals will be included. To begin building the agent-based model, we must define the spatial context (environment), define the agents, establish our parameters and behavioral rules, and establish our time intervals, denoting when movement will occur in the model.

4.5.1   Spatial Context

The spatial context is the artificial landscape represented in the model, and we can refer to the landscape as a county, with plots within the county, where individuals may live and food stores are located. Our county is represented on a 50×50 landscape, thus having 2,500 plots, where individuals live and food stores are located. [It is important to note that our agent-based modeling software (NetLogo) allows for the importation of actual geographical information system (GIS) shape files. We can then actually import X and Y coordinates for individuals and food stores we include in the model, which can provide greater detail of spatial context.] The characteristics of the plots in our county are extremely important to our model. An individual's choice of where to live and a food store's choice of where to locate are based on the agent parameters we define in the next section, specifically socioeconomic status. Lower-income individuals live in areas they can afford, and stores that sell lower-quality foods tend to locate in similar areas. Thus, we specify that a plot's characteristics are a function of the socioeconomic status of residents and quality of stores located there. A plot's value diminishes as the number of lower-income residents living nearby increases and as the number of stores selling low-quality foods located nearby increases. This phenomenon also will allow us to explore the emergence of food deserts, as food deserts are defined as communities, particularly low-income areas, in which residents do not live in close proximity to affordable and healthy food retailers (USDA 2011).

4.5.2   Agent Types: Parameters

There are two types of agents that we include in our model: individuals and food stores. We randomly assign individuals in our model with a binary score for socioeconomic status (1 = high income, 0 = low income), a health utility score (1 = excellent health, 0 = poor health), and a food preference score (1 = healthful food preference, 0 = unhealthful food preference). To keep the model simple, we randomly assign 25% of the individuals in our model with low income, poor health, and unhealthful food preferences. Individuals may then select to live on plots within the county. Next, we specify our food stores and assign quality settings for each food store. We specify that there are two types of food retail stores: (1) traditional food retailers, such as supermarkets and grocery stores, and (2) alternative food retailers, such as convenience stores and corner markets. We establish that traditional food retailers are sellers of high-quality (healthful) food and alternative food retailers are sellers of low-quality (unhealthful) food and assign a binary score for each (1 = sellers of high-quality food, 0 = sellers of poor-quality food). To keep the model simple, our food stores provide either high-quality food or low-quality food. We randomly assign 50% of the stores as sellers of low-quality food and establish that low-quality foods are expensive and high-quality foods are inexpensive[3] (binary scores of 1 = expensive, 0 = inexpensive).

---

[3] Traditional food retailers on average are able to offer lower prices for foods as compared to similar foods available in convenience stores and corner markers (Ver Ploeg et al. 2009).

4.5.3   Interactions Among Agents: Rules

Now that we have set parameters, we establish a utility function for each individual to determine how the agent chooses where to shop for food. The individuals aim to balance the distance they travel to the store with their preference type and income. Thus, the individuals' utility function is based on the distance the individuals travel to the store, their income characteristic and corresponding store quality (iqual), and their food preference and corresponding store quality (pqual) and is written as:

$$\text{Utility} = \left(\frac{1}{\text{distance}}\right)^{\alpha} \cdot \left(\frac{1}{\text{iqual}}\right)^{\beta} \cdot (\text{pqual})^{\gamma}$$

where α, β, and γ are balancing parameters and are initially set at 0.5 in the simulation, indicating that individuals evenly balance shopping at a store that sells the type of food they prefer with a close distance they must travel and lower price they must pay.

4.5.4   Time

At every ten time steps in our model (ten time steps is considered as one shopping trip), individuals will choose a store from which to shop for food. At every ten time steps, stores will calculate and reset statistics of customers shopping in their store based on those customers' characteristics and food preferences, and stores may adapt and change in response. Because our model will measure interactions occurring simultaneously over time, stores will be able to change the type of food they sell. Individuals may then adapt their behaviors and preferences. At ten time steps, the model can also calculate the average health scores of shoppers by the type of store they have chosen to shop in. At every 180 time steps (180 time steps is considered as 1 year), stores may make decisions to relocate or close based on the model's statistics (few customers, low-income customers, etc.). This dynamic process can continue as long as we allow in the model. As the model continues to run and produce statistics, we can use those results to explore alternative scenarios.

4.5.5   Scenarios

As stated earlier, the purpose of our agent-based model is to explore the emergent food desert environment and aggregate dietary choices and health outcomes of individuals living in food deserts and further explore if policies may reduce any dietary and health disparities between residents living in food deserts and those living in non-food deserts. In our model, we explore the interactions between individuals and food stores and observe the environment and dietary choices and health outcomes of individuals. Following observation of the initial setup of the model, we can make changes to the initial parameters we have set and introduce policies to explore if changes in outcomes emerge. With each policy that we introduce, we can explore how effective each may be in addressing the aggregate dietary choices and health outcomes of individuals living in food deserts. For example, one policy may be to introduce a junk food tax. To do this, we can change store quality settings and make unhealthy foods substantially more expensive than healthful foods and observe if individuals with unhealthful food preferences will then change and consume healthful foods and if the aggregate diet choices and health of individuals with unhealthful preferences change. Perhaps, we may observe that a junk food tax would result in less consumption of unhealthy foods. This may also lead to changes in the social environment with aggregate preferences for unhealthy food diminishing as a result of the policy intervention.

A second policy scenario could be to gradually introduce new healthful food stores in the food deserts and observe if the presence of the store caused shopping patterns to change from unhealthful to healthful. After the introduction of a new healthful food store, a pre-intervention/post-intervention examination of individuals' shopping patterns could be observed to examine if improved healthful food retail access would lead to improved changes in the diets and subsequent health of residents. Perhaps, we may observe that increased availability of a healthful food store would result in more consumers choosing to shop there. While a regression (and qualitative) study of this nature would take years to conduct as we would have to gather years of data before and after the introduction of the food store, the agent-based model allows us to simulate this phenomenon in real time. A third policy scenario may be to provide subsidies to those stores selling unhealthful foods to incentive them to provide a range of healthful food products. We could do this by setting parameters that establish that all stores sell a range of foods from healthful to unhealthful and observe shopping statistics of consumer purchases to see if diet choices change. Perhaps, we may observe that providing incentives to stores to begin providing a range of healthful foods would result in a change in dietary preferences of consumers.

Each of the proposed policy interventions can alter the physical food landscape, thus altering the social environment and subsequently altering the behavior of individual consumers interacting within these environments. The purpose of introducing these scenarios is to explore how individuals and environments may react to changes brought about by policy interventions. The expected outcomes of our agent-based model can help us understand the differences in diet choices and health based on interactions of socioeconomic status, preferences and characteristics and locations of food stores, and the environment that can emerge from individual and food store decisions, thereby not only explaining what happened but also explaining how spatial disparities in diet and health have happened.

4.6   Multilevel Modeling vs. Agent-Based Modeling: Conceptual and Methodological Advantages and Challenges

Analysis with our multilevel model allows us to use data to estimate the independent effects of individual-level variables (income) and environmental-level variables (neighborhood and census tract) on individual-level outcomes (health) at one point in time. We are provided with an explanation of what happened by identifying the effects of the various levels of the environment on health. By distinguishing different levels, the multilevel model provides context of the variability in health utility across different levels of analysis and allows us to observe effects (in the data) as they flow from one level to the next. We are able to identify the effect of space, so that we can infer the spatial disparity of food deserts from the perspective of its influence.

Using observed data, our multilevel model has the ability to provide statistical information of the variation in health outcomes between food desert and non-food desert communities and help inform public policy. The observed data used in the model provides a necessary reference, meaning it provides information contained in a well-defined collection of physical things that have been produced by an environment. People, places, and characteristics are all physical things contained in a data set, and our goal is to use the information they provide (i.e., to describe, analyze, estimate, and make inferences). Empirical observation of the data can lead to theory building, through the testing of theories (we can accept and use the theory in practice or reject and seek a better alternative theory), ultimately providing support for the conceptual models that we construct based on the data.

In addition to the advantages of observed data, we must also recognize data limitations, particularly with the collection process and availability of survey-based health data. Problems with data in the survey context include errors in sampling and coverage and errors in the accuracy of responses, which leads to reduced validity in analyzing the results. In addition, we are often limited to the data that is available to explore a subject of interest. In other words, the only answers we can get are the ones in which the data is available to answer. This can also lead to reduced validity in results that are generated from the data. As we will discuss later, an agent-based model is an alternative methodological tool when faced with these types of data limitations.

While our multilevel regression model is able to isolate independent effects and provide us with explanations of variability of health across different levels of analysis, it cannot give us the full explanation of the interrelated relationships between these levels. The assumptions of standard regression models limit the opportunity to explore multidirectional feedback among variables. With regression models, we assume that no explanatory variables are a function of any other explanatory variables in the model. We also assume linearity, and even when we have a regression model that is nonlinear, such as a model with a dichotomous dependent variable, we still use probability functions that allow us to transform equations in order to linearize those inherently nonlinear relationships.

Additionally, while the multilevel model does provide data that explains what happened, it does not provide a basis to explore how it happened. As stated, the spatial patterning of diet and health evolves over time as individuals and their environments adapt and change. Because there may also be an element of emergence where macro-level factors, such as food deserts, emerge as a result of micro-level interactions and behaviors, such as the decisions and preferences of individuals and food stores, this creates difficulty as our multilevel model is incapable of handling such processes. The challenge is that standard statistical approaches are incapable of incorporating multiple feedback and adaptive mechanisms between people and their environments over time.

By using an agent-based model we can actually explore the interactions and interdependencies among variables and possibly provide an explanation of how food deserts have happened. It can be argued that understanding how food deserts have happened can enhance our understanding of their effects on health. In other words, if you know how it happens, you can better explain the effects. The major advantage of our agent-based model is that it can model the dynamic processes related to environmental effects on health, which focuses attention on interdependent processes rather than just independent associations between variables. Agent-based modeling allows for feedback between the micro- and macro-level and allows us to examine how macro-level processes emerge from micro-level actions, and subsequently how those macro-level processes can then influence micro-level actions. This feedback is important in understanding that each level influences the other and contributes to the patterns that we detect.

As we build the agent-based model, we can model the interactions between individuals and food stores and observe the emergent food environment and subsequent diet and health outcomes of individuals. This allows us to understand the spatial disparity as an outcome of social interactions in the environment. Understanding how food deserts have emerged can provide greater context of the phenomenon and thus greatly enhance the development of policies to alleviate the disparities associated with them.

Returning back to a discussion of our multilevel model, with the model, we use statistical analysis in which we simplify what is naturally complex and assume that there are no dynamic processes. In our example, we would be able to use multilevel regression to explain variation in health and model the likelihood that health utility at the individual level is a function of variables defined at the social and physical environment level; however, we would not be able to model that individual-level characteristics may influence the nature of the social or physical environment, nor would we be able to model that the social and physical environments influence individual-level behaviors, with all of these factors influencing health.

Likewise, our agent-based model must also simplify that which is naturally complex (Axelrod 1997) in order to generate a model that is understandable and interpretable. However, the process of simplification still allows us to incorporate interactions and feedbacks between the micro- and macro-levels. The validity issues in statistical modeling are also not lost in the agent-based model. Because we must simplify in order to generate a model that is understandable and interpretable, realism in our simulated environment can be constrained, and this makes validation difficult.

Table 4.2 Side-by-side comparison of methods

	Multilevel modeling	Agent-based modeling
Purpose	Observe and estimate the independent effects of variables as they flow from one level of the environment to the next	Observe interdependent relationships among variables as they flow from one level of the environment to the next
	Can observe the spatial inequality from the perspective of its influence on health	Can observe the spatial inequality as the outcome of social interactions in the environment, as well as from the perspective of its influence on health
Underlying assumptions	Models statistical interactions among variables	Models social interactions among entities
	Can explain what has happened by showing the consequences	Can explain how it has happened by showing the inception
Structure	Micro and macro	Micro and macro
	Establish specific functional forms of the relationships among variables at the micro- and macro-levels	Establish entities at the micro-level and observe patterns of micro interactions that produce macro outcomes
Data	Model produces results observed in the data	Model produces results that generate the data
Integration of models	Building and simulating the emergence of an environment can enhance our understanding of the consequences associated with the environment. To this end, building the agent-based model can help us better explain the results that we observe in the multilevel model	
	Data from the multilevel model can be used to set parameters in the agent-based model, and data produced from the agent-based model can lead to improvements in the quality of data collected for future research using multilevel modeling	

In addition, validation is difficult in agent-based models because no algorithm exists to determine what techniques or procedures to use in determining the correctness of the model (Sargent 2007).

To ensure a valid linkage to reality, the agent-based model must base its parameters and decision rules on observed data patterns and prior empirical research. Since the lack of observed data within the model is a methodological hiccup for those new to understanding agent-based models, the parameters, decision rules, and scenarios that we build in the model must be grounded in theory and based on what we learn from prior empirical research. As such, the results from our multilevel model can aid in the development of our agent-based model.

Lastly, agent-based models allow us to simulate a theoretically realistic environment and generate synthetic data, allowing for evaluation of hypothetical policies that may potentially be introduced in the real world. What we learn from our agent-based model can provide greater insight into additional data needed for statistical research and new areas of research for policy researchers, further expanding theory in the field. Table 4.2 provides a summary side-by-side comparison of the conceptual and methodological distinctiveness of each method.

4.7 Conclusion

The increasing use of computer simulations in policy research is not a replacement for regression modeling, but simulations do offer advantages in exploring complex policy problems. Multilevel regression is a statistical tool that provides greater validity over standard regression when modeling micro- and macro-level factors; however, when modeling dynamic processes involving micro- and macro-level factors, agent-based modeling is better suited for analyzing the interrelated nature of policy problems. In its time, multilevel modeling has advanced the study of spatial differences in health outcomes, and now agent-based modeling must take the baton and run with it in further advancing our understanding of spatial differences in health. While both methods have advantages and challenges, agent-based modeling has important capabilities that multilevel modeling lacks. Multilevel modeling cannot incorporate interaction between the individual and their environment; however, agent-based modeling should still be viewed as a complement to multilevel regression. Because multilevel modeling applies statistical methods to observed data, there is still a place for it in our analytical universe, and because the agent-based model must base its parameters and decision rules on observed data patterns and prior empirical research, we still need methods that can provide that information. Both conceptual and methodological approaches have the ability to help inform our understanding and lead to policies that will alleviate diet and health inequalities in food deserts.

References

American Heart Association. (2009). Retrieved June 20, 2009, from http://www.americanheart. org/presenter.jhtml?identifier=4973

Auchincloss, A.H., & Roux, A.V.D. (2008). A New Tool for Epidemiology: The Usefulness of Dynamic-Agent Models in Understanding Place Effects on Health. *American Journal of Epidemiology* 168(1), 1–8.

Auchincloss, A.H., Riolo, R.L., Brown, D.G., Cook, J., & Roux, A.V.D. (2011). An Agent-Based Model of Income Inequalities in Diet in the Context of Residential Segregation. *American Journal of Preventive Medicine* 40(3), 303–311.

Axelrod, R. (1997). Advancing the Art of Simulation in the Social Sciences. In.: Conte R, Hegselmann R, Terna P (eds.) Simulating Social Phenomena. Berlin: Springer.

Bingenheimer, J.B., & Raudenbush, S.W. (2004). Statistical and Substantive Inferences in Public Health: Issues in the Application of Multilevel Models. *Annual Review of Public Health* 25, 53–77.

Blanchard, T., & Lyson, T. (2002). Access to Low Cost Groceries in Nonmetropolitan Counties: Large Retailers and the Creation of Food Deserts. Paper Presented at the Measuring Rural Diversity Conference, Washington D.C. Retrieved May 6, 2006, from http://srdc.msstate.edu/ measuring/blanchard.pdf.

Blanchard, T., & Lyson, T. (2003). "Retail Concentration, Food Deserts, and Food Disadvantaged Communities in Rural America." Final Report for Food Assistance Grant Program, Southern Rural Development Center, Economic Research Service, U.S. Department of Agriculture. Retrieved April 14, 2006, from http://srdc.msstate.edu/focusareas/health/fa/blanchard02_final.pdf.

Brooks, W.T., & Redlin, M. (2009). Occupational Aspirations, Rural to Urban Migration, and Intersectionality: A Comparison of White, Black, and Hispanic Male and Female Group Chances for Leaving Rural Counties. *Southern Rural Sociology* 24(1), 130–152.

Bourdieu, P. (1984). *Distinction: A Social Critique of the Judgment of Taste*. Cambridge: Harvard University Press.

Carter-Pokras, O., & Baquet, C. (2002). What is a "Health Disparity"? Public Health Reports 117, 426–434.

Centers for Disease Control and Prevention. (2011). National Center for Health Statistics. VitalStats. Retrieved September July 16, 2011 from http://www.cdc.gov/nchs/vitalstats.htm

Centers for Disease Control and Prevention. (2011). CDC Health Disparities and Inequalities Report – United States, 2011. Morbidity and Mortality Weekly Report Supplement/Vol. 60. Retrieved July 28, 2011 from http://www.cdc.gov/mmwr/pdf/other/su6001.pdf

Curtis, S., & Jones, I.R. (1998). Is There a Place for Geography in the Analysis of Health Inequality? *Sociology of Health and Illness* 20(5), 645–672.

Domina, T. (2006). What Clean Break? Education and Nonmetropolitan Migration Patterns, 1989–2004. *Rural Sociology* 71(3), 373–398.

Duncan, C., Jones, K., & Moon, G. (1998). Context, Composition and Heterogeneity: Using Multilevel Models in Health Research. *Social Science and Medicine* 46(1), 97–117.

Food Deserts.Org. (2006). Retrieved April 20, 2006, from http://www.fooddeserts.org/images/whatisfd.htm.

Frank, L.D, & Engelke, P. (2001). The Built Environment and Human Activity Patterns: Exploring the Impacts of Urban Form on Public Health. *Journal of Planning Literature* 16, 202–218.

Fulfrost, B., & Howard, P. (2006). Mapping the Markets: The Relative Density of Retail Food Stores in Densely Populated Census Blocks in the Central Coast Region of California. Report to the Second Harvest Food Bank of Santa Cruz and San Benito Counties and the Agriculture and Land Based Training Association. Retrieved July 15, 2011 from http://www.escholarship.org.proxy.lib.ohio-state.edu/uc/item/34j371tf

Godwin, S., & Tegegne, F. (2006). Lack of Easy Accessibility as a Potential Barrier to Adequate Fruit and Vegetable Consumption by Limited-Resource Individuals. *Journal of Food Distribution Research* 37(1), 81–86.

Gorman, D.M, Mezic, J., Mezic, I. & Gruenwald, P.J. (2006). Agent-Based Modeling of Drinking Behavior: A Preliminary Model and Potential Applications to Theory and Practice. *American Journal of Public Health* 96(11), 2055–2060

Kauffman, P. R. (1998). Rural Poor Have Less Access to Supermarkets, Large Grocery Stores. *Rural Development Perspectives* 13(3), 19–26.

Kearns, R.A., & Joseph, A.E. (1993). Space in its Place: Developing the Link in Medical Geography. Social Science and Medicine 37(6), 711–717.

Kuo, S. H., & Lin, B.H. (2000). Estimation of Food Demand and Nutrient Elasticities from Household Survey Data. Food and Rural Economics Division, Economic Research Service, U.S. Department of Agriculture. (Technical Bulletin. No. 1887). Washington, DC.

Luke, D.A. (2004). Multilevel Modeling. Sage University Paper Series. Quantitative Applications in the Social Sciences: Series 143. Thousand Oaks: Sage Publications.

Lobao, L., Hooks. G., & Tickamyer, A. (2007). Advancing the Sociology of Spatial Inequality in The Sociology of Spatial Inequality. Albany: State University of New York Press.

Lyson, T.A., & Raymer, A.L. (2000). Stalking the Wiley Multinational: Power and Control in the U.S. Food System. *Agriculture and Human Values* 17, 199–208.

Mancino, L., Lin, B.H., & Ballenger, N. (2004). The Role of Economics in Eating Choices and Weight Outcomes. Economic Research Service, U.S. Department of Agriculture. (Agricultural Information Bulletin. No. 791). Washington, DC.

Mari Gallagher Research and Consulting Group. (2006). Examining the Impact of Food Deserts on Public Health in Chicago. Retrieved June 10, 2007, from http://www.marigallagher.com/site_media/dynamic/project_files/Chicago_ Food_Desert _ Report.pdf.

Morland, K., Wing, S., Roux, A.D., & Poole, C. (2001). Neighborhood Characteristics Associated with the Location of Food Stores and Food Service Places. *American Journal of Preventative Medicine* 22(1), 23–29.

Morton, L.W., Bitto, E.A., Oakland, M.J., & Sand, M. (2005). Solving the Problem of Iowa Food Deserts: Food Insecurity and Civic Structure. *Rural Sociology* 70(1), 94–112.

Neckerman, K.M. (2004). *Social Inequality*. New York: Russell Sage Foundation.

Rice, K. (2010). Measuring the Likelihood of Food Insecurity in Ohio's Food Deserts. *Journal of Food Distribution Research* 41(1), 101–107.

Rose, D., Bodor, J.N., Swalm, C.M., Rice, J.C., Farley, T.A., & Hutchinson, P.L. (2009). Deserts in New Orleans? Illustrations of Urban Food Access and Implications for Policy. Paper prepared for University of Michigan National Poverty Center/USDA Economic Research Service, USDA Conference "Understanding the Economic Concepts and Characteristics of Food Access.'

Roux, A.V.D. (2000). Multilevel Analysis in Public Health Research. *Annual Review of Public Health* 21, 171–192.

Sargent, R.G. (2007). Verification and Validation of Simulation Models. Proceedings of the 2007 Winter Simulation Conference.

Sharkey, J.R., & Horel, S. (2009). Characteristics of Potential Spatial Access to a Variety of Fruits and Vegetables in a large Rural Area. Paper prepared for University of Michigan National Poverty Center/USDA Economic Research Service, USDA Conference "Understanding the Economic Concepts and Characteristics of Food Access.'

Snijders, T.A.B. (2005). Fixed and Random Effects. In Everitt, B.S., and Howell, D.C. eds. Encyclopedia of Statistics in Behavioral Science. Hoboken, NJ: John Wiley and Sons.

Story, M., Kaphingst, K.M., Robinson-O'Brien, R., & Glanz, K. (2008). Creating Healthy Food and Eating Environments: Policy and Environmental Approaches. *Annual Review Public Health* 29, 253–272.

United States Department of Agriculture. (2011). Retrieved February 8, 2011, from http://www.ers.usda.gov/Briefing/FoodSecurity/

Ver Ploeg, M., Breneman, V., Farrigan, T., Hamrick, K., Hopkins, D., Kaufman, P., Lin, B.H., Nord, M., Smith, T., Williams, R., Kinnison, K., Olander, C., Singh, A., & Tuckermanty, E. (2009). Access to Affordable and Nutritious Food: Measuring and Understanding Food Deserts and their Consequences, [Administrative Publication No. (AP-036)] Retrieved September 23, 2010, from http://www.ers.usda.gov/Publications/AP/AP036/

Yang, Y., Roux, A.V.D., Auchincloss, A.H., Rodriguez, D.A., & Brown, D.G. (2011). A Spatial Agent-Based Model for the Simulation of Adult's Daily Walking Within a City. *American Journal of Preventive Medicine* 40(3), 353–361.

Chapter 5
Urban Renaissance or Invasion: Planning the Development of a Simulation Model of Gentrification

Adam Eckerd and Tony Reames

Abstract Gentrification has gone from being perceived as a process that cities should avoid at all costs to a welcome result of sound economic redevelopment policy. This transformation in perception is rooted in the recent decoupling of the inflow of high-status residents to the urban core from the outflow of low-status residents. However, it is unclear whether this decoupling is based on an actual lack of a relationship between displacement of the poor and urban resettlement by the rich or is rather a relic of the empirical difficulty of empirically tracking the movements of displaced populations. In this chapter, we propose assessing the extent to which the decoupling of gentrification and displacement is warranted by deriving an agent-based residential sorting model to represent the dynamics of urban neighborhood change.

5.1 Introduction

Urban neighborhoods are dynamic. The communities in which people live are constantly in flux, with multiple processes interacting—residents move in and out, businesses open and close, the housing stock ages and is replaced, and the larger city and region evolve and adapt. While some neighborhoods may remain relatively stable, others change dramatically over short periods of time. Gentrification is one such change, wherein neighborhoods transition from comparatively low socioeconomic status to comparatively high socioeconomic status (Kennedy and Leonard 2001). Although common in urban areas, the complexity of gentrification has engendered a variety of different explanations and implications that are attributed

A. Eckerd (✉) • T. Reames
Center for Public Administration and Policy, School of Public and International Affairs, Virginia Polytechnic Institute and State University, 1021 Prince Street, Alexandria, VA 22314
e-mail: aeckerd@gmail.com; tonyreames@ku.edu

A. Desai (ed.), *Simulation for Policy Inquiry*, DOI 10.1007/978-1-4614-1665-4_5,
© Springer Science+Business Media, LLC 2012

to the process (Hamnett 1991). In recent years, there have been two opposing perspectives in gentrification research; either the displacement of lower socioeconomic status residents is an integral and assured feature of the process, or it is a possible, but by no means guaranteed, side effect of gentrification (Slater 2006; Lees and Ley 2008; Freeman 2008). There is little doubt that at least some displacement occurs, but the difficulty collecting aggregate data on displaced residents makes these findings difficult to generalize.

At its root, the problem is definitional. Two sets of scholars have proposed different definitions of what actually constitutes gentrification. One camp describes gentrification in two parts—first, high-status residents move in and then low-status residents move out (Slater 2006). The other camp has decoupled these two concepts, with gentrification constituting only high-status move in and referring to potential low-status move out as displacement (Hamnett 2003). The implications of this decoupling, however, are much more than simply definitional. The efficacy of policies intended to spur neighborhood redevelopment may hinge upon answering the question of how prevalent displacement is (Vigdor 2002; O'Sullivan 2002; Lees 2008; Wacquant 2008; Eckerd 2011). If redevelopment efforts can create incentives to bring new, wealthier residents and businesses to urban neighborhoods without displacing existing residents, then the process may be worth encouraging. If, however, creating such incentives worsens the condition of low-status residents by forcing them to relocate, then urban governments must be careful about how neighborhood redevelopment occurs (Newman and Wyly 2006).

In this chapter, via a description of the process used in the early planning stages of a simulation model, we will propose an agent-based model to help understand the extent to which lower socioeconomic status residents are likely to be displaced in the gentrification process and explore whether it is appropriate to conceptually decouple gentrification from displacement. To begin, we describe the conditions under which simulation models can help us understand complex policy areas and elaborate on how a study of gentrification fits these conditions. We then discuss how such a model is planned and developed, describing the various decisions that must be made in the conceptualization and operationalization of a simulation model.

5.2   Simulating Public Policy

Isolating the effects of any particular public policy is a complicated exercise. Policies are implemented in social systems that are affected by any number of other policies as well as interactions between individuals, groups, organizations, governments, and their contexts. At best, we can usually only roughly gage whether a policy has had some positive or negative effect upon the intended beneficiaries and whether there are a large number of unintended consequences. For some policy areas, this level of knowledge is sufficient to aid in policy making, but when policy is intended to address *ill-structured* or *wicked* problems, the consequences of applying faulty assumptions to policy designs may, at best, be inconsequential or, at worst, severe

(Rittel and Webber 1973). Wicked problems are problems whose causes and therefore solutions are unclear, with today's solutions often leading to new sets of problems (Balint et al. 2011). With an inability to isolate the overall, system-wide effects of a policy in a wicked problem area, solutions may be contributing to, or even exacerbating, the problematic situation rather than solving it. The concern regarding gentrification and displacement is that policy efforts that are intended to revitalize or redevelop areas could potentially overshoot the mark. The benefits of revitalization are usually intended to be received by existing residents of a community; but if existing residents are forced to leave such areas as a result of the move in of higher socioeconomic status residents and subsequent escalating rents, then the intended beneficiaries of the policy may actually end up being worse off (Vigdor 2002).

Economic development policies are not the only types of policies implemented in complex social systems. In many policy realms, there are too many variables interacting in too many different ways to enable us to differentiate what is caused by a policy incentive versus what is caused by a myriad of other seemingly exogenous factors. Nevertheless, policy analysts still must attempt to disaggregate these effects and determine the extent to which the policy solution has been effective at addressing the problem. With advances in computational capacity, simulation has become one way that policy analysts can isolate the specific effects of a policy, while also gaining some understanding of the dynamic nature of complex policy areas (Johnston et al. 2007). Simulation techniques have been used to assess policies related to traffic patterns and flows, land use (Engelen et al. 1995) and urban dynamics (Batty et al. 1999), in addition to gentrification (O'Sullivan 2002; Torrens and Nara 2007).

A variety of different simulation techniques can be useful to contribute to our understanding of complex policy systems. The other chapters of this text cover several of the more common approaches, but all of these simulation techniques share some common aspects. Like other attempts to model social reality, simulation models are simplifications of reality and, as such, reveal trends from which we can infer causes, but cannot determine causality (Davis et al. 2007). Because of their dynamic but self-contained nature, simulations are useful for exploring the potential effects of tweaking assumptions or variables within the context of the simplification of the model, but are not necessarily useful for deriving actual estimates of policy effects (Berger 2001). Simulation approaches are useful in cases where experimentation or point estimation is difficult or ethically problematic (Gass 1983; Casti 1997; Johnston et al. 2007), and through comparative trials, simulations can enable researchers to isolate effects of policy within the model structure (Davis et al. 2007). Simulation trials absent policy can be compared to those incorporating policy (or different policy alternatives) to determine the relative efficacy of policy in achieving stated goals and also for exploring some of the potential unintended consequences (Davis et al. 2007; Eckerd 2011).

Agent-based modeling is a simulation approach that can be used in policy analysis to explore how the decisions that individuals make can affect social structures and policy outcomes. An agent-based model is a "bottom-up" operationalization of social interaction (Axelrod 1997), wherein individual, autonomous agents interact with one another according to a set of decision rules defined by model developers. Agent interactions are dynamic through time, enabling a view of the macrolevel social structures and processes that emerge as a result of these individual decisions and interactions (Holland 1998; Axelrod 1997; Epstein and Axtell 1996). Schelling's (1978) study on residential segregation was among the first widely known agent-based models deployed in an urban dynamics context. Schelling's simple model showed how relatively benign individual preferences for having neighbors similar to themselves can accumulate to substantial residential segregation on the macrolevel. O'Sullivan (2002) and Torrens and Nara (2007) both simulate the context of gentrification, arguing that gentrification is a complex process that is not easily understood through statistical analysis, nor are case-based results sufficiently generalizable to draw meaningful policy conclusions. As a process that is intertwined with a multitude of other social systems, neighborhood evolution is an excellent example of a complex process that is difficult to study empirically or generalize across different contexts (Beauregard 1986) and is thus a process ideally suited for exploring via simulation.

5.3   Gentrification and Displacement

Broadly, gentrification is the process through which formerly lower socioeconomic status neighborhoods become higher socioeconomic status neighborhoods (Hamnett 1991). The causes and results of this process are not especially clear; there may be a variety of reasons why lower status neighborhoods transition to higher status, and the results of that process likely spill beyond the borders of one single neighborhood (Wyly and Hammel 1999; Torrens and Nara 2007). Given this lack of clarity with respect to causes and consequences, there are several different definitions of the phenomenon used throughout the extant literature and much disagreement regarding the extent to which gentrification is a problem (Smith 1987; Ley 1987; Redfern 2003; Slater 2006). While there is general agreement that the influx of higher socioeconomic status residents is part of the process, the displacement of lower socioeconomic status residents is sometimes conceived of as an integral feature of gentrification, but also viewed as a possible, but not assured, result of the process (Slater 2006). Some representative definitions of gentrification are provided in Table 5.1, illustrating the range from more benign, noncausal definitions to explicitly normative, ideological descriptions of the process.

Table 5.2 presents a sample of means by which displacement has been defined in past studies, again illustrating a wide range of views from the purely procedural to a process imbued with meaning.

Beyond these definitional issues, it is also unclear exactly where, when, and under what circumstances gentrification will occur and whether that process is beneficial or not (Sullivan 2007; Freeman 2008; Lees and Ley 2008). There are a multitude of potential causes, ranging from regional characteristics endemic to the urban system (Sanchez and Dawkins 2001), to policy efforts that affect

Table 5.1 Definitions of gentrification

Author	Definition
Glass et al. (1964)	"[T]his process of 'gentrification' starts in a district it goes on rapidly, until all or most of the original working-class occupiers are displaced and the whole social character of the district is changed"
Nelson (1988)	"The process by which reinvestment in urban neighborhoods leads to an inflow of residents of higher socioeconomic status than the original residents of the community"
Smith (1979)	"[P]oor and working-class neighborhoods in the inner city are refurbished by an influx of private capital and middle-class homebuyers and renters"
Hamnett (1991)	"[G]entrification commonly involves the invasion by middle-class or higher-income groups of previously working-class neighbourhoods"
Hackworth (2002)	"[T]he production of space for progressively more affluent users"

Table 5.2 Definitions of displacement

Author	Definition
Grier and Grier (1978)	"Displacement occurs when any household is forced to move from its residence by conditions that affect the dwelling or its immediate surroundings, and; (1) are beyond the household's reasonable ability to control or prevent; (2) occur despite the household's having met all previously imposed conditions of occupancy; and make continued occupancy by that household impossible, hazardous, or unaffordable"
Lee and Hodge (1984)	[Displacement occurs only via] "private action including abandonment, demolition, eviction, condominium conversion, mortgage default and the termination of a rental contract"
LeGates and Hartman (1986)	"Gentrification will force low-income minority groups out of desirable inner-city neighbourhoods to less desirable areas, thus reducing their quality of life and defusing their political power"
Ellen and O'Regan (2011)	"[D]isplacement is not simply about exiting a unit, it is about why the exit occurs"

neighborhood characteristics (Wyly and Hammel 1999). There is also a dynamic interaction of different social systems from the economic (London et al. 1986; Smith 1982) to the social (London et al. 1986; Papachristos et al. 1984) and political (London et al. 1986: Rose 1984). And with a set of potential detrimental outcomes, such as displacement and destruction of historic communities (Abu-Lughod and Janet 1999; Chernoff 1980; Levy and Roman 1980; Pattillo 2007; Perez 2004; Rymond-Richmond 2007; Smith 1996), and beneficial outcomes, such as enhanced livability and an influx of jobs (Clay 1979; Florida 2002; Freeman 2006; McKinnish et al. 2010), gentrification is a quintessential example of a complex process (Beauregard 1986). As such, there are several, not necessarily congruent, theoretical points of view that appear equally valid to apply to the study of gentrification, and the process is not easily attributable to one set of causal drivers, nor one set of results (Freeman 2008). Differentiating between these causal mechanisms and results is important in a policy context because the line differentiating gentrification from a policy-oriented goal of economic redevelopment is fine (Clark 1992). Ideally, economic redevelopment is the driver for ensuring that benefits flow to city residents most in need. Through redevelopment, cities hope to provide poor residents with jobs, better access to services, and safer communities (Bartik 1991; Valler and Wood 2010). However, there is a risk that this redevelopment will overshoot its goal and spur a rapid escalation in rents as demand for property by higher socioeconomic status residents in the neighborhood increases (Brueckner and Rosenthal 2009). As property values rise and rents increase, long-time residents may not be able to afford to stay and are displaced to neighborhoods that have not yet been redeveloped, potentially leaving the intended policy beneficiaries worse off than before redevelopment plans were implemented (Vigdor 2002). Depending upon one's point of view, this displacement is either an integral feature of gentrification or a possible result (Slater 2006) and the question hinges upon the extent to which lower socioeconomic status populations are actually displaced by incoming higher socioeconomic status residents (Palen and London 1984; Zukin 1987). In either case, the goal of economic redevelopment is usually not to benefit incoming new residents who likely already have stable employment and wealth, but to benefit residents of communities where access to jobs and services is limited (Bartik 1991).

The decoupling of gentrification and displacement in the literature points to the complication of understanding the process (Slater 2006; Freeman 2008). Viewed as one process, most urban analysts would agree that gentrification should be avoided to the extent possible in order to not displace low socioeconomic status individuals (Clark 2005). If, however, these two concepts are decoupled, then the influx of higher socioeconomic status individuals is not necessarily problematic provided that there is not subsequent displacement of low socioeconomic status residents in turn (Sullivan 2007). Unfortunately, throughout nearly 40 years of study, there is little definitive evidence regarding the extent of or nature of displacement of lower socioeconomic status residents that occurs (Slater 2006). Anecdotal evidence of displacement can be found, but there has been little generalizable evidence of the extent or costs of this displacement (Lyons 1996; Vigdor 2002; Sullivan 2007). Such data are difficult to acquire; incoming residents to a focal community are easier to find than outgoing residents. New residents can be interviewed and surveyed, inventories of neighborhood business and service growth can be tracked, and new building permits can be assessed. However, unless a researcher was studying the community before the gentrification cycle began, he or she is unlikely to know who lived in the area before higher status residents began moving in and she is unlikely to be able to track the potentially disparate movements that those who leave the community take after gentrification has begun. While the decoupling has been treated as an ideological divide in the literature (Slater 2006), it may also be the case that the decoupling is a result of a practical data problem: exiting residents are hard to track (Vigdor 2002).

Gentrification is a complex, multifaceted issue (Freeman 2006), but the question of whether its benefits outweigh its costs hinges on the extent of displacement that occurs (Vigdor 2002; Freeman 2005). With a complex process at play and data that are difficult to collect, this is a question ideally suited for exploration through simulation. Throughout the remainder of this chapter, we will describe the conceptual development of an agent-based simulation model to assess the extent to which displacement of original neighborhood residents appears to occur as a result of an influx of incoming, wealthier residents.

5.4 Agent-Based Models

The key factors that underlie an agent-based model are the spatial context, the sets of agents, and temporal rules of behavior. The spatial context is a visualized landscape consisting of the computer display pixels that make up the representation in the model. Each pixel is spatially defined relative to all other pixels in computer memory and as such form the basis for the spatial context of the agent-based model. In the model, cells (or patches) are set according to a predefined number of pixels (for instance, 25 pixels make up one cell), and each cell is, in turn, defined spatially relative to all other cells in a Cartesian plane. We will refer to these landscape demarcations as either *patches* or *plots* through the rest of this chapter. The heterogeneous agents, sometimes called *turtles*, in an agent-based model can be representations of any individual and/or autonomous actor. Agents need not be representations of sentient actors, although many agent-based models focus on the behavior of people or animals. The common theme of agents is that they either act or are acted upon according to a set of predefined rules that allow researchers to assess model outcomes over time. Rules can apply to the behavior of individual agents, or they can apply globally to the model's context. As the model proceeds in time, agents adapt according to the rules applied to them and the context changes in response to the aggregation of those adaptations. Time intervals can be defined according to any specified frame, and each time interval is referred to as a *tick*, which is the term we will use going forward.

Agent-based models are useful beyond exploring the types of behavior that emerge within the model; the development of the model itself can be a valuable generative learning experience for model developers as well (Epstein 2006). The process of building an agent-based model requires a careful derivation of the rules of behavior (and rules for changing those rules) underlying the agents' decisions. Model developers must anticipate each decision situation that agents will be faced with during the model's simulations and operationalize these assumptions mathematically. This requires developers to mathematically formalize theoretical behaviors for the purposes of exploring social implications in a simulated world that is a representation of society that is a balance between parsimony and realism. The assumptions that are made in the derivation process dictate how the agents in the model will behave, and as such, developers must be clear about what assumptions have been made and why.

A model of gentrification must account for variables at different levels of social interaction. There are potentially important characteristics of the metropolitan region (Wyly and Hammel 1999), the neighborhood (Brueckner and Rosenthal 2009; Smith 1979), and the individuals that live in, or could potentially have interest in living in the community (Ley 1986). Moreover, as an urban dynamics model, it will function according to broader understanding regarding neighborhood cycles and individual preferences (Brueckner and Rosenthal 2009; Schelling 1978). The model will include individual agents who select a place to live, plots of land with different prices and attributes that the agents may choose from, collections of plots that define different neighborhoods, rules for how agents make decisions, and the effects that these decisions have on plot attributes, neighborhood characteristics, and subsequent agent decision rules. In the remainder of this chapter, we will describe how we made these choices for a model of urban gentrification, detail the theoretical assumptions to which we hewed, and point out some the advantages and limitations of the approaches taken.

5.5 Model Planning

5.5.1 The Region

Different regions at different times have seemed more prone to gentrification than others (Lees 2000; Kennedy and Leonard 2001). Regional considerations may be very important for the propensity of neighborhoods in such areas to gentrify, which could partially explain difficulties in determining the important causal factors that influence the occurrence of gentrification. Using an agent-based simulation model, these regional characteristics could be tweaked and compared. Different types of regions with different economic and geographic characteristics could be compared over simulation trials. With the goal of this model aimed at determining the extent of the relationship between high-status move in and low-status move out, however, regional characteristics are less integral to the project's focus. Taking advantage of the bottom-up nature of agent-based models, the gentrification model developed focuses instead on neighborhood characteristics and individual preferences. This is an important modeling decision that fundamentally focuses the model on one aspect of gentrification, while leaving aside some potentially important gentrification considerations. Nevertheless, to keep the model tractable and programmable, such bounds must be set early in the development process.

This decision relates to one of the core debates in the gentrification literature. Although it is almost certainly the case that there are both a set of individuals who desire to live in redeveloping urban areas as well as a stock of undervalued properties in the urban core, much of the debate regarding the key causes of gentrification have focused on the determination of which of these two influences is a comparatively more important cause of the phenomenon (Smith 1979; Ley 1986; Hamnett 1991). Given the focus in the literature on neighborhood and individual characteristics, the decision was made to hold the regional characteristics constant. While

Fig. 5.1 Visual representation of the agent-based model

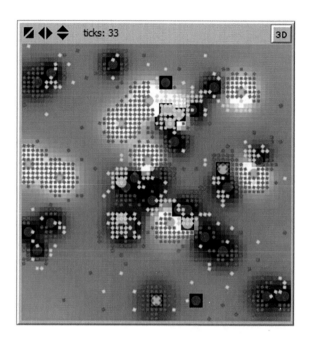

in the model development stage, we could have constructed the model in such a way as to run sets of simulations varying regional characteristics, it was our choice to focus instead on assessing the relative prevalence of gentrification-related displacement through the lens of the housing supply (Smith 1979) and the residential demand (Ley 1986) gentrification hypotheses (see Hamnett 1991 or Lees 2000 for an in-depth discussion). Since regional variables will not change during the simulation trials, the regional context is effectively held constant. The model explores the displacement of low socioeconomic status residents in an unchanging regional context.

The spatial region, as shown in Fig. 5.1, consists of 2,500 plots upon which individual agents can settle. No more than one agent may occupy one plot at any given time, and there are no barriers to movement on the spatial plain. The advantage of this approach is that we are able to assess relocation absent any of the constraints that actual relocation could pose. The effort is an exploration of relocation and displacement that assumes relocation is as easy as it possibly can be, which will likely make both gentrification and displacement as prevalent as they can be. The disadvantage of this is that it defies reality. There are always costs and constraints limiting relocation, including moving costs and zoning regulations that eliminate many properties from residential consideration. Nevertheless, if displacement is relatively rare even in a simulation model where there are no costs to relocation, the result could suggest that the decoupling of gentrification and displacement in the literature is appropriate.

5.5.2   *Plots*

Patches, or the plots of space upon which agents may locate, are an integral aspect of the model. Plots are conceived of as representations of the homes that agents select, with aggregations of plots constituting neighborhoods. Plots are kept parsimonious, but must be sufficiently complex to build appropriate confidence in the model's realism (Forrester and Senge 1980). As such, each plot should possess unique characteristics, while also belonging to neighborhoods of plots. Much like the real estate of which the model's plots are representations, plots have interdependent relationships with other nearby plots, their neighborhood, and the region as a whole. While the model cannot possibly encompass all of the aspects that make selecting a place to live a complicated endeavor, plots should have a sufficient difference of characteristics to approximate the actual real estate system. The next set of development decisions therefore relate to the extent to which the model's plots will approximate a true real estate market.

At a minimum, since the model is, at its root, a model of a real estate market with a supply of and demand for homes, each plot must have some relative price or value level. One of the key gentrification hypotheses posits that gentrification is more likely in areas with a rent gap (Smith 1979)—areas where the price of homes is well below the potential value of the homes. In real estate research, there are many aspects of a home that are posited to affect the prices—its location in the region, the reputation of the neighborhood in which it is located, the amenities and disamenities located in the neighborhood, characteristics of the home itself including architectural style, square feet, number of rooms, and condition of the home, and characteristics of the lot itself, such as acreage, frontage, and access to transportation (Can 1990; Li and Brown 1980; Zietz et al. 2008). Any or all of these characteristics could be operationalized and included in the agent-based model, but this extent of heterogeneity is not necessary to explore the gentrification process, and inclusion of all of these variables would complicate interpretation of results.

To make analysis manageable, it was therefore determined that all structures on all plots would be treated as homogenous, and analysis would focus instead on location and past settlement patterns. Therefore, no variation in structure size, condition, or architectural character was programmed into the model. The only aspect of structure that is considered is the plot's "age," which is simply counted from the time that the first agent selects the plot in question. This assumption then requires a subsequent assumption that once an agent occupies a plot for the first time, the next agent that occupies the plot "lives" with the same set of conditions as the previous occupant, albeit at a later time. This effectively represents the age of a structure, and a home's age is often a good approximation for other characteristics of the property (Zietz et al. 2008). Using this as a proxy enables a simpler interpretation of the effect of housing characteristics on gentrification and displacement. Achieving simplicity, however, requires some simplifying assumptions. As such, in order to keep prices relatively simple, age will affect price rather simply; as a home's age increases, its price decreases (Zietz et al. 2008), all else equal.

Arguably more important in the consideration of a home's characteristics is its location (Smith 1979). The neighborhood in which a plot is located is likely to have a substantial effect on its price and value regardless of the structure's age (or other characteristics). Therefore, the price of plots in the model should be functionally based on the neighborhood in which the plot is located and the prices of other plots in its immediate vicinity. Since neighborhoods are the focus of most gentrification studies, neighborhood characteristics are especially important to characterize appropriately in the model. Finally, the price of a plot must also be some function of residential demand.

The price of a plot therefore will be a function of the length of time that the plot has been occupied, the demarcated neighborhood in which it is located, the prices of plots in its immediate vicinity, and the residential demand for the plot itself. Although these variables do not encompass the totality of the factors that determine home prices, in the simplified world of the model, these should adequately encompass the range of price factors necessary for agent decision making.

5.5.3   Agents

The crux of an agent-based model is that the focus of decision making for the model's behavior is on autonomous, heterogeneous individuals, or agents. The agents in an agent-based model can be as heterogeneous as the model developer desires, but they are always autonomous decision makers that assess the current circumstances (at some given point in time, t) and make decisions accordingly. In a model of gentrification, as with many urban dynamics models, agent behavior will tend to focus on location decision making and the emergence of neighborhood impacts through the aggregation of those decisions. Thus, model development decisions for agent behaviors focus on how location decisions will be made and how much variety there is in the agents' characteristics. Once again, these decisions must factor model tractability with realism and ensure that agents are sufficiently complex and heterogeneous for the model to inform policy, but not so complex as to render multiple or very complex explanations for the results equally plausible.

Given the discussion above with regard to plot characteristics, some of the keys to agent decision making have already been effectively made. In designing the plots, the decision was made that agents will, in part, base location decisions on the price and characteristics of plots and the characteristics of neighborhoods. However, agents may also have preferences regarding demographic characteristics of the agents located nearby as well as varying interests in locating near certain amenities or away from disamenities. At this stage in the development of the model, it must be determined which factors will influence the location decision and at what relative weights. In other words, we must derive some utility function that agents will use in selecting their optimal location.

At the same time, decisions must be made regarding how heterogeneous agents should be. The extent of heterogeneity possible is bounded only by computational power; agents could be programmed to be quite complex, with a host of variables that can change over time during each simulation trial. However, as with plots, making agents too heterogeneous can constrain the ability to attribute model behavior to any specific variable (Dean et al. 1999). Conversely, if agents are too homogeneous, variations in decision making may be so few that no emergent behavior is visible through the simulation trials (Dean et al. 1999). The power of dynamic models is their ability to set a circumstance based on behavioral assumptions and allow patterns to emerge as a result of the aggregation of these behaviors (Epstein 2006). Therefore, agents need to be heterogeneous enough to produce meaningful differences in outcomes, but homogeneous enough that those outcomes can be attributed to some key differences in agents' characteristics or behavior. The choice is whether to create a less realistic model by making agents relatively homogenous, thereby holding many potential explanatory variables constant, or to make the model more realistic by making agents relatively heterogeneous, thereby potentially making model outcomes attributable to a host of factors beyond the scope of the research in question.

The extent to which agents are homogeneous will affect the scope of decision making rules built into the program. For a model of gentrification, at minimum, agents must vary in one key respect. Since gentrification is defined as the influx of high socioeconomic status residents to low socioeconomic status neighborhoods, agents must, at the very least, be categorized as either low socioeconomic status or high socioeconomic status, for example, by having some agents be *rich* and some be *poor*. A simple, dichotomous categorization of socioeconomic status seems insufficient to capture a social construct as complex as *socioeconomic status*, however. Given competing explanations of gentrification, socioeconomic status may be determined by a host of characteristics beyond just wealth. While wealth or income factors in, racial/ethnic characteristics may be important for socioeconomic status, as may be the level of education, type of employment, or any individual characteristic that can affect the extent to which others view that individual's level of status (Ladd 1977; Slater 2006; Wacquant 2008). No model can truly capture the full scale of socioeconomic status, so the choice centers on determining the appropriate way to simplify and operationalize socioeconomic status. Looking to the gentrification literature, two key characteristics have been posited as being particularly relevant: race and wealth.

Gentrification has been described throughout the extant literature as a class-based phenomenon whereby the wealthy move into poor communities (Banzhaf and Walsh 2008) and as race based whereby whites move into minority, particularly African-American, neighborhoods (Mohai and Bryant 1992). Although it is an oversimplification of socioeconomic status to limit the construct to two characteristics, this limitation makes sense in light of existing theory and literature. Agents in the model will therefore be defined as being members of either the majority or the minority, with each agent possessing a scaled wealth attribute. Socioeconomic status is operationalized as a scale consisting of both wealth and race, with each individual agent possessing one of two possible racial identities with a unique level of wealth. Since gentrification literature tends to view these race and wealth characteristics as definitional for the phenomenon, agents will be homogenous in all other respects. That is, they will make decisions according to the same utility function, albeit within constraints associated with their race and wealth, and all other potential individual characteristics that may important for understanding gentrification will be held constant through the simulation trials.

5.5.4   Rules

With these broad characteristics of the region, plots, and agents in mind, the model development tasks turn to actually formalizing and operationalizing the behavioral rules and decision criteria that agents will use as the model ticks forward through time. Two key mathematical relationships must be formalized: how the real estate market functions via prices of plots and how agents make their location decisions. Within this framework, interactions must be formalized to establish how the relationships between plot and plot, between plot and agent, and between agent and agent actually operate.

Shifting to the development stage requires a change in focus from a theoretical perspective regarding which variables are expected to interact with one another, to a focus on validating the model whereby those theorized relationships are calibrated to observed behavior in actual urban settings. The process at this stage becomes iterative—operationalizing relationships in different ways and assessing whether the behavior that emerges in each functional form approximates what has actually been observed (Forrester and Senge 1980). That is, the model should converge on instances where it looks like the real world. Confidence is built as the model increasingly shows that it is able to accurately approximate or retrodict what has been historically observed. By comparing model results with past, observed behavior in the actual system, the model can gain credibility over time. Although the ability to accurately re-create the past does not confer the ability to predict the future, accurate retrodiction is seen as an indicator of model validity and therefore usefulness.

Forrester and Senge (1980) described a battery of tests, falling into three broad areas: model structure, model behavior, and policy implications. By confirming that the structure of the model matches the structure of the real system and the behavior predicted by the model matches behavior in the real system, the odds increase that the model will be viewed as a relatively valid representation of the real system. To that end, the Forrester and Senge (1980) tests, shown in Table 5.3, are comparative in nature, with the expectation that a model is more valid to the extent that it compares favorably to the structure and behavior of the real system.

By calibrating a model with observed data from the past, we ensure that the model is a valid representation of past system behavior, but one of the key complications for modeling social science behaviors is that past behavior is an uncertain predictor of future behavior (Epstein 2006). It is a probabilistic predictor to be sure, but it is far from certain that modeling assumptions that accurately retrodict past behavior will lead to accurate predictions of future behavior. Nevertheless, if we

Table 5.3 Forrester and Senge's (1980) tests for building confidence in models

Category	Test	Description
Model structure	Structure verification	Does model structure correspond with structure of real system?
	Parameter verification	Do model parameters correspond conceptually and numerically with real system parameters?
	Extreme conditions	Does the model remain stable under extreme variation?
	Dimensional consistency	Do model units of measure correspond with actual units?
	Boundary adequacy	Does the structure satisfy the model's purpose?
Model behavior	Behavior reproduction	Does behavior in the model match observed behavior in the real system?
	Behavior prediction	Does the model predict plausible behavior in the future?
	Behavior anomaly	Do model assumptions produce any behaviors that are anomalous to behavior in the real system?
	Family member	Is the model generalizable to related systems or is it only applicable to one unique situation?
	Surprise behavior	Does the model predict the same unexpected behavior that has occurred in the real system?
	Extreme policy	If an extreme policy is followed in the real system, does the model accurately predict the actual outcomes?
	Boundary adequacy	Are all necessary elements in place for the model to address the policy problem?
	Behavior sensitivity	Do plausible changes in model parameters lead to implausible results?
Policy implications	System improvement	Does the model provide results that are beneficial to policy makers?
	Changed behavior prediction	Does the model accurately predict changes in behavior brought about by changes in policy?
	Boundary adequacy	If model structure is changed, do the policy recommendations change dramatically?
	Policy sensitivity	How uncertain are the policy recommendations?

accept that past can be prelude, then calibrated simulation models can provide a great deal of insight into what sorts of social processes are comparatively more likely to emerge if certain policies are adopted.

The actual operationalization of the relationships proposed in the model is, therefore, an iterative process of calibration rather than simply a formalization of theorized dependencies. In the proposed model, there must be a price function for plots of land, a utility function for agent preferences, and spatial functions regarding neighborhood desirability and settlement patterns. While theory can guide model development regarding which variables should be included, the actual functional form of these calculations will change throughout the development process as the simulation is tested and steps are taken to ensure that the model approximates the sorts of behaviors and outcomes that we have actually observed in cities. Where such calculations start is less relevant than where they end, although it is usually useful to look to the relevant extant literature for estimates of the numerical nature of the relationships that are being modeled.

5.6 Conclusion

Simulation models can be a useful asset to policy researchers and policy makers. Through the development of simulation models, we can learn about and explore policy contexts where the complex nature of interdependent relationships between systems and actors make policy prescriptions difficult. Through the calibration of models to real systems, we learn how to functionally codify the nature of those relationships and explore how different policy prescriptions might affect outcomes of interest.

In this chapter, we described the process through which an agent-based model was planned for the purposes of exploring the extent to which it is appropriate to decouple the gentrification and displacement concepts. Urban systems are inherently complex (Beauregard 1986), and the causes and consequences of neighborhood changes have historically been difficult to assess. To address these complications, we proposed an agent-based model of a simple urban area. The model will continue through the development process ultimately resulting in a tool that enables researchers and decision makers to explore the extent to which it appears likely that lower socioeconomic status residents will be forced to relocate as a result of higher socioeconomic status residents relocating into their neighborhoods. While it would be inappropriate to rely solely on a simulation model to design specific aspects of an eventual policy that addresses the negative aspects of gentrification, the project will provide insight into the larger questions of who benefits from neighborhood redevelopment and who does not. In a complex policy area where empirical results have not led to clear conclusions, such an exercise can be of tremendous value. The agent-based model planned through this chapter will not definitively show whether or not we should consider gentrification and displacement to be two independent processes, but it will add to our field of knowledge by explicitly exploring the underlying structure of these neighborhood processes based on what we currently know about gentrification. By simulating simplified alternative worlds, we can gain insight into how policies can both encourage economic development and ensure that the benefits of such development flow to those most in need.

References

Abu-Lughod, Janet L. (1999). *New York, Chicago, Los Angeles: America's Global Cities.* Minneapolis, MN: University of Minnesota Press.

Axelrod, R. (1997). *The Complexity of Cooperation: Agent-Based Models of Competition and Collaboration.* Princeton, NJ: Princeton University Press.

Balint, P., Stewart, R. Desai, A., and Walters, L. (2011). *Wicked Environmental Problems: Managing Uncertainty and Conflict.* Washington, DC: Island Press.

Banzhaf H., and Walsh, R. 2008. Do People Vote with Their Feet? An empirical test of Tiebout's mechanism. *American Economic Review.* 98(3): 843–863.

Bartik, T. J. (1991). *Who Benefits from State and Local Economic Development Policies?* Kalamazoo, MI: W.E. Upjohn Institute for Employment Research.

Batty, M., Xie, Y., and Sun, Z. (1999). Modeling urban dynamics through GIS-based cellular automata. *Computers, Environment and Urban Systems*, 23(3), 205–233.

Beauregard, R. (1986). The chaos and complexity of gentrification. In N. Smith and P. Williams eds. *The gentrification of the city* (pp. 35–55). Allen and Unwin, Boston.

Berger, T. (2001). Agent-based spatial models applied to agriculture: A simulation tool for technology diffusion, resource use changes and policy analysis. *Agricultural Economics*, 25, 245–260.

Brueckner, J, and Rosenthal, S. (2009). Gentrification and neighborhood housing cycles: Will America's future downtowns be rich? *Review of Economics and Statistics*, 91(4), 725–743.

Can, A. (1990). The Measurement of Neighborhood Dynamics in Urban House Prices. *Economic Geography,* 66(3), 254–272.

Casti, J. (1997). *Would-Be Worlds: How Simulation is Changing the Frontiers of Science.* Toronto: Wiley.

Chernoff, Michael. (1980). Social displacement in a renovating neighborhood's commercial district: Atlanta. In Shirley B. Laska and Daphne Spain eds. *Back to the City: Issues in Neighborhood Renovation* (pp. 208–18). New York: Pergamon Press.

Clark, E. (1992). On blindness, centrepieces and complementarity in gentrification theory. *Transactions of the Institute of British Geographers*, (17)3, 358–362.

Clark, E. (2005). The order and simplicity of gentrification: A political challenge. In eds Atkinson, R., and Bridge, G. *Gentrification in a global context: The new urban colonialism.* London: Routledge.

Clay, P., 1979. *Neighborhood Renewal: Middle-class Resettlement and Incumbent Upgrading in American Neighborhoods.* Lexington Books, Lexington, MA.

Davis, J., Eisenhardt, K., and Bingham, C. (2007). Developing theory through simulation methods. *Academy of Management Review*, 32(2), 480–499.

Dean, J., Gumerman, G., Epstein, J., Axtell, R. Swedlund, A., Parker, M., McCarroll, S. (1999). Understanding Anasazi culture change through agent-based modeling. In eds Kohler, T., and Gumerman, G. *Dynamics in Human and Primate Societies.* Oxford: Oxford University Press.

Eckerd, A. (2011). Cleaning up without clearing out? An assessment of environmental gentrification. *Urban Affairs Review*, 47(1), 31–59.

Ellen, I.G., and O'Regan, K.M. (2011). How low income neighborhoods change: entry, exit, and enhancement. *Regional Science and Urban Economics,* 41, 89–97.

Engelen, G., White, R., Uljee, I., and Drazan, P. (1995). Using cellular automata for integrated modeling of socio-environmental systems. *Environmental Monitoring and Assessment*, 34(2), 203–214.

Epstein, J. (2006). *Generative Social Science: Studies in Agent-Based Computational Modeling.* Princeton, NJ: Princeton University Press.

Epstein, J., and Axtell, R. (1996). *Growing Artificial Societies: Social Science from the Bottom Up.* Washington, DC: Brookings Institution Press.

Florida, R. (2002). *The Rise of the Creative Class: And How It's Transforming Work, Leisure, Community and Everyday Life.* New York: Basic Books.

Forrester, J., and Senge, P. (1980). Tests for building confidence in system dynamics models. *TIMS Studies in Management Sciences*, 14, 209–228.

Freeman, L. (2005). Displacement or succession? Residential mobility in gentrifying neighborhoods. *Urban Affairs Review*, 40(4), 463–491.

Freeman, L. (2006). *There Goes the 'Hood: Views of Gentrification from the Ground Up.* Philadelphia, PA: Temple University Press.

Freeman, L. (2008). Comment on 'The eviction of critical perspectives from gentrification research'. *International Journal of Urban and Regional Research*, 32(1), 186–191.

Gass, S. (1983). Decision-aiding models: Validation, assessment, and related issues for policy analysis. *Operations Research*, 31(4), 603–631.

Glass, R., et al. (1964). *London: Aspects of change*. London: MacGibbon and Kee.

Grier, G., & Grier, E.E. (1978). *Urban displacement: a reconnaissance*. Washington, DC: U.S. Department of Housing and Urban Development.

Hackworth, J. (2002). Post-recession gentrification in New York City. *Urban Affairs Review*, 37, 815–843.

Hamnett, C. (1991). The blind men and the elephant: The explanation of gentrification. *Transactions of the Institute of British Geographers*, 16(2), 173–189.

Hamnett, C. (2003). *Unequal City: London in the Global Arena*. London: Routledge.

Holland, J. (1998). *Emergence: From Chaos to Order*. Reading, MA: Perseus.

Johnston, E., Kim, Y., and Ayyangar, M. (2007). Intending the unintended: The act of building agent-based models as a regular source of knowledge generation. *Interdisciplinary Description of Complex Systems*, 5(2), 81–91.

Kennedy, M. and Leonard, P. (2001). Dealing with neighborhood change: A primer on gentrification and policy choices. Discussion paper prepared for The Brookings Institution Center on Urban and Metropolitan Policy.

Ladd, E. (1977). Liberalism upside down: The inversion of the New Deal order. *Political Science Quarterly*, 91(4), 557–600.

Lee, B. A., & Hodge, D.C. (1984). Spatial differentials in residential displacement. *Urban Studies*, 21, 219–231.

Lees, L. (2000). A Reappraisal of gentrification: Towards a 'geography of gentrification'. *Progress in Human Geography*, 24(3), 389–408.

Lees, L. (2008). Gentrification and social mixing: Towards an inclusive urban renaissance? *Urban Studies*, 45(12), 2449–2470.

Lees, L., and Ley, D. (2008). Introduction to special issue on gentrification and public policy. *Urban Studies*, 45(12), 2379–2384.

LeGates, R., and Hartman, C. (1986). The anatomy of displacement in the U.S. In N. Smith and P. Williams (eds) *The Gentrification of the City* (pp.178–200). Boston: Allen and Unwin.

Levy, P. R., and Roman A. C. (1980). The hidden dimensions of culture and class: Philadelphia. In Shirley B. Laska and Daphne Spain eds. *Back to the City: Issues in Neighborhood Renovation* (pp. 143–153). New York: Pergamon Press.

Ley, D. (1986). Alternative explanations for inner-city gentrification: A Canadian assessment. *Annals of the Association of American Geographers*, 76(4), 521–535.

Ley, D. (1987). The rent-gap revisited. *Annals of the Association of American Geographers*, 77, 465–468.

Li. M.M., and Brown, H.J. (1980). Micro-neighborhood externalities and hedonic housing prices. *Land Economics*, 56(2), 125–141.

London, B., Lee, B. A., and Lipton S. G. (1986). The determinants of gentrification in the united states: a city-level analysis. *Urban Affairs Review*, 21, 369–387.

Lyons, M. (1996). Gentrification, socioeconomic change, and the geography of displacement. *Journal of Urban Affairs*, 18(1), 39–62.

McKinnish, T., Walsh, R., White, T.K. (2010). Who gentrifies low-income neighborhoods? *Journal of Urban Economics*, 67 (2), 180–193.

Mohai, P. and B. Bryant. (1992). Environmental racism: Reviewing the evidence, in B. Bryant and P. Mohai eds., *Race and the Incidence of Environmental Hazards*. Boulder, CO: Westview Press.

Nelson, K. (1988). *Gentrification and Distressed Cities.* University of Wisconsin Press: Madison, WI.

Newman, K., and Wyly, E. (2006). The right to stay put, revisited: Gentrification and resistance to displacement in New York City. *Urban Studies,* 43, 23–57.

O'Sullivan, D. (2002). Toward micro-scale spatial modeling of gentrification. *Journal of Geographic Systems,* 4, 251–274.

Palen, J. J., and London, B. (1984). *Gentrification, Displacement and Neighborhood Revitalization.* Albany: SUNY Press.

Papachristos, A., Smith, C., Scherer, M., and Fugiero, M. (1984) More Coffee, Less Crime? The Relationship between Gentrification and Neighborhood Crime Rates in Chicago, 1991 to 2005. *City & Community,* 10(3), 215–240.

Pattillo, M. (2007). *Black on the block: the politics of race and class in the city.* Chicago, IL: University of Chicago Press.

Perez, G. M. (2004). Gentrification, intrametropolitan, migration, and the politics of place. In *The Near Northwest Side Story: Migration, Displacement, and Puerto Rican Families* (pp. 142–152). Berkeley, CA: University of California Press

Redfern, P. (2003). What makes gentrification 'gentrification'? *Urban Studies,* 40(12), 2351–2366.

Rittel, H., and Webber, M. (1973). Dilemmas in a general theory of planning. *Policy Sciences,* 4, 155–169.

Rose, D. (1984). Rethinking gentrification – beyond the uneven development of Marxist urban theory. *Environment and Planning D: Society and Space,* 2(1), 47–74.

Rymond-Richmond, W. C. (2007). "Habitus of Habitat: Mapping the History, Redevelopment, and Crime in Public Housing." Dissertation Thesis. Chicago, IL: Northwestern University.

Sanchez, T.W., and Dawkins, C.J. (2001). Source Distinguishing city and suburban movers: Evidence from the American housing survey. *Housing Policy Debate,* 12(3), 607–631.

Schelling, T. (1978). *Micromotives and Macrobehavior.* New York: W.W. Norton and Company.

Slater, T. (2006). The eviction of critical perspectives from gentrification research. *International Journal of Urban and Regional Research,* 30(4), 737–757.

Smith, N. (1979). Toward a theory of gentrification: A back to the city movement by capital not people. *Journal of the American Planning Association,* 45, 538–548.

Smith, N. (1982). Gentrification and uneven development. *Economic Geography,* 58(2), 139–155.

Smith, N. (1987). Gentrification and the rent-gap. *Annals of the Association of American Geographers,* 77(3), 462–465.

Smith, N. (1996). *The new urban frontier: gentrification and the revanchist city.* New York: Routledge.

Sullivan, D. (2007). Reassessing gentrification: Measuring residents' opinions using survey data. *Urban Affairs Review,* 42(4), 583–592.

Torrens, P., and Nara, A. (2007). Modeling gentrification dynamics: A hybrid approach. *Computers, Environment and Urban Systems,* 31, 337–361.

Valler, D., & Wood, A. (2010). Conceptualizing local and regional economic development in the USA. *Regional Studies,* 44(2),139–151.

Vigdor, J. (2002). Does gentrification harm the poor? *Brookings-Wharton Papers on Urban Affairs.* Brookings Institution Press. Washington, DC: 133–174.

Wacquant, L. (2008). Relocating gentrification: The working class, science and the state in recent urban research. *International Journal of Urban and Regional Research,* 32(1), 198–205.

Wyly, E., & Hammel, D. (1999). Islands of decay in seas of renewal: Housing policy and the resurgence of gentrification. *Housing Policy Debate,* 10(4), 711–771.

Zietz, J., Zietz, E. N., and Sirmans, G. S. (2008). Determinants of house prices: a quantile regression approach *The Journal of Real Estate Finance and Economics,* 37(4), 317–333.

Zukin, S. (1987). Gentrification: Culture and Capital in the Urban Core. *Annual Review of Sociology,* 13, 129–147.

Chapter 6
Simulating Life Cycle Costs
for Nuclear Facilities

Adam Eckerd, Peter Lufkin, Bernard G. Mattimore,
Jon Miller, and Anand Desai

Abstract An agent-based model was developed to simulate the cost consequences of maintaining or deferring maintenance of facilities as they move through their life cycle, under different funding scenarios. The model incorporates measures of risk and makes explicit assumptions about the interdependent nature of hazardous facilities.

6.1   Introduction

In this chapter, we illustrate how an agent-based model can assist in decision making for facilities management. We describe how the model can be used to simulate potential costs under scenarios incorporating alternative assumptions regarding funding, risks, and operating costs associated with managing facilities. As a demonstration, we use data provided by a US National Laboratory (Covello et al. 1989; Fullwood and Hall 1988).

A. Eckerd (✉)
Center for Public Administration and Policy, School of Public and International Affairs, Virginia Polytechnic Institute and State University, 1021 Prince Street, Alexandria, VA 22314
e-mail: aeckerd@gmail.com

P. Lufkin • J. Miller
Whitestone Research, 2050 Alameda Padre Serra, Santa Barbara, CA 93103, USA
e-mail: plufkin@whitestoneresearch.com; jmiller@whitestoneresearch.com

B.G. Mattimore
Lawrence Livermore National Laboratory, 1216 Cheshire Circle,
Danville, CA 94506, USA
e-mail: berniemattimore@sbcglobal.net

A. Desai
John Glenn School of Public Affairs, The Ohio State University,
Page Hall, 1810 College Road, Columbus, OH 43210, USA
e-mail: desai.1@osu.edu

A. Desai (ed.), *Simulation for Policy Inquiry*, DOI 10.1007/978-1-4614-1665-4_6,
© Springer Science+Business Media, LLC 2012

A primary concern for facility managers is the allocation of resources necessary to maintain the productive capacity of facilities throughout their intended service life. Our model anticipates the costs associated with a facility as it goes through the sequential states of its life cycle: acquisition, operations, maintenance and repair, recapitalization, and decommissioning.

Our approach recognizes two complications in modeling life cycle costs, at least with respect to potentially hazardous facilities. First, the facility condition and its state of operation are treated as interrelated. For instance, a laboratory in poor condition and no longer capable of contamination containment or maintaining a precise temperature might be recapitalized and returned to operation, or shifted to a path toward decommissioning. Second, the model assumes a spatial interdependence among facilities. If, for example, maintenance is deferred at one building and leads to an increase risk of contamination, then the risk to the operational capability of other buildings in the vicinity is increased.

6.2   The Problem of Managing US Nuclear Facilities

The National Nuclear Security Administration (NNSA) is responsible for ensuring the safety and security of the US nuclear stockpile. There are eight NNSA sites, some in operation since the 1940s. These facilities are becoming increasingly expensive to maintain and operate as they approach the end of their service life. Decisions must be made about how to maintain, recapitalize, or dispose of often highly contaminated facilities. And these decisions must be made in the uncertain context of changing weapons strategies, strained federal budgets, and the risk of natural calamity or accident.[1] In its planning, each site has a spectrum of options with regard to individual facilities:

1. Full maintenance—maintain facilities at recommended levels, fulfilling their expected lifespan.
2. Deferred maintenance—some part of recommended maintenance is deferred to the future while facilities remain operational, based on current "as built" design.
3. Recapitalization—restore facilities to original productive capacity or modify to meet changing program needs.
4. Safe storing—cease operations but remain in a "cold, dark, and dry" state with potential for some future use.
5. Entombing—deactivate and encase facilities in a secure containment structure, rendering them inaccessible but relatively secure.
6. Decommissioning—shut down and demolish facilities with contamination remediated to such a point that the physical site could be used for some other purpose.

---

[1]The NNSA approach to maintaining the nuclear stockpile and its related infrastructure is described in the *FY 2011 Stockpile Stewardship and Management Plan.*

The best managerial option for a given facility can change as missions evolve and the facility ages. Although cost considerations are often paramount, the selection of a course of action must also consider the present and future risk of system failure. The ever-present problem, then, is to balance costs and risk while meeting organizational objectives.

6.2.1 Risk for Facilities

Risk is commonly calculated as the product of the probability and consequences of failure (Dietz et al. 2001; Fullwood and Hall 1988). In the case of facilities, failure can be defined as the inability to perform as intended: e.g., an office that loses power, or a warehouse with faulty refrigeration. In conventional economic analysis, such risk of failure is assumed to be constant and isolated from the condition of other facilities (DOD 1995). However, our view is more complex. We argue that the risk of facility failures can be related to the state of other facilities, and that the risk of failure is variable over time and circumstance (Dietz et al. 2001; Fone and Young 2000).

As the recent disaster at Fukushima Daiichi plant in Japan shows, the risk of facility failure is hardly constant. There, the infinitesimal threat of damage by earthquake was amplified by the tsunami that threatened a core meltdown and eventually forced the closure of the facility.

The probability of failure can increase or decrease depending on the proximity of other facilities. For instance, although only one of the three power plants at both Three Mile Island and at Fukushima Daiichi was severely damaged, the other two reactors at each location were shut down because the perceived risks of continuing to operate them were considered to be high simply because of their proximity to the damaged plant. Conversely, the proximity effect can be positive. If a toxic facility is decommissioned, it might decrease the probability of an undesirable event at a neighboring facility, as well as diminish the magnitude of the consequences.

6.2.2 The Facility Life Cycle

Our model evaluates costs and risks as facilities pass through successive states of their life cycle. The life cycle of a nuclear facility is functionally the same as that of any other facility: the facility is constructed and it passes through an operational period during which decisions are made to sustain some level of maintenance and repair (M&R). As the facility ages, it might be recapitalized to restore its productive capacity or change its use. At the end of its productive life, the facility must be stored in a secure fashion or demolished. The length of time each facility spends in each of these states is determined, in large part, by mission responsibilities. Figure 6.1 identifies the states of a facility over its lifecycle.

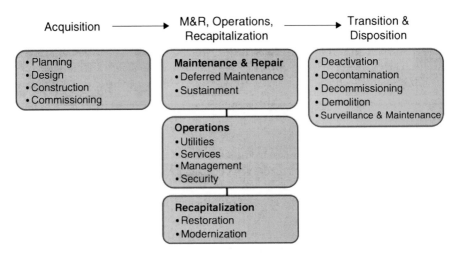

Fig. 6.1 States in a facility life cycle. *Source*: Whitestone Research

Each state of the life cycle involves a number of decisions. The transition and disposition (T&D) state, the last in a facility's life, provides a useful example to illustrate such decisions.

Once a facility loses its mission or purpose and has no immediate alternative use, it enters the T&D phase: this phase includes surveillance and maintenance procedures, transfer of programmatic responsibilities, deactivation, and decommissioning including decontamination and demolition.[2] T&D takes on added complexity when the facilities have been part of the nuclear industry (Church and Nakamura 1993). For nuclear facilities, T&D is burdened by enormous costs, the external risk to human and environmental health, and the internal risk to the controlling agency and its workers. The general T&D process is shown in Fig. 6.2.

During the transition period, operations at a facility are ceased and the facility is placed in a stable state (DOE 2001), while disposition corresponds to a host of steps after a facility has been transitioned (DOE 1999). As part of disposition, facilities are observed and maintained and generally fully deactivated, decontaminated, and potentially dismantled with all equipment disposed of (DOE 2000). Ultimately at the end of the T&D process, there are three disposition options (Taboas et al. 2004). First, the facility can be fully decommissioned. When a facility has been fully decommissioned, entailing the full scale clean up and removal of hazardous material, the site can be usable for other purposes, or at least pose substantially less risk to human health (Taboas et al. 2004). The Rocky Flats site in Colorado has been undergoing a full decommissioning process, with the removal of all buildings and development on the site. While the site is not expected to be usable for future development, it is being transitioned for use as a wildlife refuge.

---

[2] For terms and definitions see DOE (1999, 2000, 2001).

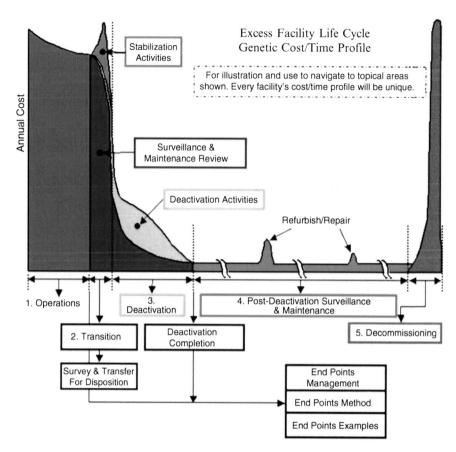

Fig. 6.2 Cost levels in the transition and disposition process. *Source*: Department of Energy

As a second option, an entombed facility is encased in some long-lived stable material, such as concrete. The failed reactor at the Chernobyl site in Ukraine is a good example of an entombed facility. Although the site cannot be used for other purposes, entombing can achieve a sufficiently safe (although not completely safe) level of risk mitigation (Taboas et al. 2004). Entombment costs, to the extent that they can be estimated in advance are surely significant, but likely not as high as decommissioning costs; however, it is also likely that ongoing surveillance costs at entombed sites will be higher than at decommissioned sites (Solomon 1982).

The third option is to safe store a facility. The safe storing process is essentially a delay tactic undertaken when a facility has reached the end of its life cycle, but a decision has not been made as to whether entombing or decommissioning is the more appropriate end point. A safe stored facility is placed in a stable, relatively safe state, short of entombing, enabling time to detail the ultimate disposition option, as is the case with Unit 2 at Three Mile Island in Pennsylvania.

Each option has advantages and disadvantages for future costs, risks to external populations, risks to systems or facility failures, and risk to the integrity of the larger site and safety of its workers. Given this complexity, the full scope of possible risks cannot be known, yet, we can at least simulate the T&D state and explore the possible cost outcomes.

6.3   Agent-Based Facility Life Cycle Model

An agent-based model was developed to simulate the cost consequences of sustaining or deferring maintenance of facilities as they move through their life cycle, under different risk assumptions and funding scenarios.[3] The model incorporates measures of risk and makes explicit assumptions about the interdependent nature of facilities. We conceive of individual facilities as autonomous but interdependent entities, existing both as independent structures and as components within a landscape of interdependent facilities with a common organizational mission. Therefore, decisions to defer present maintenance can have a cumulative temporal effect as well as a spatial effect on facilities across the landscape. The unit of analysis or the agent in these simulations is an individual facility (such as a building), referred to as the focal facility.

We created this simulation using NetLogo, an agent-based modeling software program developed at Northwestern University.[4] Data informing the model were derived from Program of Record (POR), or baseline cost projections at a sample site. The POR is developed using data from the Department of Energy Facility Information Management System (FIMS).

Each year, a 10-year site plan is created by overlaying projected facility management needs on information from the current physical property database. These plans, developed the site level, include information on acquisition, operations, M&R, recapitalization, and T&D expenses by year. Site-specific plans are aggregated by the Department of Energy to yield the POR necessary to meet stockpile support requirements. We used the 2010 POR data with the annual 2011 fiscal year projections incorporating policy recommendations for maintenance and recapitalization expenditures.

The MARS system (MARS 2010), a software tool for forecasting facility maintenance and repair, operations, and capital costs, to obtain a 20-year projection of the cost expectations for each of the years from 2010 to 2030. These data serve as the basis for the simulation model, which runs for 20 periods (years) assessing the effects of different user-defined budget assumptions and stochastic exogenous events, so that a facility manager might freely explore different scenarios.

With the model's graphical user interface (GUI), users can adjust the level of funding relative to the recommended baseline amount for acquisition, operations,

---

[3] http://glenn.osu.edu/phd/aeckerd/mars/m&r.html.

[4] http://ccl.northwestern.edu/netlogo/.

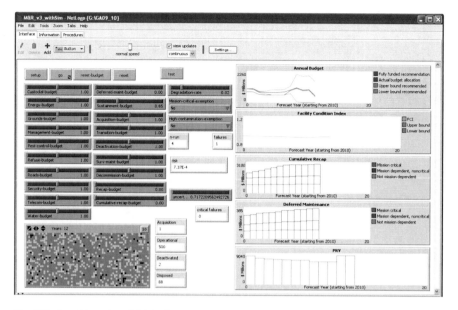

Fig. 6.3 Agent-based model interface

and transition and decommissioning (Fig. 6.3). The first column of "sliders" shown in the GUI allows the user to manipulate the level of funding for different cost categories in the operations budget. The second column allows the user to allocate funds specifically to reduce the backlog due to earlier decisions to defer maintenance, as well as determine the level at which various major budget categories such as acquisition, transition, and decommissioning should be funded. The third column of sliders has a yes/no option to give priority to mission critical and highly contaminated sites. Mission critical facilities are essential for the site to fulfill its mission (GAO 2008).

As the simulation runs, present and future costs for each focal facility (agent) are affected by a number of different factors, both relating to the focal facility, and to stochastic influences. Baseline costs for each facility are derived from the data where a facility's costs are a function of the facility's (1) size, (2) mission criticality, (3) level of contamination, (4) hazard potential, and (5) current use. The type of costs attributed to a facility depends on the particular state of its life cycle, as shown in Table 6.1.

In general, the various costs are computed according to the following rules:

1. Acquisition costs are expressed as a single value apportioned equally over a 3-year construction period.
2. Operational costs are incurred on a yearly basis, following the completion of construction.
3. M&R costs are determined by a set of scheduled tasks specific to each facility.

Table 6.1 Cost and corresponding facility phases

Cost	Phase
Acquisition	Acquisition
Custodial	Operational
Energy	Operational
Grounds	Operational
Management	Operational
Pest control	Operational
Refuse	Operational
Roads	Operational
Security	Operational
Telecommunications	Operational
Water	Operational
M&R	M&R
Deferred maintenance	M&R
Recapitalization	Recapitalization
Cumulative recapitalization	Recapitalization
Transition	Transition and disposition
Deactivation	Transition and disposition
Surveillance	Transition and disposition
Decommission	Transition and disposition

4. Deferred maintenance costs accrue if M&R costs are not fully funded during the period in which they are incurred.
5. Recapitalization costs are incurred whenever facilities move through their life cycle, and POR assessments suggest that restoration and modernization, retrofitting or altering the use of the facility would constitute the most economically feasible option. Failure to allocate resources to recapitalization results in the accumulation of such costs into cumulative recapitalization.
6. T&D costs are incurred in sequence from transition to decommissioning.
7. Facilities can remain in one or another of these states for multiple time periods depending upon the expected length of time that the data suggest is required for the specific tasks. Costs are allocated accordingly in each time period until such time as the phase is complete. After a facility has been decommissioned, it incurs no costs going forward.

Beyond the costs typically related to the facilities life cycle we add a random variable to account for risk. In the model, a global (site level rather than facility level) risk factor is defined in terms of two types of risk. One risk of failure is due to deferred maintenance, that is, if the facility is not properly maintained, its risk of failure varies according to the amount of deferred maintenance. So, when M&R costs have been deferred (i.e., if required maintenance has been deferred), global risk increases by a factor of the proportion of M&R that has been deferred, as shown in (6.1) (the total risk function), where S_t is the proportion of M&R costs deferred at time t.

The second risk component varies over time, according to how external risks are perceived. For this simulation we have not explicitly modeled how external risks such as acts of god, changes in security threat levels, and so forth interact to result in changes in the risk of failure. For the time being we have set it such that at each successive time period, the risk of facility failure increases linearly annually. Thus, for each passing year, the risk of failure is increased slightly (0.00001) as shown in (6.1). In effect, the model accounts for exogenous risks due to changes in the environment as well as endogenous risks due to factors such as deferred maintenance to influence global risk, R_t, which is capped at 0.01, lest the probability of failure rise to unlikely levels.

$$R_t = R_{t-1} + (R_{t-1} \times (1 - S_t))$$ (6.1)
$$R_t \leq 0.01$$

The probability of any individual building failing varies at each time period according to the global risk calculation. At each time interval t, we model the failure of a facility as a random outcome of a Bernoulli process with probability of failure being R_t. Thus, in the simulation, to determine whether the facility survives to the next time period, each facility is assigned a random value (0 or 1) derived from a Bernoulli distribution with mean R_t. If the random number is 0, the facility does not fail at t and continues to function until another random value is determined via the same process at time $t+1$. If the value is 1, then the facility fails at time t. When a facility fails, costs for that building increase by a factor determined by the level of contamination at the facility, as shown in (6.2) where C_{ijt} is the cost factor j (those factors listed in Table 6.1) for facility i at time t, PC_{ijt} is the proprietary POR data projection at time t of cost j for facility i, and X_{it} is the contamination level of facility i, a categorical variable ranging from 1 to 4 with 1 indicating no contamination and 4 indicating high contamination.

$$C_{ijt} = (PC_{ijt} \times X_{it})$$ (6.2)

When the facility that fails is highly contaminated, the costs for other facilities located in its proximity also increase (6.3) by a factor of the global risk level R, where D is the Euclidean distance from the focal facility i to the nearest highly contaminated facility that has failed.

$$C_{ijt} = \left(PC_{ijt} \times X_{it} \times \left(\frac{1}{D_{it}} \right) \right)$$ (6.3)

Additionally, when a facility that fails is critical to the organizational mission of the site, subsequent costs for all facilities increase, according to the extent of contamination present at that facility (6.4). Failures at uncontaminated, non-mission critical facilities thus have little effect on facility costs, while the effect of highly contaminated and/or mission critical facilities can be very large.

$$C_{ijt} = (PC_{ijt} \times X_{it} \times R_t)$$ (6.4)

Figure 6.3 shows the user interface that is updated at each time period in the simulation, allowing users to track the budgetary and facility condition consequences of the funding strategies chosen over time. The full-fund amount shown is the total of all POR recommendations for each year excluding deferred maintenance and cumulative recapitalization costs. Hence, the fully funded budget B_t at time t is

$$B_t = \sum_{i,j} C_{ijt} \tag{6.5}$$

The budget for each year is the summation of all costs actually allocated according to the scenario being tested. Any operational or M&R costs not covered in a time period accumulate into deferred maintenance, as shown in (6.6) where DM_t is the site level total deferred maintenance, PC_{ijt} is the data cost projection for cost j for facility i, and A_{jt} is the proportional allocation level selected for by the model user for cost category j, at time t.

$$DM_t = \sum_{ij} (PC_{ijt} - (PC_{ijt} \times A_{jt})) \tag{6.6}$$

Similarly, any recapitalization expenses not covered in a time period accumulate into cumulative recapitalization (6.7), where CR_t is the site-wide cumulative recapitalization amount and Y_t is the recommended recapitalization cost for facility i. If for the scenario being tested, any of the allocation choices are set over 100%, excess funds allocated to any operations or M&R categories are used to pay down deferred maintenance, while excess recapitalization allocations are used to pay down cumulative recapitalization. The amount of recapitalization required is addressed in Lufkin et al. (2005).

$$CR_t = \sum_i (Y_{it} - (Y_{it} \times A_{jt})) \tag{6.7}$$

Any costs not fully covered each year are subject to a penalty, as shown in (6.8) and (6.9), where DP is the deferral penalty.

$$DM_t = DM_{t-1} + (DM_{t-1} \times DP) \tag{6.8}$$

$$CR_t = CR_{t-1} + (CR_{t-1} \times DP) \tag{6.9}$$

On the dashboard, the first plot on the top right-hand side in Fig. 6.3 shows the level of recommended funding (full-fund) and the amount actually allocated by using the slider options (budget). Below that, the second plot shows the facility condition index (FCI) for all buildings, as shown in (6.10) where PRV is the replacement value for facility i at time t.

$$FCI_t = \sum_i FCI_{it} = \sum_i 1 - \left(\frac{DM_{it}}{PRV_{it}} \right) \tag{6.10}$$

The third and fourth plots track the accumulation of unfunded recapitalization and deferred maintenance expenses, respectively, presenting the total amounts, as well as differentiating the accumulation of expenses for mission critical, mission-dependent, and non-mission-dependent facilities. The final plot, at the bottom right of Fig. 6.3, shows total plant replacement value (PRV) level through the simulation (6.11).

$$PRV_t = \sum_i PRV_{it} \qquad (6.11)$$

6.4   Risk and Alternative Cost Scenarios

The model is an exploratory device, enabling a comparison of the future costs and risks of alternative funding scenarios for facilities. While we draw upon data from NNSA facilities, the results obtained are relevant to any large organization. This effort is a first step to understanding the systemic relationships among funding, risk, and facility condition. A later step would build on this understanding and refine the model for the purpose of guiding future decisions. However, these model scenarios can be used to compare outcomes of different funding strategies.

To illustrate how the model can be used, we ran a series of simulations varying our assumptions about exogenous factors — global risk and energy costs — that are outside the control of the decision makers and endogenous factors, such as funding levels and priorities, which can be influenced by the decision makers. We constructed scenarios from alternative assumptions regarding exogenous variables, considering two levels of risk and three levels of energy prices. Exogenous risk was assumed to be high or low, and energy costs were assumed to be: (1) as expected, (2) 25% higher than expected, or (3) 75% higher than expected. Low risk was defined as a failure rate of less than or equal to 0.001 on a scale of 1–0; high risk exceeded that value. Risk of failure is capped at 0.001 on a scale of 0–1 and it could be as high as 0.01 when the risk is high.

Potential policy decisions, regarding the endogenous factors, consisted of three different alternatives: (1) fully funding M&R; (2) funding it at 90% of recommended levels; and (3) funding it at 95% of recommended levels while maintaining full funding for mission critical and highly contaminated facilities. For comparison purposes, we also considered the NNSA POR as a baseline scenario wherein M&R was fully funded and we assumed that there was no exogenous risk and thus facility failure was not possible.

The number of simulations that can be potentially run quickly becomes large as one considers all the possible combinations of values of exogenous and endogenous variables. We ran a number of scenarios by varying the M&R funding level (100%, 95%, and 90%), whether mission critical facilities were exempt from funding cuts (yes or no) and whether highly contaminated facilities were exempt from funding cuts (yes or no). We also considered different contexts for these scenarios. We considered three different levels of exogenous risk of failure (high, medium, and low) and considered the cost of fuel to be as projected in the POR, as well as the costs being 25% and 75% higher. For the purposes of illustration, we focus on three and compare them with the POR to illustrate the consequences of different levels of deferred maintenance. The scenarios we discuss are:

1. *100% M&R.* Under this scenario M&R is funded at 100% of the required amount.
2. *90% M&R, no exemptions.* Under this scenario M&R is funded to 90% of the required amount, a cut equally shared by critical, noncritical facilities, and highly contaminated facilities.
3. *95% M&R of noncritical facilities and 100% of mission critical and highly contaminated facilities.* Under this scenario, M&R is funded at 95% of the required amount for noncritical facilities. M&R for mission critical and highly contaminated facilities is maintained at 100%.
4. *POR: projection of 2010 data for 20 years.* The baseline data represent 100% funding M&R costs without any consideration of external risks or changes in energy costs.

The outcomes for each of these scenarios show the broad potential impact of relatively small changes given alternative risk and energy cost environments.

6.5   Failures and Costs

The simulated numbers for failures and costs for three scenarios and POR are shown in Figs. 6.4–6.7 For example, in a low risk environment (Fig. 6.4) the number of failures can multiply rapidly in the absence of full funding over a 20-year horizon. Note that the number of failures shown in Figs. 6.4 and 6.5 are not true estimates, but are generated by a Bernoulli process where the probability of failure at time t is R_t, as defined in (6.1). Because there are no risks or energy costs associated with the POR, which represents a fully funded scenario, the number of failures associated with it is zero throughout the 20-year period of the simulation and therefore not shown in Figs. 6.4 and 6.5.

Scenarios other than the POR have alternative levels of exogenous and endogenous levels of risk and different levels of M&R funding. Risk is updated in the simulation according to (6.1), where exogenous risk is simply increased by a small amount each year and endogenous risk is a function of deferred maintenance. Thus, it is not surprising that more failures are anticipated when M&R is funded at the 90% level even when the exogenous risk is assumed to be relatively low.

Assumptions of slightly higher exogenous risk lead unsurprisingly to slightly higher rates of failures as shown in Fig. 6.5. Note that even with full funding (100% M&R), the probability of facility failure increases with exogenous risk. Considerations of risk aside, as maintenance is deferred, more facilities fail.

The ultimate objective of the simulation, however, is not to account for facility failures, per se, but to account for the costs of those failures. In Fig. 6.6, annual budgetary trend lines show the total budget for the three alternative scenarios compared to the POR cost assumptions. The total budget includes all life cycle costs,

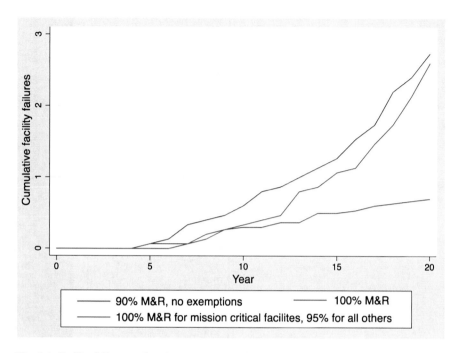

Fig. 6.4 Facility failures under a low exogenous risk assumption

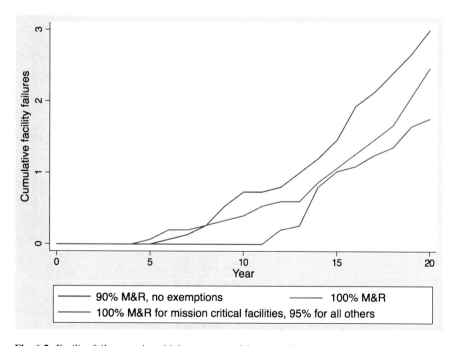

Fig. 6.5 Facility failures under a high exogenous risk assumption

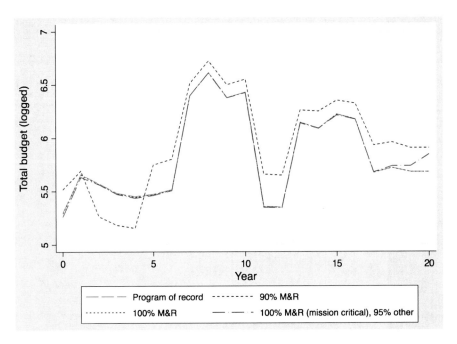

Fig. 6.6 Annual budget trends under a low risk assumption

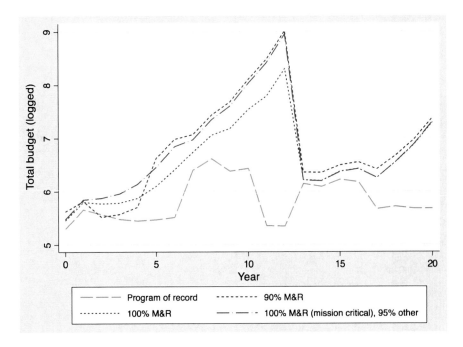

Fig. 6.7 Annual budget trends under a high risk assumption

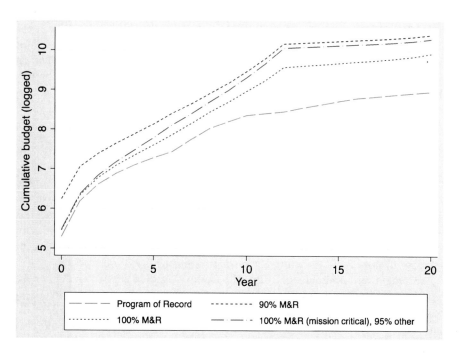

Fig. 6.8 Cumulative budget trends under a high risk assumption

from acquisition to decommissioning, including failures in a given year. Cost variation is not extreme in any of the scenarios under a low risk assumption; there are clear increases in costs for the scenarios in which some level of maintenance is deferred. For each case, costs rise and fall as new facilities are acquired and move through the life cycle, but there are no dramatic alterations for the POR or full M&R scenarios. These two are almost indistinguishable from one another and from the 95% funding for M&R with exemption for mission critical facilities throughout the low risk context (Fig. 6.6). After a few initial years of cost savings, these three cost scenarios are consistently lower than the scenario with 10% deferred costs.

Another view of simulated costs focusing on annual (marginal) costs is shown in Fig. 6.7. We find dramatic divergence in the cost trends between POR and the other scenarios. For example, between years 10 and 16 the simulation projects decline POR costs and rapidly increase costs for the other scenarios. This divergence is because there are no failures under our assumptions regarding POR. Aside from the POR, facilities still fail in the simulation even under full M&R due to exogenous risks.

As might be expected, the highest costs in any given year tend to be those where M&R had been funded at only 90% of recommended levels, even though this strategy is initially less expensive. Despite short-term savings, in the long-term deferring more maintenance appears to be less cost effective because of the accumulation of penalties for deferring maintenance. Costs for full M&R are generally lower than other choices, and fewer facility failures occur. The cumulative costs of the different strategies (Fig. 6.8) under a high risk scenario show that while the costs at the outset might be similar, the costs of deferring maintenance quickly outpace the 100% funding scenarios, and cumulative savings are not realized even in the short term for deferred scenarios. Except for the POR data, facilities fail in each of the simulation scenarios, and the cost of those failures clearly outpaces the savings realized through deferring maintenance.

6.6 Discussion

Our simulations have shown how different strategies can affect the probability of facility failure and the related costs; they also show their sensitivity to key assumptions. Under different assumptions regarding external risk, budgetary outcomes can be quite different, even when using the same funding strategy. Similar sensitivities exist with respect to energy prices and the state (acquisition, operational, deactivated, or disposed) of the facility at a given time during the 20-year period.

A strength of this simulation is that the facilities studied are allowed to age, be repurposed, or decommissioned. Figure 6.9 shows the part of the simulation dashboard that illustrates the spatial location and life cycle status of each facility as the simulation runs through the study period. This specific screenshot from the GUI shows the state of the facilities in year 13. A yellow dot represents a facility in operation, a black dot is a facility in state "disposed," a red dot is a facility that has been deactivated, and a green dot represents a facility in the state of being acquired. The numbers of facilities in each state are shown in the boxes on the right.

An additional strength of this model is that it explicitly takes risk associated with proximity into consideration. This is a novel concept that deserves more discussion. Three examples are instructive. Decommissioning a contaminated site would in the process of decontamination raise the risk of failure for its neighbors, but once the cleanup is complete the neighborhood becomes safer (lower risk). To represent this risk in the model, we modeled the risk levels of each facility as well as the effect of

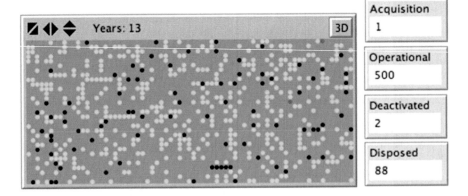

Fig. 6.9 State of the facilities in year 13

this risk level on its immediate surroundings. Although we did not utilize sensitive information regarding actual spatial locations, geo-coded location data for each facility would allow us to obtain density measures, which could then be modeled to explore the effects of density and building proximity on the ability to secure the facilities and protect them in case of a fire or a flood. Taking a broader perspective on facility condition to include productivity and efficiency as indicators of the facility's ability to achieve its intended purpose, we can also model how proximity affects the supply chain by including the locations of supply and production facilities in the simulation.

From the simple illustration in Fig. 6.9, the importance of considering these spatial and temporal changes is clear. For example, note the bottom center portion with several black dots in a row. In this space, five facilities had all been decommissioned and disposed over time, and this process surely has implications for overall site risk given the spatial proximity and localized risk reduction achieved in this area. Under a linear cost projection, such results would be unexplored.

We view these simulations as a first step in representing the complexity of trading off deferred maintenance and risk. The next steps require replacing simplifying assumptions with a more sophisticated understanding of the model interactions. We do not want to underestimate the effort entailed in developing such enhancements of the simulation; each explicit sub-model could be the topic of a separate study.

This exercise does, however, point to the types of data that must be collected to provide a sound basis for the models in actual managerial experience. More sophisticated modeling of the failure rates coupled with actual data series on failures of different facility components can potentially yield forecasts of the number of failures under different scenarios. There is little publicly available empirical evidence to guide assumptions regarding the levels and consequences of exogenous contamination and other sources of risk. However, with a better understanding of the underlying phenomena and additional information, the decision makers can be given better guidance on how to adjust these factors under different contexts. Such information, perhaps from other programs within NNSA, can help develop a richer characterization of contamination and a better understanding of exogenous risks so as to enhance the users' confidence in the robustness of the simulations.

Similarly, full comprehension of the penalties associated with deferring maintenance will require additional data collection. Unfortunately, there is little guidance in the literature for setting these penalties and how the different expenditures on various maintenance operations interact with each other to mitigate or exacerbate the consequences of deferring maintenance in the different cost categories shown in Table 6.1. No systematic data exist that can be used to estimate the rate at which costs increase as degradation occurs due to deferred maintenance. Indeed, sophisticated models for deferred maintenance exist (Moore et al. 2007; Sanford Bernhardt and McNeil 2008), but there is little empirical evidence for comparing penalties in terms of increased failures or costs associated with deferring maintenance. What data should be collected first and what should be next set of enhancements to the simulation model will depend upon the priorities of the users of this decision support tool. Setting such priorities will require continued close collaboration between facility managers and model developers.

6.7 Confidence Through Collaboration

Simulations are a blend of practice and theory. Neither the facility decision makers nor the model builders are capable of independently generating a comprehensive model on their own. Success is best achieved through collaboration between communities of inquiry (Shields 2003) and communities of practice (Wenger 1998); for practitioners the simulation must reflect the culture of the workplace and address their immediate concerns (Richardson and Anderson 1994).

The intensity of interaction between researchers and practitioners varies according to the stage of development and implementation of the model. The two do not need to be shoulder to shoulder throughout the process. The closest interaction is required at the outset when the simulation is being conceptualized. It is important for the model builders to grasp how the users perceive the nature of the decisions and the environment in which they are to be made. The researchers can independently develop the model, but its use and the interpretation of the outcomes must again be done in collaboration with the users.

In the absence of a well-defined theory to inform model development, the validity of a simulation is defined largely in terms of the confidence its developers and potential users place in its ability to meet their purpose (Worren et al. 2002; Forrester and Senge 1980; Kim et al. 2011). To achieve that user perspective as well as academic rigor, this project involved a close collaboration among academics, decision makers, and technical consultants. Our confidence in this simulation is based on having worked on its development over a multiple year period in collaboration with facility managers as well as modelers who had extensive knowledge and experience of NNSA facilities and the facilities data.

6.8 Conclusion

In this chapter, we have described a model that simulates the costs of operating a hazardous facility. The model is novel in a number of ways. It recognizes that costs differ according to state in the facility life cycle. It incorporates measures of risk, and it assumes that facilities are related geographically.

With this tool, we can begin to think systematically about the decisions that confront facility decision makers. With high levels of dangerous contamination, there is considerable uncertainty regarding the consequences of the decisions made each year about whether to defer or sustain maintenance, whether to retrofit and reuse facilities, or whether to shutter and decontaminate them. Although the simulation does not provide "answers" to these quandaries per se, it can provide a simplified world free of actual consequences in which to test the potential consequences of management choices.

Acknowledgments Funding support in the form of a research fellowship from Lawrence Livermore National Laboratory and Whitestone Research to Ohio State University is gratefully acknowledged. Without attributing any remaining shortcomings of the paper to him, we thank Cliff Shang for his comments and insights. The views presented here are those of the authors and do not represent the official position of the Lawrence Livermore National Laboratory, the National Nuclear Safety Administration, or the U.S. Department of Energy.

References

Church, T., and Nakamura, R. 1993.*Cleaning Up the Mess: Implementation Strategies in Superfund*. Washington, DC: Brookings Institution Press.

Covello, V., P. Sandman, and P. Slovic. 1989. Risk Communication, Risk Statistics, and Risk Comparisons: A Manual for Plant Managers in V. Colvello, D. McCallum, and M. Pavlova, (eds) *Effective Risk Communication: The Role and Responsibility of Government and Nongovernment Organizations*. New York: Plenum Press.

Dietz, T., S. Frey and E. Rosa. 2001. Risk Assessment and Management. In ed S. Frey, *The Environment and Society Reader*. Needham Heights, MA: Allyn & Bacon.

DOD. 1995. Economic Analysis for decision Making. DOD Instruction 7041.3 Nov 7 1995 Washington DC: Department of Defense.

Department of Energy (DOE). 1999. *G 430.1-4: Decommissioning Implementation Guide*, September, 1999.

Department of Energy (DOE). 2000. *DOE/EM-0383: Decommissioning Handbook: Procedures and Practices for Decommissioning*, January, 2000.

Department of Energy (DOE). 2001. *G 430.1-5: Transition Implementation Guide*, April, 2001.

Fullwood, R. and R. Hall. 1988. *Probabilistic Risk Assessment in the Nuclear Power Industry*. Elmsford, NY: Pergamon Press.

Forrester, J., and P. Senge. 1980. Tests for Building Confidence in System Dynamics Models. *TIMS Studies in Management Sciences*,14, 209–228.

Fone, M., and P. Young. 2000. *Public Sector Risk Management*. Oxford: Butterworth-Heinemann.

Government Accountability Office (GAO). 2008. *Federal Real Property: Government's Fiscal Exposure from Repair and Maintenance Backlogs is Unclear*. Report to the Committee on Oversight and Government Reform, House of Representatives.

Kim, Y., D. Landsbergen and A. Desai. 2011. Negotiated Space: A Framework for Building Confidence in the Pragmatic and Consequential Validity of Policy Models. Working paper. John Glenn School of Public Affairs, Columbus, Ohio.

Lufkin, P., A. Desai, and J. Janke. 2005. Estimating the Restoration and Modernization Costs of Infrastructure and Facilities. *Public Works Management and Policy*, vol. 10, no. 1, pp. 40–52.

MARS 2010. *Facility Cost Forecast System*. Santa Barbara, CA: Whitestone Research.

Moore, C., M. Tjioe, A. Manzella, K. L. Sanford Bernhardt, and Sue McNeil. 2007. Agent Models for Asset Management. In LucioSoibelman and BurcuAkinci. (eds) *Computing in Civil Engineering: Proceedings of Proceeding of the 2007 ASCE International Workshop on Computing in Civil Engineering*. pp. 176–183.

Richardson, G. and D. Anderson. 1994. Teamwork in Group Model Building *System Dynamics Review*, Vol. 11, no. 2, pp. 113–137.

Sanford Bernhardt, K. L. and S. McNeil. 2008. Agent-Based Modeling: Approach for Improving Infrastructure Management. *Journal of Infrastructure Systems*. Vol. 14, no.3, pp. 253–261.

Shields, P.M. 2003. The Community of Inquiry: Classical Pragmatism and Public Administration. *Administration & Society*. Vol. 35, no. 5, pp. 510–38.

Solomon, B. 1982. US Nuclear Energy Policy; Provision of Funds for Decommissioning. *Energy Policy*, 11, 109–119.

Taboas, A., A. Moghissi, and T. LaGuardia, 2004. *The Decommissioning Handbook*. New York: ASME Press.

Wenger, E. 1998. *Communities of Practice: Learning, Meaning, and Identity*. New York: Cambridge University Press.

Worren, N., K. Moore, and R. Elliott. 2002. When Theories Become Tools: Toward a Framework for Pragmatic Validity. *Human Relations*, 55(10), 1227–1250.

Chapter 7
Simulating a Fraud Mechanism in Public Service Delivery

Yushim Kim

Abstract This chapter illustrates a use of agent-based modeling to simulate how the dynamics of fraud occur in a public service delivery program. While fraud is a well-known problem in the public sector, the study of fraud is challenging because the behavior is subtle and adaptive. Underlying mechanisms are often not explicitly revealed. Crime data collected from investigations are biased downward because they include only those who are detected. In this chapter, I focus on modeling a fraud mechanism based on theories of crime and compare simulation outputs with results from a previous empirical study. I end this chapter with the discussion of the utility of agent-based modeling for policy inquiry.

7.1 Introduction

Fraud[1] is a well-known problem in the public sector. Government and state-owned enterprises consist of the largest proportion of organizations reporting fraud worldwide.[2] In the USA, state and local governments are found to be very reactive

---

[1] In the seminal paper of white-collar crime, Sutherland (1940) defined fraud as "a misrepresentation of asset values" (p. 3). This economic crime has been found in various sectors. In a public service delivery program such as WIC and Food Stamps, trafficking and overcharging are identified as common examples of fraud (USDA 2001). The program performs regular monitoring activities and has established various sanction mechanisms (e.g., warning letter and civil penalties).

[2] Global Economic Crime Survey is a worldwide study conducted by PwC to "to assess corporate attitudes to fraud in the current economic environment" (see http://www.pwc.com/gx/en/economic-crime-survey/data/index.jhtml for the 2009 survey).

Y. Kim (✉)
School of Public Affairs, Arizona State University,
411 N. Central Avenue, Suite 400, Phoenix, AZ 85004, USA
e-mail: ykim@asu.edu

A. Desai (ed.), *Simulation for Policy Inquiry*, DOI 10.1007/978-1-4614-1665-4_7,
© Springer Science+Business Media, LLC 2012

compared to the federal government in terms of how they deal with fraud.[3] Despite the significance of the problem and its implications for society, fraud in public service delivery programs largely remains a practical matter rather than an issue that receives systematic scholarly attention. In fact, the study of fraud itself is challenging. The underlying behavior is subtle and adaptive, its occurrence is often not explicitly revealed, and crime data collected from investigations are biased downward because they include only those who are detected.

This chapter explores how fraud reveals itself through the interactions of its key players within a system. The focus is on modeling the interaction between program recipients and vendors using an agent-based model (ABM). The simulation models a public health service delivery program, the Women, Infants, and Children (WIC) program in Ohio. The underlying mechanism of the rule-breaking behavior of some players in the model is informed by government reports and theories of crime. The substantive research task is to examine whether the model's underlying mechanism can lead to the empirically observed patterns of fraud.

I first briefly describe the research context and an issue of fraud in the context. To inform the simulation model, I summarize a systemic perspective on crime. In line with this perspective, theories of crime are also explained to provide a theoretical foundation for the process that some players in the program may confront. I then explain how an ABM is designed in the particular context. Based on the simulation outputs, I evaluate whether the model performs in the way it was conceptually laid out and what patterns emerge from the artificial system. I end with a discussion of why this approach is useful for policy inquiry.

7.1.1 Research Context

There are thousands of public service delivery programs in the USA, including the food stamp program, unemployment insurance programs, and the WIC program. Each program serves a distinct purpose for specific target populations. For example, the WIC program aims to safeguard the health of low-income women and their nutritionally at-risk children from birth to age five. The program provides nutritious supplemental foods, nutritional education, and referrals to health care and other social services, and is available in all 50 states, the District of Columbia, 34 Indian Tribal Organizations, and all US territories. There are 90 WIC state agencies that administer the program through 2,200 local agencies and 9,000 clinics.

In 2008, Ohio's WIC, with a budget over $240 million, served approximately 300,000 participants each month. Ohio WIC has contracts with more than 200 local clinics and 1,400 vendors, and the participants, local clinics, vendors, and state

---

[3] A white paper from SAS sponsored a TechWeb survey of 327 federal, state, and local government decision makers to examine the state of fraud in October 2010 (http://www.sas.com/reg/wp/corp/26091).

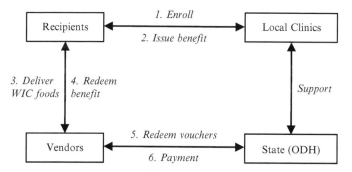

Fig. 7.1 Operation of the Ohio WIC program

agency are the major players in the system. WIC operates mainly at the state and local levels so the federal government is not explicitly modeled in the present analysis. Figure 7.1 represents the business process of the WIC program at the state level (Kim and Xiao 2008). The system consists of the *Ohio Department of Health* (ODH), which maintains the vendor management, certification, and payment management systems in support of the *local clinics* that certify *participant* eligibility. Participants, in turn, go to *vendors* to redeem benefit vouchers given to them by local clinics. Vendors are paid by the state for the vouchers used at their stores.

The abuse of such a program has been a problem for public managers. While in the private sector, theft and "shrinkage" is mainly due to customers or employees acting as individuals, fraud in public service delivery programs more often requires the active participation of the program recipients as well as the service provider. For example, overcharging is the main source of fraud for vendors in the WIC program. Trafficking—the exchange of public service benefit for cash—requires multiple players to participate in the illegal exchange of benefit vouchers. Some other illegal activities include forcing unwanted purchases and the substitution of WIC foods for unauthorized items. Each of these actions is illegal in the WIC program. For simplicity of modeling, fraud here refers to an act of illegal benefit exchanges, such as trafficking and overcharging, between vendors and recipients.

7.2 A Systemic Perspective on White-Collar Crime

To study the fundamental building blocks of social inquiry, Bunge (2006) suggests taking a systemic perspective on crime as an alternative to the traditional social philosophies that focus on either individuals or society as a whole. Like any systems view, this perspective acknowledges that social systems are composed of individuals who affect and are affected by others and that their actions cannot be understood without considering the system of which they are a part.

Systems can be identified by composition, environment, structure, and mechanism, as follows:

$$\mu(s) = \langle C(s), E(s), S(s), M(s) \rangle,$$

where s is a system; $C(s)$ is a collection of the parts of the system, s; $E(s)$, the environment, is a collection of items other than those in s and on which s can act or be acted upon; $S(s)$, the structure, is a collection of relations that keep the system whole; and $M(s)$, the mechanism, is a collection of processes that allow s to perform its specific function (Bunge 2006). Each component in the quadruple above is dynamic and subject to change over time. For instance, the composition of a public service delivery program is the collection of its key players such as program recipients, local clinics, contract vendors, and public agencies. The environment includes social or natural boundaries, constraints, even the cultures that surround these players. The structure is identified by how each part is related to other parts in the delivery of public services. Mechanisms in the program may refer to processes that lead some players to break rules or lead to the deterrence of such rule-breaking behavior by a governing authority.

Unlike the clock-like image provoked by the term *mechanism*, social mechanisms are purposeful. Many criminologists are interested in social mechanisms such as criminogenesis, crime perpetration, and crime control. Criminogenesis is a society-wide mechanism that refers to "the set of pathways leading some people to habitual law-breaking" (Bunge 2006, p. 12). Crime perpetration is "the process individual delinquents and criminal gangs face" (Bunge 2006, p. 12). Crime control is the set of informal and formal management approaches used to prevent and correct crime.

Wikström (2005) emphasizes crime as an act that results from interactions at the intersection between individuals and settings and that "what links the individual and the setting to act is the individual's perception of alternatives and process of choice" (p. 217). In other words, Wikström (2010) proposes that "*the convergence* (in time and space) of a person's propensity (P) and exposure (E) initiates a perception-choice process ($\rightarrow$) whose outcome is an action (or inaction), for example, an act of crime (C)" (p. 61). Wikström (2005) makes a distinction between crime propensity and acts of crime:

> … *crime propensity* may be conceptualized as the individual tendency to see crime (the breaking of a moral rule) as an alternative and to choose that option. Propensity is thus not individual characteristics and experiences (which causes propensity) and it is not action (which is the outcome), but the process that links the two (the *tendency* to see and choose in particular ways). … Crime is an act of moral rule breaking, committed by an individual, in a particular setting. (p. 213)

Key arguments of this theory are (1) *propensity* (P) moves an individual to commit a crime; it is the nature of the intersection with a setting that consists of opportunity, friction, and monitoring; (2) *exposure* (E) results from interaction between the individual and the setting leads to acts of rule breaking for *some* individuals; and

Fig. 7.2 Interaction of key elements

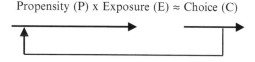

Propensity (P) x Exposure (E) ≈ Choice (C)

(3) as individual crime propensities change as a result of their *choice* (*C*) in a setting, the characteristics of the setting also change as a result of what individuals choose. Figure 7.2 illustrates this distinction and process (Wikström 2010, p. 61).

It is worth of noting that the behavioral setting that defines "exposure" consists not only of opportunities but also of *fraction and monitoring*. Deterrence has been a key topic in the economics of crime literature (Becker 1968). Substantial empirical research has been conducted to examine the effect of punishment on crime and criminal behavior (Cooter and Ulen 2007). In a recent study, Pogarsky et al. (2004) argue that a process of offender decision-making consists of two linkages—how official sanction and information affect a would-be offender's perception of the risks of criminal conduct and how such perceptions influence the actual decision to offend.

Wikström's (2009, 2010) follow-up studies focus on the empirical testing of situational action theory in the UK. He operationalizes people's crime propensity based on the morality of individuals and their ability to exercise self-control, examining how crime propensity interacts with exposure and changes as a result of that interaction. While I am aware of the difference in research contexts, subjects, and objectives between Wikström's work and the current study, several findings from his empirical studies inform the design of the ABM in this study.

7.3   An Artificial Public Service Delivery System

ABM is slowly gaining a foothold in the social and policy sciences, particularly with the explosion of computational technologies and innovations (Epstein 2006; Miller and Page 2007). One significant feature of ABM is that researchers can work with primitive data—numbers and characters—as is the case with any simulation; however, more importantly, ABM allows the inclusion of entities (e.g., individuals, schools, stores, public agencies) as objects. This provides a unique opportunity to introduce an individual entity as an autonomous decision-making unit in social simulations. In other words, researchers can frame problems as dynamic social processes among heterogeneous and purposeful actors who make autonomous decisions. Doing so requires careful specification of the social actors, interactions, interdependencies, and processes among these decision makers. Also, the careful synthesis of existing knowledge from traditional disciplines is necessary and critical for enhancing the fidelity of simulation models and helps us to better understand the nature of complex social and policy problems.

In the ABM, the delivery of services and behaviors of the players can be modeled as a series of interdependent transactions among agents. As described in Fig. 7.1, recipient agents redeem their vouchers at vendors responsible for delivering food and nutritional supplements to recipient on behalf of the public agency. The model distinguishes between the propensity toward fraud, opportunities for fraud, and the actual decision to engage in rule-breaking behavior. The window of opportunity for illegal activities occurs during the benefit exchange between program participant and vendor, but agents with different levels of criminal propensity take the opportunity to engage in illegal exchanges differentially. As a result, the fraud decision outcomes vary, producing distinct vendor–participant interaction patterns. This interaction pattern is organized for vendors because they are a primary focus of WIC programs' fraud monitoring activities.

7.3.1 The "Simulation" Landscape

The artificial world is a finite landscape referred to in ABM parlance as patches (33×33 grid cells) where two different types of agents—program participants and vendors—explicitly reside. The simulation can run with a fixed number of vendor and participant agents or with a varying numbers of agents to reflect their entry and exit in the program over time. The current simulation makes the simplifying assumption that the number of each type of agent is fixed.

7.3.2 Agents and Their Attributes

7.3.2.1 Program Recipients

The key attribute of each recipient and vendor in the model is the "risk propensity," a hypothetical property used for modeling the distribution and change of an agent's tendency toward fraudulent behavior. During a benefit exchange, this propensity influences agents' decision-making related to illegal voucher exchanges (fraud involvement) and is recursively influenced by their involvement in the illegal process. Using the Peterborough Adolescent and Young Adult Development Study data in the UK, Wikström (2010) found that "… the crime propensity score is approximately normally distributed" (p. 69) when a composite score is constructed based on a morality scale and a scale measuring the generalized ability to exercise self-control. Similarly, recipients' risk propensities are assigned as random draws from a Gaussian normal distribution, with a mean of 0.40 and standard deviation of 0.30, with values ranging from a minimum of 0.00 to a maximum of 1.00. The assumption is that the higher the assigned risk propensity, the higher the probability of engaging in illegal behavior.

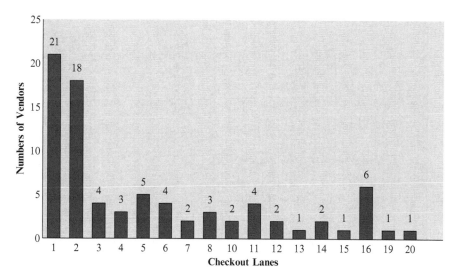

Fig. 7.3 The distribution of simulated vendors by the number of checkout lanes

7.3.2.2 Vendors

When considering vendors as decision-making units, two attributes are introduced: store size and risk propensity. Store size is considered a proxy of business type and is represented by the number of vendor checkout lanes. Large vendors are most likely to be national chains, while small vendors with one or two lanes are generally family-owned. In the simulation, store size ranges from 1- to 20-lane vendors. Figure 7.3 presents the distribution of vendors with their checkout lanes after running the simulation ten times, which replicates the distribution of an empirical observation in an Ohio WIC county (Kim 2006). A similar distribution pattern of national WIC store size is also found in a USDA report (2001, p. 31).

The store size is used (1) to calculate each store's utility for participants when they redeem their benefits and (2) to assign initial risk propensities for vendors. Larger vendors are more influential in calculating the utility of a vendor for participants (as can be seen from the store choice rule below). Regarding the latter, fraud occurs more frequently among small vendors relative to large vendors (USDA 2001), so the smaller the vendor, the greater the tendency of that vendor to engage in illegal activities: "The number of cash registers was categorized into three levels to create small (0–2 registers), medium (3–7 registers) and large-sized vendors (more than 8 registers) (p. 31)... more overcharges occurred for small-size vendors compared to medium-size or large vendors (p. 79)" (USDA 2001). In the simulation, therefore, the initial risk propensities for vendors are assumed to be normally distributed differently depending on store size (i.e., <3 checkout lanes: a mean of 0.50; 3–5 checkout lanes: a mean of 0.40; and >5 checkout lanes: a mean of 0.30) with a standard deviation of 0.30 for all three groups.

7.3.2.3 Public Agency

A public agency is not explicitly located in the landscape. The role of the public agency in monitoring, preventing, and sanctioning fraudulent vendors can be performed as part of the simulation toolkit's own function. Thus, it is assumed that these activities are performed implicitly by the public agency agent.

7.3.3 Interaction and Decision Rules

Once these attributes are endowed with the initialization of the simulation, agents go through a series of interactions and decision-making processes. First, the participant faces a decision regarding which vendor to choose for benefit voucher redemption. The participant's store choice is modeled using the Huff spatial interaction model (1964).

Formally, the Huff model can be written as

$$P_{ij} = \frac{U_{ij}}{\sum U_{ij}} = \frac{S_j^\alpha \cdot D_{ij}^\beta}{\sum S_j^\alpha \cdot D_{ij}^\beta},$$

where P_{ij} is the probability of the ith consumer visiting the jth store. The utility (U) consists of two decision factors: size (S_j) of store j and distance D_{ij} between i and j. Sensitivity parameters are often assigned with $\alpha = 1$ and $\beta = -2$ following the Newtonian analogy, where the square of the distance is an appropriate exponent in gravity models (Haynes and Fotheringham 1984). A longer distance is associated with the lower utility of a store for a participant. In the Huff model, the probability of a consumer visiting a particular store is calculated as a relative measure that is equal to the ratio of the utility of that store to the sum of the utilities of all stores considered by the consumer. Using this rule, participant agents in the simulation would have a preference ordering for selecting their vendor.

When participants visit a vendor according to the store choice rule, they exchange benefit vouchers. The initial decision on the type of benefit exchange (fraudulent or normal) is made as a result of a coin toss for both agents because they do not have information on each another. In other words, they do not know whether the other party is willing to engage in an illegal exchange. Thus, the first decision outcome is a function of the risk propensities of the two agents and random chance at the moment of their first encounter. In his study, Wikström (2010) defined low, medium, and high propensity using standard deviations: "Low propensity is defined as one standard deviation or more below the mean and high propensity as one standard deviation or more above the mean" (p. 69). Similarly, vendors and participants are grouped by the agent's risk propensity (extremely low: <0.10; low: 0.10–0.33; medium: 0.34–0.66; high: 0.67–0.90; and extremely high: >0.90). An agent with a risk propensity >0.90 will have a 50% chance of engaging in an illegal benefit exchange during the first interaction. The chance of engaging in an illegal exchange for the next group diminishes to approximately half the chance of the previous group, that is, 25% for those with a high risk propensity, 12% for those with a medium risk propensity, 6% for those who with a low risk propensity, and only 3% for those with an extremely low risk propensity.

The above decision rule yields four possible exchange outcomes between a participant and vendor: (1) the vendor wants an illegal voucher exchange while the participant does not; (2) the vendor does not want an illegal voucher exchange while the participant does; (3) both agents agree to an illegal voucher exchange; and (4) both agree not to be involved in an illegal voucher exchange. If there is agreement [outcome (3) or (4)], participant agents continue to visit the vendor and use their benefits in different ways (fraudulent or normal) throughout the simulation except one case. For participants who do not become involved in fraudulent exchanges [outcome (4)] but have a relatively high risk propensity (>0.66), a 10% random chance of moving to other vendors is introduced in order to consider high-risk participants' search for alternative fraud opportunities. If the fraud negotiation fails [outcome (1) or (2)], participant agents move to the next vendor selected by the store choice rule and continue going through the benefit exchange process until a successful exchange outcome occurs [i.e., (3) or (4)].

Decisions regarding illegal benefit exchanges trigger a small change in the risk propensity for participants and vendors during each interaction with the exception of case (4). In the normal benefit exchange (4), the risk propensity for both agents remains the same as in the previous simulation step. In other decision outcomes, the risk propensities change. When a participant engages in an illegal exchange, the risk propensity increases by 0.1, whereas when they refuse to engage in an illegal exchange, the risk propensity decreases by 0.1. When a vendor engages in an illegal exchange, the risk propensity increases by 0.01, whereas when they fail or refuse to engage in an illegal exchange, the risk propensity decreases by 0.01 for every ten incidences, considering the uneven ratio of vendors to participants in the system. This rule assumes that (1) those who are exposed to the situation of having to decide whether to participate in an illegal benefit exchange are considered to be would-be offenders; and (2) agents who refuse to engage in the illegal activity are the ones who take seriously the possibility of being punished. So in this indirect modeling of the deterrence effect of monitoring and regulation, an agent's risk propensity decreases upon refusal to engage in illegal benefit exchanges.

7.3.4 Model Setup

NetLogo is used as the simulation platform. In a single run, the population of 200 program recipients and 8 vendors is randomly initialized. The simulation ran ten times so a total of 2,000 participants and 80 vendors are generated from the simulation runs. During the simulation, vendors are monitored by the public agency based on the percentage of illegal benefit exchanges that occur relative to the total number of exchanges. When a vendor's illegal benefit exchange percentage exceeds 10%, the public agency function recognizes the abnormal sales activities and tags the vendor as *fraudulent*. The simulation continues tracking the number of *fraudulent* vendors in the system.[4]

7.4 Analysis

Analysis begins with visual evaluation of model performance followed by a comparison of the simulation outputs and observations from an earlier empirical study (Kim 2007). Visualization not only provides a quick evaluation of simulation outputs but also helps check whether the model is implemented as conceptualized. Programming errors are also easier to identify from the graphical outputs than attempting to debug the software program. Comparison of the simulation output with empirical observations improves confidence and grants some empirical validity to the model.

7.4.1 Visual Examination

Figure 7.4 shows the graphical user interface (GUI) that allows the user to interact with the simulation. On the left side of Fig. 7.4a, the "sliders" allow the user to adjust key input parameters such as the number of vendors and participants. The right panel illustrates the interactions between program recipients and vendors. The house symbols represent vendors and indicate their location. This symbol varies in size to reflect store sizes. Colored dots represent the participant locations, where the size of the circles reflects the participants' risk propensity: small dots for extremely low or low risk propensity (<0.33), a medium circle for medium risk propensity (0.34–0.66), and a large circle for extremely high or high risk propensity (>0.67). The colors indicate the results from the Huff model linking participants to vendors. For example, the yellow circles indicate participants who shop at the medium-sized vendor in the top left of the picture in the GUI in Fig. 7.4a.

Figure 7.4b presents what happens during the first interaction between participants and vendors after program participants decide which vendor to visit. In the left panel, a link highlights the case of illegal benefit exchanges between a vendor and a program participant. For example, the yellow vendor at the top is involved in fraudulent benefit exchanges with a program recipient at the bottom. On the right side of

---

[4] Technically, every transaction in the simulation can be examined so that the public agency agent can detect every illegal benefit exchange. However, in practice, the public agency cannot observe every transaction eye to eye and largely relies on high-risk vendor identification methods to regulate the program. Thus, I assume that the public agency agent can identify fraudulent vendors using transaction data only as an aggregate volume as state WIC programs do.

a Initial choice based on the Huff model

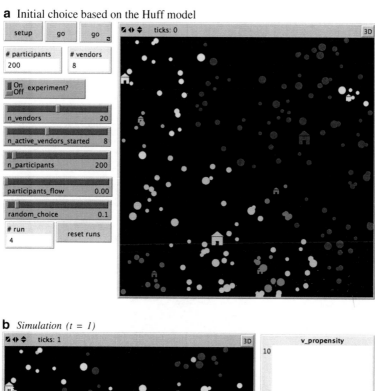

b *Simulation (t = 1)*

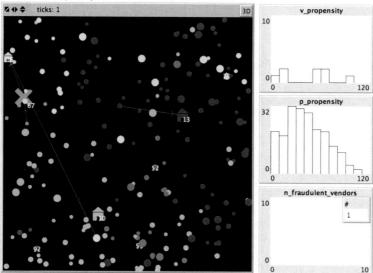

Fig. 7.4 Visual examination of the simulation model

C Simulation *(t = 70)*

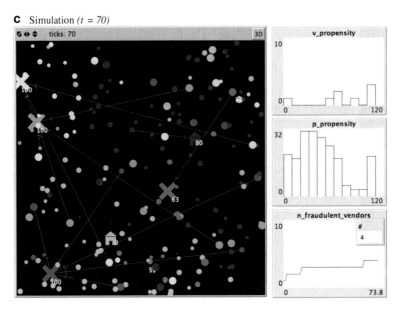

Fig. 7.4 (continued)

Fig. 7.4b, the output panels start to report the initial risk propensity distributions of the vendor and participant agents. The bottom chart reports the number of *fraudulent* vendors identified. One fraudulent vendor (i.e., the vendor with an X mark on the left side) was reported here, requiring the attention of a governing authority.

There are two things to note here. First, for the yellow participant at the bottom, the vendor was not the participant agent's preferred store. In Fig. 7.4a, the participant was assigned a light blue color, which indicates that the light blue vendor above the recipient agent was the simulated choice. The participant agent moved to the yellow vendor because of the failed exchange with the light blue store. Second, the sizes of the circles linked to the light purple vendor are the largest, which indicates that the risk propensity for the light purple participants linked to the light purple X (i.e., the vendor tagged as "fraudulent") is high (between 0.67 and 1.0). Also, note that the number attached to each vendor is the vendor's risk propensity (multiplied by 100 for easy interpretation).

Figure 7.4c shows the snapshot of the interaction at $t = 70$. The interaction panel shows that three other small vendors became fraudulent vendors by the end of the simulation. All four were relatively small vendors. These vendors are also not attracting participants who were expected to exchange their benefits at that vendor as predicted by the theory. The risk propensity distribution of vendors and participants in Fig. 7.4c also changed from the initial distribution in Fig. 7.4b, as agents with high risk propensity actively began to engage in fraudulent benefit exchanges. More agents appear on the right side of the scale (100), which indicates an increase in the number of vendors or participants with higher risk propensities due to vendor–participant interactions during the simulation.

7.4.2   Vendor–Participant Interaction Patterns

Kim (2007) reports empirical findings based on transactions data from the Ohio WIC program's vendors and participants. This analysis includes 78,236 voucher transactions from 22,874 participants at 78 vendors in an Ohio county during April 2004. Kim's analysis shows that the interaction patterns of vendors identified as high-risk (or fraudulent) vendors are different from the patterns of vendors identified as normal vendors. This analysis found that *while fraudulent vendors attracted program participants who had a low probability of visiting the vendor, these vendors also dispelled participants in their neighborhoods who were supposed to redeem their benefits there.*

Kim constructs measures that capture the interaction between vendors and participants. The theoretical probability of each participant choosing a specific vendor in the Ohio county was calculated using the Huff spatial interaction model and empirical data. The average (MEAN) and maximum (MAX) were constructed to indicate the general characteristics of the clients the vendor attracted and the highest probability of a client visiting the vendor.

Given the focus of WIC's vendor monitoring, the interaction patterns were summarized for vendors. From the previous analysis, two empirical observations were made: (1) a scatterplot of the measures of the 78 vendors and (2) the distribution of the measures by vendors' risk levels. Here, the simulation output is examined at step 70 (almost 6 years, as each simulation step is a month).

Figure 7.5a shows a scatterplot of the 78 vendors from the empirical data. Both values (MEAN on the x-axis and MAX on the y-axis) could range between a minimum of 0 and a maximum of 1. The chart shows that the 78 vendors vary in terms the types of program participants they attracted in April 2004. For example, at the bottom of the chart are several vendors whose majority of clients had a very low probability of visiting their store (extremely low MEAN). Even the participant with the highest probability of choosing a particular vendor is the one who does not have much chance of visiting the vendor in theory (extremely low MAX). Therefore, these vendors' interactions with participants are distinctively different from other vendors in the chart.

The five charts in Fig. 7.5 illustrate how the distributions of MEAN and MAX changed during the simulation. If all participants choose a vendor to maximize their relative utility as in Fig. 7.4a, then the distribution of the measures in the simulation looks like Fig. 7.5b in the current simulation. This is far from the observed interaction pattern in Fig. 7.5a.

In the simulation, because some participant agents engage in illegal benefit exchanges over time, the distribution of vendors where these participants exchange their benefits also changes. Here, I report scatterplots at $t = 1, 24, 47$, and 70. While the scatterplot at $t = 70$ in Fig. 7.5f is not identical to the empirical pattern in terms of the numerical estimates, the general pattern based on the interaction and decision rules described earlier is close to the patterns observed in the empirical analysis in Fig. 7.5a. In other words, a majority of vendors interact with participants who have

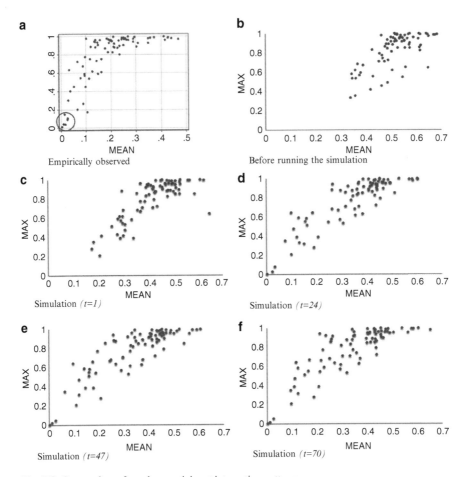

Fig. 7.5 Scatterplots of vendor–participant interaction patterns

a relatively high probability of visiting the vendor in their neighborhood. However, some simulated vendors at the left bottom of each chart appear to abnormally interact with participants with low probabilities of visiting them, as in the observed pattern. Scatterplots at $t = 1$, 24, and 47 present three different stages of this progression of the interaction patterns in the simulation.

Second, the descriptive statistics of the measures for the 78 vendors and the results from the present simulation are compared (Table 7.1). In the empirical analysis, the mean value of MEAN at the vendors was 0.19, and the mean of MAX among the Ohio WIC vendors was 0.77. In the simulation output, the mean value of MEAN for the 80 artificial vendors was 0.33, and the mean value of MAX was 0.77. At $t = 70$, the simulation produced slightly higher values than the empirical data, but the general distributional pattern is similar. Several factors could influence the difference, such as the use of different high-risk vendor identification methods.

Table 7.1 Comparison of vendor–participant interaction patterns

Empirical observation (April 2004)				
$N=78$	Mean	SD	Min	Max
MEAN[a]	0.19	0.11	0.01	0.47
MAX[b]	0.77	0.29	0.11	0.99
Simulated output ($t=70$)				
$N=80$				
MEAN	0.33	0.14	0.01	0.65
MAX	0.77	0.25	0.01	0.99

[a] Average probability of WIC customers at vendors
[b] The highest probability of a WIC customer at vendors

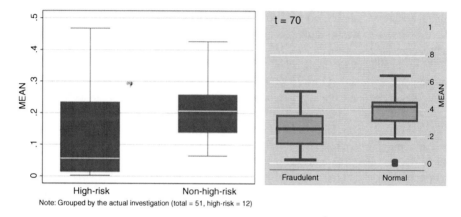

Note: Grouped by the actual investigation (total = 51, high-risk = 12)

Fig. 7.6 Comparison of MEAN distributions (*left*: empirical; *right*: simulated)

Finally, the distribution of the empirical and simulated MEAN values by vendor type (fraudulent vs. normal) is reported with box plots in Fig. 7.6. The top section, reprinted from Kim (2007), shows that vendors were categorized as a result of an actual field investigation in the Ohio WIC program. Note that in this figure, the "high-risk" vendors are "fraudulent" and the non-high-risk vendors are "normal." The distribution of MEAN was relatively lower among vendors identified as fraudulent (*high risk*) as compared with normal (*non-high-risk*) vendors.

The right box plot in Fig. 7.6 shows the corresponding output information from the simulation. The box plot at $t=70$ can be compared with the empirical distribution. In general, the MEAN distribution among fraudulent vendors ($N=32\%$ and 40%) shown on the left is lower than that of normal vendors ($N=80\%$ and 60%) shown on the right. Note that the empirical distribution was obtained from the actual program in which regular monitoring and regulation policies were in place, whereas the simulation introduced deterrence components (or mechanisms) in a very limited manner. One would expect the simulated values to be different because the simulations do not incorporate these policies.

7.5 Discussion

Newspaper stories about fraud in public service delivery programs seem to be fairly common. For example, a Waukegan, Illinois, couple was accused of cheating the food stamp program of more than $500,000 (August 2009 and April 2011) and redeeming more than $1.175 million in Illinois food stamp and WIC coupons, with more than half of the redemption obtained through fraud (Chicago Sun Times, June 26, 2011). Also, four people in Savannah, Georgia, were charged in July 2011 in a federal indictment in a store-front scheme to illegally exchange cash for food stamps and WIC program benefits at a reduced rate (Savannahnow.com, July 20, 2011). While fraudulent transactions may be a fraction of the budget of public service delivery programs, the social implications are nontrivial. Zero fraud may not be achievable in human society, but efforts to reduce adverse activities can be strengthened by better understanding the nature, structure, and processes of public service delivery systems.

This chapter has focused on modeling a plausible mechanism of fraud in public service delivery and has developed a simulation model. The analytical processes and outcomes show that the underlying mechanism does help in gaining an understanding of how differential vendor–participant interaction patterns between fraudulent and normal vendors in the Ohio WIC emerge. While the simulation output is not identical to the empirical pattern (and will not ever be), the results show that there is enough similarity in general interaction patterns between the empirical data and simulation output to make the study valuable. One possible reason for the higher simulation values could be the difference in deterrence mechanisms. The empirical data were collected from a program that regularly monitored program activities and implemented established sanction mechanisms for over 40 years, whereas such a mechanism was only introduced indirectly in the simulation by decreasing the risk propensity of agents who refuse to engage in fraudulent activities due to the fear of being sanctioned.

In describing a behavioral setting, situational action theory (Wikström 2006) includes a deterrence factor along with opportunity and friction. This inhibiting mechanism is defined as the perceived risk of intervention or associated risk of sanction if individuals act unlawfully. Deterrence also occurs in response to monitoring. In fact, monitoring as a form of deterrence has been a primary argument in the economics of crime literature (Becker 1968). Researchers have studied the effect of deterrence mechanisms such as the certainty, severity, and celerity of criminal punishment in various settings. Therefore, situational action theory itself utilizes a synthesis of routine activity theory, self-control theory, and the economics of crime to explain crime's pathway. In this chapter, the simulation tracked the number of fraudulent vendors; however, the results of monitoring were not fed back to vendor or participant agents. An obvious question that arises is as follows: How can we connect rules for policy changes with rules for social processes, and what insights can be generated from the process to inform policy decision-making in public service delivery programs?

A question often asked by policy analysts is "So what?" This impulse is closely tied to the nature of the field that aims to inform policy decision-making. However, some answers to the "So what?" question based on simulation models can be premature or meaningless—as is true for any analytical model—unless there is some confidence that the simulation model is robust. Having confidence in an ABM may be more challenging than having confidence in a traditional equation-based simulation model because ABMs are designed for different purposes. Here, I present a way to gain some confidence in ABMs for policy analysis. After all, an ABM can be informed by theory and practice as well as have an empirical basis.

Possible extensions of the current study include but are not limited to:

- Can alternative underlying mechanisms on fraud based on different theories (e.g., social network theory) also lead to the observed patterns?
- Can other types of fraud mechanisms (e.g., organized crime by a third party) be introduced and examined? How will they alter the systemic patterns?
- How will different combinations of deterrence mechanisms (certainty, severity, and celerity of sanctions) alter the dynamics of fraudulent exchanges and the level of fraudulent vendors in the program?
- Does the model's explanatory power extend to WIC programs in other states?
- Does the simulation-based decision support a change in approach or enhance the quality of decision making and the perception of decision makers in public service delivery programs?

References

Bunge, M. (2006). A systemic perspective on crime, In P. H. Wikström and R. J. Sampson (eds.), *The Explanation of Crime: Context, Mechanisms and Development* (pp. 8–30). Cambridge: Cambridge University Press.

Becker, G. S. (1968). Crime and punishment: An economic approach. In R. Febrero & P. S. Schwartz. (eds.), *The Essence of Becker* (pp. 463-517). Stanford: Hoover Institution Press.

Cooter, R.D., & Ulen, T. (2007). *Law and economics* (5th ed.). Boston: Pearson Addison Wesley.

Epstein, J. M. (2006). *Generative social science: Studies in agent-based computational modeling*. Princeton: Princeton University Press.

Haynes, K. E., & Fotheringham, A. S. (1984). *Gravity and spatial interaction models*. Beverly Hills, CA: Sage Publications, Ltd.

Heath, B., Hill, R., & Ciarallo, F. (2009). A survey of agent-based modeling practices (January 1998 to July 2008). *Journal of Artificial Society and Social Simulation, 12*(4), 9. http://jasss.soc.surrey.ac.uk/12/4/9.html

Huff, D. L. (1964). Defining and estimating a trading area. *Journal of Marketing, 28*(3), 34–38.

Kim, Y. (2006). *Analysis for adaptive complex public enterprises*. Doctoral Dissertation. Columbus: Ohio State University.

Kim, Y. (2007). Using spatial analysis for monitoring fraud in a public delivery program. *Social Science Computer Review, 25*(3), 287–301.

Kim, Y., & Xiao, N. (2008). FraudSim: Simulating fraud in a public delivery program. In L. Liu & J. Eck. (eds.). *Artificial Crime Analysis Systems: Using Computer Simulations and Geographic Information Systems* (pp. 319–338). Hershey, PA: IGI Global.

Miller, J. H., & Page, S. E. (2007). *Complex adaptive systems: An introduction to computational models of social life*. Princeton: Princeton University Press.

Pogarsky, G., Piquero, A.R., & Paternoster, R. (2004). Modeling change in perceptions about sanction threats: The neglected linkages in deterrence theory. *Journal of Quantitative Criminology, 20*(4), 343–369.

Sutherland, E. H. (1940). White-collar criminality. *American Sociological Review, 5*(1), 1–12.

USDA. (2001). *WIC vendor management study 1998* (Report No. WIC-01-WICVM).

Wikström, P. H. (2005). The social origins of pathways in crime: Towards a developmental eco-logical action theory of crime involvement and its changes, In D. P. Farrington (ed.), *Integrated Developmental & Life-Course Theories of Offending* (pp. 211–245). New Brunswick: Transaction Publishers.

Wikström, P. H. (2006). Individuals, settings, and acts of crime: Situational mechanisms and the explanation of crime, In P. H. Wikström and R. J. Sampson (eds.), *The Explanation of Crime: Context, Mechanisms and Development* (pp. 61–107). Cambridge: Cambridge University Press.

Wikström, P. H. (2009). Crime propensity, criminogenic exposure and crime involvement in early to mid adolescence. *MschrKrim, 92*, 253–266.

Wikström, P. H. (2010). Activity fields and the dynamics of crime: Advancing knowledge about the role of the environment in crime causation. *Journal of Quantitative Criminology, 26*, 55–87.

Chapter 8
Exploring Assumptions Through Possible Worlds: The Case of Homeownership

Roy L. Heidelberg

Abstract Simulations provide an ideal setting for exploring the logical entailments of assumptions through computational modeling. When constructing simulations about the social world, researchers are building what essentially are possible worlds based on the assumptions under consideration. In this chapter, we discuss these two concepts, possible worlds and assumptions, as they pertain to simulation through the case of homeownership. Homeownership has developed as an important social construct in American society, and its place has been reinforced through many forms of direct policy intervention. Research about homeownership posits a causal effect between it and desirable social outcomes, but the logical consequences of this relationship are rarely discussed. We use an agent-based model to explore the assumption that homeownership itself improves communities and demonstrate what this entails for lower-quality areas.

8.1 Introduction

Many studies on housing and community development place a strong emphasis upon the value of ownership as a mechanism for improving the status and quality of communities (DiPasquale and Glaeser 1999; Rohe et al. 2002a, b; Gale et al. 2007; Friedrichs and Blasius 2009). Studies of this posited causal relationship depend upon the correlative nature of ownership with desirable qualities, such as low crime, high levels of childhood opportunity and performance in school, and high civic engagement. There are rational reasons presented to support these claims. For example, homeowners have more to lose (financially) when crime is high, so they

R.L. Heidelberg (✉)
The Ohio State University, 1810 College Rd., Columbus, OH 43210, USA
e-mail: royheidelberg@gmail.com

A. Desai (ed.), *Simulation for Policy Inquiry*, DOI 10.1007/978-1-4614-1665-4_8,
© Springer Science+Business Media, LLC 2012

are motivated to form neighborhood watch groups. Likewise, they have more to gain from high-quality services, so they involve themselves more in civic activity. There is some dispute about these relationships (Rohe and Stegman 1994; Shlay 2006; Reid 2007), but the construct that homeownership undergirds the American way of life is a notion that dates back to the early part of the twentieth century, and it is an assertion worth taking seriously. Policy has traditionally encouraged ownership and done so to the financial and social detriment of renters. The tax code, for example, incentivizes ownership by reducing the cost of loans by granting a deduction for the interest paid on mortgages (Gale et al. 2007). The 30-year fixed-rate mortgage is an instrument developed in the USA used to make ownership affordable, but in other countries, such as Canada, such a lengthy fixed rate is unused. In Canada, the longest fixed rate that a borrower can typically attain is 10 years. In the USA, some regions, such as Southern California, are forced to use 50-year term mortgages to make the payments affordable for the average family, and qualified borrowers can actually get it at a fixed rate.

As policy seems committed to considering ownership itself as a good, we as researchers should consider what that logically entails. What does it actually mean to assert that *ownership* influences neighborhoods? What would the world look like if ownership did achieve what it is charged, namely, an effective way of improving quality of neighborhoods and improving individual life courses? These questions require us, in many respects, to exercise our imagination and try to carry out a scenario consisting of a series of assumptions to a logical conclusion. We do this constantly, despite the practical and computational challenge of thinking through all the possible iterations and interdependencies, but in this chapter, we will discuss how using simulation enables us to explore arguments of this sort directly and with greater ease.

An important quality of simulation is that it enables researchers to explore possible worlds through the extrapolation of assumptions. The two main aspects of this quality, assumptions and the idea of possible worlds, are important in policy, from design through implementation and evaluation. As such, an ability to study them and conduct research, no matter how speculative, is valuable to discourse. The purpose of this chapter is to elaborate on the meaning of the statement that simulation enables researchers to explore possible worlds through the extrapolation of assumptions by way of an exemplar model, namely, the ownership construct in housing and community development. This requires first a focus upon two concepts: assumptions and possible worlds.

8.2   On Assumptions

Policies are designed around constructs that we *hold* to be true but may not, in fact or deed, persist as universally reliable truth; these holdings are what we will refer to as assumptions.

This axiomatic approach to policy design is at the foundation of equal democratic systems; for example, a careful reading of the Declaration of Independence suggests that the notion of equality is not a natural state imbued within us biologically, but a construct that is held to be true in order to justify the actions that follow, namely, a declaration of independence from the British crown: "[…] we *hold* these truths to be self-evident, that all men are created equal […]" (Arendt 1993).

In the Declaration of Independence, Jefferson was not interested simply in a single truth, but a series of truths that provide the framework through which a particular action is taken, all of which are important justificatory aspects of radical revolution. The first of these is that all men are created equal, but other relevant truths provide the architecture of revolution, such as that there are rights endowed by a Creator and that, importantly, "governments are instituted among Men, deriving their powers from the consent of the governed." These normative notions of equality, fairness, and accountability have been used historically to justify national revolutions, but they are also important aspects of domestic policy and important evaluative criteria in policy. We hold fairness and equality to be important qualities that must be maintained in the policies that are produced by our governance system; in this manner, the assumption of equality can be both a necessary precondition for design as well as a metric for determining the quality of the policy outputs. Either way, we assume that individuals deserve a certain level of equality.

Let us now turn to a case that is more relevant contemporaneously. Housing has recently found a place in public consciousness as a driver of economic growth and decline, but it has always been a critical concern of domestic policy. At least since the 1950s and growing out of the Great Depression, home ownership has been the preferred policy approach of the United States federal government (Saunders 1990; Bratt 1997; Green and White 1997; Bratt 2002; Gale et al. 2007), although some popular sentiment is now turning against this policy (Kiviat 2010) in the wake of scholars questioning the rationale of low-income ownership policies (Shlay 2006). Nevertheless, this emphasis upon ownership as the preferred tenure option not just for individuals but also for communities has marginalized nonowners, including renters and low-income public assistance recipients.

A large body of literature evaluates the potential positive externalities of homeownership at both the aggregate level for the community and for individual households (Rohe and Stegman 1994; Rossi and Weber 1996; DiPasquale and Glaeser 1999; Aaronson 2000; Rohe et al. 2002a, b; Dietz and Haurin 2003; Engelhardt et al. 2010). At the individual level, research suggests that homeowners are more involved in civic activities such as activism (Cox 1982) and voting (DiPasquale and Glaeser 1999) as well as general involvement in social and political institutions (Rohe and Stegman 1994). On a related note, homeowners have a greater incentive to join associations that aim to maintain and improve the social and physical conditions of their community because of their reduced mobility (Rohe et al. 2002a, b). Homeowners may be more likely to improve and maintain their homes (Saunders 1990), actions that may benefit their neighbors (Dietz and Haurin 2003).

The belief that ownership is good for communities has important ramifications for policy design. A basic intent of policy is to make ownership easier through making it more affordable. The 30-year fixed-rate mortgage is a hallmark instrument of American housing policy, and the mortgage deduction is an important rationale in the deliberation over the cost of ownership. These policies, dedicated to individual ownership, are intended to encourage the positive externalities that help to improve communities by reducing crime, improving early childhood development opportunities, and encouraging, through individual homeownership, ownership within and of the community.

Moreover, ownership is associated with improved local institutions and governance, which in turn reduces crime and other social problems (Hoff and Sen 2005). There is also evidence that high levels of ownership are associated with positive child outcomes. Children who are raised in neighborhoods with high levels of ownership or in owner-occupied homes stay in school longer than children of renters, and teenage girls who live in owner-occupied homes are less likely to become pregnant (Green and White 1997). Neighborhoods seem to have at least a modest impact upon childhood educational and behavioral outcomes (Leventhal and Brooks-Gunn 2000).

That ownership is good for individuals and families as well as communities can be thought of as an assumption for modeling just as equality of opportunity and the basic framework of democracy are; they are, however, assumptions of a different sort. Ownership as a general good presents itself as an empirically evaluable claim, no matter the difficulty of actually evaluating it as an independent cause. The claim that all persons are equal is less evaluable; indeed, if it is subjected to evaluation, it may seem obvious to note that all people are not equal based on our present social structure. Some people are born into poor households, with disabilities, or in restrictive conditions. Nevertheless, in each case, these characteristics (equality or the goodness of ownership) are instituted as rules for behavior, some that we believe to be empirically true (such as that ownership has positive effects upon communities and individual well-being) or intend to be true (such as equality or fairness). We may witness that some phenomenon occurs and infer it to be a general rule, and this is where simulation becomes an effective tool. Essentially, we can take that rule and manipulate it under varying conditions that we ourselves control. In doing so, we are constructing what can be considered possible worlds in our dedicated scenarios.

8.3   On Possible Worlds

The claim that a simulation is a representation of a possible world can be ambiguous, so let us be clear about what this means. A possible world is possible in the sense that it is a logical extension of the specifications within the model, specifications that are (or at least should be) manifestly representative of assumptions that we are interested in exploring. A possible world can be practically *improbable*, but the model represents a specific view of the characteristics deemed relevant by the researcher for the argument that he or she seeks to make. For example, in classical and neoclassical economics, we abide by the assumption of self-interest, but we know that behaviorally, individuals act sometimes altruistically. Consequently, any model that portrays behavior as essentially and uniformly selfish is practically improbable, but the world portrayed is a possible world in the sense that nothing necessarily restricts individuals from all behaving according to self-interestedly derived principles, and this characteristic is instituted in the model.

To discuss this further, let us return to the example of the Declaration of Independence. Jefferson's text outlines what amounts to a possible world that is not feasible. It is an unattainable ideal in which the government has power by virtue of the consent of the governed and in which all persons are equal, a case that has never been in actuality. Indeed, the objective of the Constitution as an ever-evolving document is to achieve those ends (and many others) within a context of practical constraints. Laws and rules are established and reformed to ensure that the ideals are more apparent than less. When we talk about a possible world, we are not necessarily restricting ourselves to only that which seems presently feasible—we employ our imaginative capacities to expand the breadth of our future worlds. Simulation enables this capacity through the modeling of conditions and assumptions within a defined context.

Consider housing within a community as a dynamic system of agents making decisions based on preferences and perceptions. For policy design, we do not evaluate the unique characteristics of each particular household but instead make assumptions about the decisions we can expect them to make given certain conditions. For example, we might expect all households to pursue a strategy in which they are able to satisfy all their preferences in a sufficient manner (satisfice) or they seek to maximize given their options. It has been well established in the social science literature that individuals are unable to do the latter, so perhaps we commit our policy to the former—that people will buy houses that satisfy all their needs and as many of their wants as is feasible. One of those wants, we assume, is a high-quality neighborhood, but this might be perceived to be a relative characteristic, so each household is actually seeking a *higher*-quality neighborhood.

Meanwhile, policies are also designed around the belief that, as mentioned, ownership improves quality. The studies mentioned above delineate the ways in which ownership seems related to improved neighborhood conditions and individual outcomes. A general policy response has been to increase levels of ownership by making loans more affordable to low-income households. What, then, are we to make of neighborhoods that have high renter rates? Presumably, because these areas have low owner rates, the quality of the neighborhood is lower or lowered.

We now have a series of assumptions about behavior and quality that are related in a system that we ourselves can define, a system that arbitrarily represents a neighborhood or community. The manifestation of these assumptions is what constitutes the possible worlds that we can use to discuss the breadth of policy design. In this case, we have two layers of assumptions—that individuals will seek ownership in a way that improves their conditions, primarily through movement to higher-quality neighborhoods, and an assumption that ownership itself improves neighborhoods. When we begin to unpack these interrelated assumptions, it is apparent that there is a paradox akin to the chicken or the egg—do people purchase in lower-quality neighborhoods thereby improving the quality or does quality attract ownership? Let us assume that, for the purposes of policy design, we are less interested right now in what people actually do and more interested in what, hypothetically, is the result of these assumptions ordered in some logical manner. Essentially, we are interested in what possible worlds emerge from individuals behaving in ways that accord with our assumptions.

8.4   The Rationale and the Design of the Model

There are many policies designed to improve communities without depending solely upon ownership. Tax increment financing is used in many communities to fund infrastructure projects or to encourage developments by granting net new tax revenues to developers after the development is constructed and functional. Community Development Block Grants (CDBG) issued through the United States Department of Housing and Urban Development (HUD) aim to improve the economic opportunities of low-income households by, in addition to providing decent housing, also providing improved facilities and services. Nevertheless, if we take seriously the arguments presented in the literature about the benefits of ownership for communities and individuals (Cox 1982; Saunders 1990; Rohe and Stegman 1994; Haurin and Brasington 1996; Rossi and Weber 1996; Green and White 1997; DiPasquale and Glaeser 1999; Dietz and Haurin 2003; Belsky et al. 2005; Hoff and Sen 2005; Brasington and Haurin 2006; Friedrichs and Blasius 2009; Engelhardt et al. 2010), then we should also consider the logical consequences of designing policy that aims to increase homeownership, such as through the tax code (Gale et al. 2007). Essentially, we are asking what might a community look like if ownership itself improved neighborhoods and if dense rentership actually was detrimental to the quality of a neighborhood. Would both of our policy objectives be satisfied: improving neighborhoods while also offering households an opportunity to improve their life chances through moving to higher-quality neighborhoods? Would low-quality neighborhoods improve through ownership in a conditional setting in which individuals sought ownership in high-quality communities? This is the basic question motivating the agent-based model developed here.

Let us quickly reiterate before proceeding to the model setup. Policy is designed with two primary objectives that appear to be at odds. First, homeownership is encouraged and made affordable under the rationale that ownership benefits *individuals and families*. Low-income households are encouraged to purchase in higher-quality neighborhoods because ownership is considered a step toward financial security and social stability, even if low-income households do not consistently enjoy such benefits (Shlay 2006; Reid 2007; Newman 2008).

In other statistical evaluations, ownership is correlated with desirable *neighborhood* characteristics such as lower crime, better-performing schools, and higher-quality amenities. Consequently, community development strategies rely upon an increase in ownership levels under the assumption that high levels of ownership will improve the quality of the neighborhood or community (Galster and Killen 1995; DiPasquale and Glaeser 1999; Belsky et al. 2005).

8.4.1 Structure of the Housing Model

So, to summarize, families are encouraged to own in order to escape the low-quality neighborhoods in which they resided as renters because neighborhoods with high renter levels have lower-quality amenities and higher levels of disamenities, such as crime. At the social level, ownership itself is intended as a catalyst for neighborhood improvement.

At the individual level, households seek to optimize or satisfice their personal desires and opportunities through moving to the best possible area, while in aggregate policies are designed with the expectation that ownership itself will improve neighborhoods. The bifold logic is thus:

If an individual seeks to move then the individual will seek a higher quality community.
A community improves in quality if and only if it develops a high level of ownership.

Now, we must consider how to model such hypotheticals. The world must consist of areas with varying levels of quality and heterogeneous agents (households), some renters and some owners, all seeking to settle in a location that satisfies a randomly assigned threshold of satisfaction. The simple construction of this world is based on the rule that owners improve the quality of neighborhoods, which ties directly into the notion adopted in policy designs that homeowners and ownership in general improve neighborhoods. This construction of the basic model is a simple explication of housing policy in which there is a world with renters and owners vying for a position in the best possible place.

Adding complexity will enhance the model and help to support the argument that the outcome is reasonable. Agents are assigned levels of wealth, income, and satisfaction thresholds, which is simply a way of granting agents a unique characteristic based on how easily they are satisfied by certain conditions. Neighborhoods are made to be dynamic, changing with each new inhabitant. Also, areas have varying levels of value, so we can also explore how income inequality potentially influences the spatial sorting (which could also enable us to explore affordability policies more directly). This model, as specified in this chapter, focuses exclusively upon the issue of ownership and rentership as it relates to changing neighborhood quality. We want to use the model to construct an argument about home ownership policies based on the prevailing assumptions through the construction of possible worlds.

With simulation, uncertainty can be accommodated through random assignment. This has already been alluded to in the assignment of wealth, income, and satisfaction thresholds—these characteristics are assigned randomly because, for the purposes of this model, it is uncertain how the characteristics are distributed. In the same respect, neighborhoods have characteristics other than ownership that might influence the quality, and ownership levels might influence some of these characteristics,

Fig. 8.1 The *darker shades of green* indicate higher-quality parcels. The *blue circles* signify initial renters, and the *red arrowheads* signify initial owners. As the model proceeds, the agents change color based on whether they are owners or renters (*blue* for renters and *red* for owners). The shapes remain the same throughout the 40 runs

Example of an Initial Setup of the Model

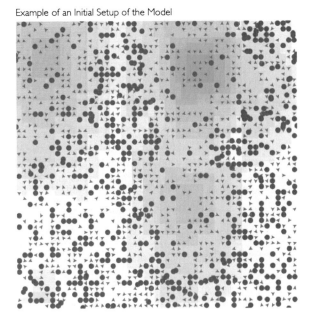

as housing scholars have argued. We are not observing those qualities here, though. Instead, we consider the affect to be evenly distributed among the groups of parcels. Essentially, the model is evaluating how ownership and rentership influence the quality of communities in an environment in which individuals are seeking to settle in the best possible place given certain constraints.

Figure 8.1 contains an initial setup of the agent-based model in NetLogo. The red arrowheads are initial homeowners, and the blue circles are initial renters. The darker shades of green indicate higher levels of initial quality. In this initial setup, the beginning homeownership rate was set at 60%, and the population consisted of roughly 1,500 agents. The world consists of 625 parcels (a 25×25 grid). At the beginning of each set of runs, the agents are assigned random location. Eighty percent of the renters are relocated outside of the high-quality areas. This setup is done primarily to mimic the initial conditions that one expects, in which the renter rate is low in high-quality neighborhoods. After the first year, each renter has an option to become immediately an owner if it is pleased with the location and satisfied with the neighborhood.

The parameters of the model collectively attempt to mimic a situation in which households seek a location to reside. There is no homelessness in this model; everyone is either a renter or an owner. The characteristics of the agents and the parcels of land are provided in Table 8.1.

As mentioned above, agents have a level of satisfaction as well as a satisfaction threshold. If the satisfaction level is below the assigned and constant threshold

Table 8.1 Parameters and characteristics of model

	Characteristics	Initial value	Dynamic value
Agents	Satisfaction	Random assignment	Function of patch quality, proximity to other owners and renters
	Satisfaction threshold	Random assignment	Constant once assigned
	Wealth	Random based on initial location	Changes with income and move
	Income	Random assignment	Constant once assigned
	Dislike of renting	Random assignment	Constant once assigned
	Move vision	Manually assigned	Constant once assigned
	Happy?	Binary	1 if satisfaction threshold is less than satisfaction
Parcel	Quality	Assigned according to constructed map of values	Changes based on renter effect and owner effect
	Value		Changes according to value of neighbors
	Category	1–3 based on initial quality	Constant once assigned
Model	Renter effect	Manually assigned	Constant: the effect of renters on the quality of the nearby households
	Owner effect	Manually assigned	Constant: the effect of owners on the quality of nearby households
	Neighborhood effect	Manually assigned	Constant: effect that the quality of parcels have on nearby parcels; influences only if the mean quality of nearby parcels is different than quality of individual patch
	Initial homeowner rate	Manually assigned	Constant once assigned

(in which the binary *happy?* is assigned a 1), then the agent seeks to move. Some agents have a higher distaste for renting than others, and this is implemented in the model through the randomly assigned constant *dislike of renting*. Wealth and income are also included: wealth is randomly assigned contingent upon initial location, and income is simply randomly assigned. Parcels of land have a level of quality and a value, each of which varies in response to the actions of the agent's movement around the world. Income increases the level of wealth, and in order for an agent to own a parcel, they must have sufficient wealth to pay for the property in full; there is no financing in this model. Moreover, renters are simply not owners; renting does not diminish their wealth. They are simply biding time before they can become owners. This model is designed so that the ownership rate increases; every agent "wants" to be an owner.

The initial setup is constructed so that every model run begins with the same world. Within the model itself, certain variables can be manipulated, including the effect that renters have upon nearby parcels, the effect that owners have, the effect of the overall neighborhood upon a particular patch, and the initial homeownership rate.

As noted above, this model is intended to be a rational reflection of residential sorting behavior. As a model, it is not empirical; on the contrary, a simulation model of this nature is speculative, an exploration of how we think about a phenomenon. The model itself is designed to favor ownership by making the agents more likely to become owners than renters under contingent circumstances. The key to the simulation is that it enables us to computationally include factors that can potentially interact with the key aspects of the phenomenon that we are interested in exploring (either randomly or deterministically, depending upon how it is programmed). In order for an agent to become an owner, the agent must have the wealth to do so, and there must be an available patch to purchase.

Programming how ownership alters quality is the most important component of the model. The simple, most straightforward manner in which to do so would be simply to base the quality of the patch solely upon whether or not it was occupied by an owner agent and to count how many owner agents were on surrounding parcels. If ownership alone is considered a *causal* impetus for quality improvement, then this might suffice. But that tells only part of the story. The alternative to ownership—renting—is equally important. Some research has focused upon the "citizenship" of renters and noted that renters are less likely to be committed to the improvement of the community. Thus, quality can be positively influenced by owners and negatively influenced by renters. It is not simply that renters are passively detrimental to quality by being not owners; they actually serve to undermine quality by, for example, not keeping properties in shape. This construct is important to consider.

The agents also respond to the space, namely, the quality of the community, in deciding whether to stay or go. If, for example, renters surround an owner, the owner parcel might be of relatively higher quality, but there is a general detrimental affect caused by the surrounding renters. This effect is programmed as a neighborhood effect, which directly impacts the satisfaction of agents. Put simply, an agent can be an owner satisfied with its parcel, but the neighborhood environment can adversely influence its satisfaction through the presence of renters.

Finally, we must consider the role of information in the model. It is unreasonable to presume that agents are aware of all available parcels in an area. In order to limit the information available, the agents are assigned a vision radius, which is designated by the variable "move vision." Agents can only see as far as the radius (move-vision value) dictates, so their options are limited to only those areas around them. Figure 8.2 depicts a five-parcel vision radius for an agent. In other runs discussed below, we varied the move vision as a way to introduce information into the model.

Fig. 8.2 Depiction of a vision radius of five parcels

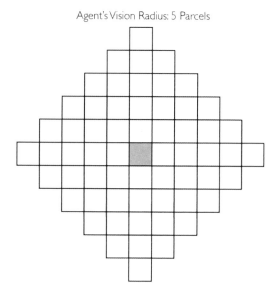

Agent's Vision Radius: 5 Parcels

8.5 Model Setup and Runs

The model is limited to 40 years, which is intended to approximate a year based on how the agents are allowed to behave. Essentially, we are evaluating a set number of households over 40 years that have an opportunity to change their residency status and/or location annually (an agent can decide to purchase the parcel that it has been renting if conditions favor such a move). Consequently, each run of the model is a run of 40 years.

The parcels were divided into three categories based on the distribution of quality: high quality, middle quality, and low quality. As depicted in Fig. 8.1, the parcels are clustered based on quality. Moreover, quality has a ceiling for all parcels. This ceiling has both structural and behavioral importance. Structurally, without a ceiling, quality would increase exponentially because ownership is encouraged so directly in this model. Behaviorally, perceptions of quality and satisfaction do not increase exponentially; just like the perceived marginal value of a dollar is less for a millionaire than for a destitute person, an increase in quality is less for residents of high-quality areas than low. Therefore, we evaluate the outcomes of the runs in two manners for comparison: change in average quality and average change in quality. The former is important because it will show us if the quality of gap is decreasing. The latter is important because it gives us insight into the effect of our variables, namely, owner and renter effects. However, because there is a ceiling and because the high-quality parcels start with a higher level of quality, focusing exclusively on the average change can be misleading.

The parameters set for the model are held constant with the exception of the owner effect, and, in later runs, move vision is varied. The initial homeownership rate for all runs is 60%, and the neighborhood effect is 0.10, which means that an agent's satisfaction level is either increased or decreased by 10% of the average quality of neighboring parcels. The renter effect for all runs is 0.04; computationally, this means that each year, if there are more renters than owners around a parcel, then the quality of the parcel is reduced by 4% of its present quality. The owner effect works in a similar manner: if there are more owners than renters around a parcel, then the quality of the parcel increases by the owner effect multiplied by the present quality. If there are no agents on neighboring parcels, then the quality remains unchanged.

8.5.1   Model Runs

The first set of runs focused upon the effect that ownership has on neighborhood quality. Three sets of 50 runs were conducted, one in which the owner effect was 50% weaker than the renter effect, one in which they were equal, and one in which it was 50% stronger than the renter effect. In all cases, the vision of the agents was set at ten parcels. The outcomes are illustrated in Fig. 8.3. These runs explore the relative difference in how the constructs are operationalized. For example, if people consider renters more detrimental than owners are beneficial, then the possible world is best illustrated by set 1a in Fig. 8.3. If renters are considered to be detrimental to quality but owners more than offset this detrimental effect through positive influences, then set 3a should be considered. If the two effects are considered to be roughly similar, then we should consider set 2a.

When renters are perceived to have an overwhelmingly negative effect, one that is not offset by the effects of owners, then neighborhoods tend to be worse off (even when the initial homeownership rate is over 60%), especially the low-quality neighborhoods. The high- and middle-quality parcels enjoy a slight increase in quality, but the low-quality parcels become worse off over the 40 years.

When the renter and owner effects offset, the low-quality parcels improve only slightly while the high- and middle-quality parcels improve in quality quite substantially. In fact, the middle-quality parcels merge with the high-quality parcels while the low-quality parcels are effectively left behind.

When the owner effect is 50% greater than the renter effect, we finally see that there is a notable improvement in the low-quality parcels. What is also clear, however, is that the high- and middle-quality parcels quickly reach the quality ceiling. So, after the first 10 years, the quality gap actually widens. It is only because of the ceiling on quality that the gap is closed somewhat by the end of the 40 years. This artificial cap on quality makes the outcome difficult to interpret. For example, if we concern ourselves with the influence that neighborhood quality can have on children, then we might be focused upon a 10–15-year horizon (roughly a generation). In this case, the gap widens. But if our concern is for the long-term prospects of neighborhoods, then the 40-year horizon might be appropriate.

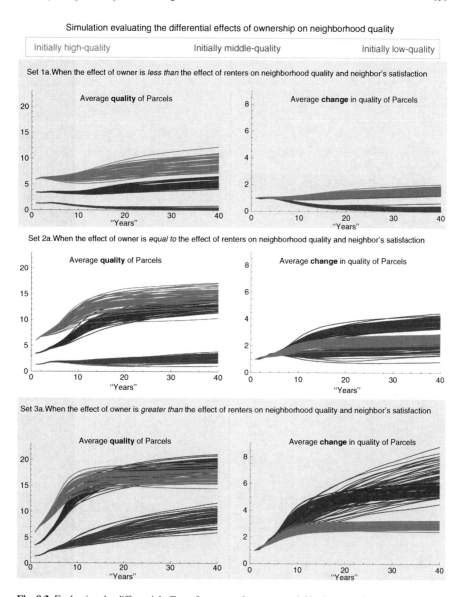

Fig. 8.3 Evaluating the differential effect of owner and renter on neighborhood quality and satisfaction

8.5.2 Adding Vision as an Information Constraint

Information is an important consideration in modeling any transaction, and in the case of an agent-based simulation, there are many ways to model information constraints. In the runs discussed in the previous section, we compared the difference in outcomes focusing upon one factor—the owner effect. We can also explore an information effect by constraining the agents in some manner. In this model, we constrain the agents by limiting the number of parcels that they can "see" as options for moving.

Effect of Owners nearby is less than the effect of Renters

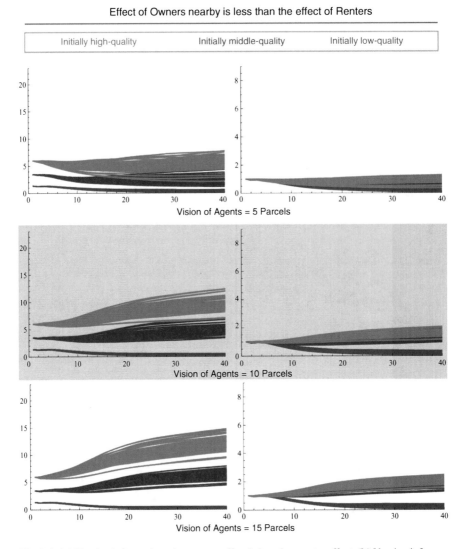

Fig. 8.4 (a) Varying information when owner effect is less than renter effect. (b) Varying information when owner effect is equal to renter effect. (c) Varying information when owner effect is greater than renter effect

This is determined by the variable "move vision." We constrain move vision in three steps: 5 parcels, 10 parcels, and 15 parcels. No agent has more information than another in any runs—so if the move vision is set at five parcels, every agent sees five parcels. None sees more or less. Practically speaking, a vision of five parcels means that an agent can see 60 parcels (approximately 10% of the parcels in the world); 10 opens up 220 parcels (approximately 35% of the world) and 15 allows them to see 480 parcels (approximately 77% of the world).

Figure 8.4a–c displays the changes in the average quality and the average change in quality over 40 years for runs when the owner effect is less than (Fig. 8.4a), equal

Effect of Owners nearby is equal to the effect of Renters

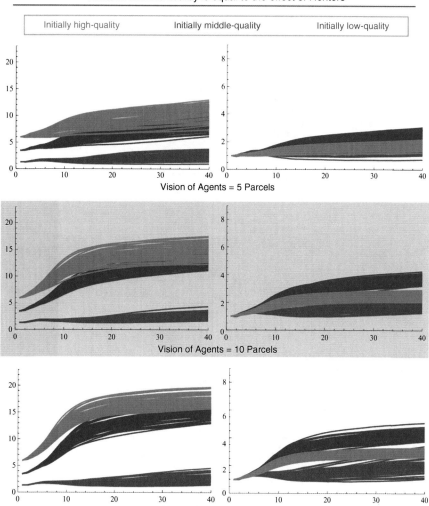

Initially high-quality   Initially middle-quality   Initially low-quality

Vision of Agents = 5 Parcels

Vision of Agents = 10 Parcels

Vision of Agents = 15 Parcels

Fig. 8.4 (continued)

to (Fig. 8.4b), and greater than (Fig. 8.4c) the renter effect. Each figure compares runs when the agents have different levels of vision.

In the case of Fig. 8.4a, we see that increasing the vision does little to improve the quality, relative or total, of the low-quality areas. The middle-quality areas do improve but not to a degree that the quality gap between them and the high-quality parcels is reduced. This outcome is reasonable when one considers that the setup of the model situates more renters in these types of parcels to begin with, so there is an immediate detriment to these areas thereby decreasing the propensity of anyone to become owners.

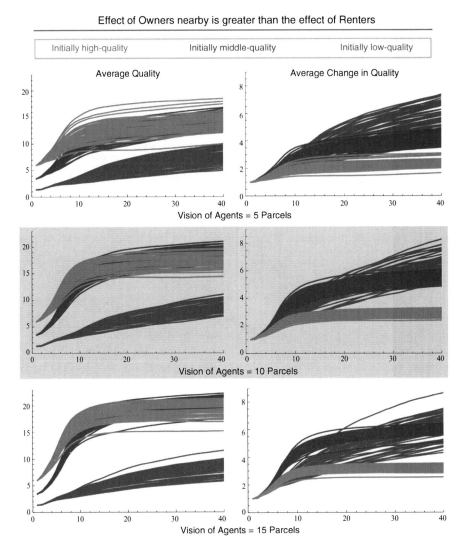

Fig. 8.4 (continued)

Figure 8.4b suggests conditions favorable for the middle-quality parcels, but the low-quality parcels do not substantially improve. The change in vision only exacerbates the quality gap between the low-quality parcels and all the other. It does, however, provide an advantage for improvement to the middle-quality parcels.

We have already discussed how the outcomes of the owner effect being 50% greater than the renter effect are difficult to interpret because of the time horizons. When the information (vision) factor is included, the story becomes even more complex. Indeed, limiting the amount of information (the vision radius) seems advantageous to the low-quality parcels. Perhaps, this is an artifact of agents in the simulation seeing the high-quality areas as a viable option when they can see three quarters of the world, whereas the agents are arguably willing to "settle" in the low-quality communities when they are unaware of what improvements in quality are available, thereby having a positive influence upon the community in aggregate because of the positive influence of ownership.

8.6 Discussion

The purpose of these model runs was to explore an idea that is widely discussed in literature on community development and housing—that ownership presents effective advantages to the quality of neighborhoods as well as to the life outcomes of children and families. The key construct that we are exploring is that of a perception in a community, the perception that renters are detrimental and owners are beneficial to communities. To begin, we ran 150 runs of a simulation model—50 when the owner effect was less than the renter effect, 50 when they were equal, and 50 when the owner effect was greater. The outcomes of these runs suggest that perceiving ownership as good (rather than of rentership as bad) is more beneficial to quality improvement, but it is not sufficient for closing the quality gap between high- and low-quality areas.

An added factor that was considered was information, which was operationalized in the models through the vision of the agents. Using the same three differences between owner effect and renter effect, the model was run to include vision radii of 5 parcels, 10 parcels, and 15 parcels. Focusing upon the condition of an owner effect that is greater than the renter effect, we noted that increasing the vision radius was actually unfavorable for reducing the quality gap between high and low-quality areas. This is perhaps a byproduct of constraining agents in the simulation to remain in the low-quality areas as homeowners—when they were unaware of the many options available, they were willing to settle on the best possible parcel, which is likely in a low-quality area when their vision was limited to five parcels around them.

Overall, the focus upon ownership as a causal factor in the improvement of quality comes down to how the models are constructed and interpreted. If we are concerned with absolute change, then the low-quality areas did indeed improve over time. However, if we consider improvement to be a relative notion, that is, dependent upon comparisons between areas, then the low-quality areas were not substantially improved through the effect of ownership. This explanation of the model results is perhaps the most behaviorally appropriate way to interpret the findings. When one considers the quality of their situation, they often compare to what else they know, a classic example of the old adage that families are always trying to "keep up with the Joneses."

8.7 Concluding Remarks

There is nothing deterministic about the models run here—that would require us to model the world as is, which is infeasible. What we have exercised here is a logical look at an idea—that the ownership society, manifested through homeownership, is inherently good for communities and individuals at the same time. What we have found is that, under the parameters that we used in our models to construct our argument, namely, income and wealth, parcel value, information, and differential effects of rentership and ownership, the outcome of relying upon ownership to improve quality does not result in substantial improvement in low-quality areas. Whether or not the idea that ownership is good for communities and rentership is bad is actually believed by researchers is irrelevant; the distinction is drawn in many research papers already cited throughout this chapter. It is important to consider that the questions we ask as social researchers contribute to the development of constructs that have the potential to be reinforced through the channels of communicating research. When we ponder such claims, it is incumbent upon us as researchers to think through the process to its logical conclusion. Sometimes this is not feasible due to the many computations that are necessary to consider alongside one another. When we present or are presented with constructs, we are inherently considering possible worlds in which these constructs hold. Simulation enables us to actualize these ruminations in such a manner that we can communicate them with other researchers and exercise a critical mind toward such ideas.

References

Aaronson, D. (2000). "A Note on the Benefits of Homeownership." Journal of Urban Economics 47(3): 356–369.

Arendt, H. (1993). Between Past and Future: eight exercises in political thought. New York, Penguin

Belsky, E. S., N. P. Retsinas, et al. (2005). The financial returns to low-income homeownership. Joint Center for Housing Studies, Harvard University. Chapel Hill, North Carolina.

Brasington, D. and D. R. Haurin (2006). "Educational Outcomes and House Values: A Test of the value added Approach." Journal of Regional Science 46(2): 245–268.

Bratt, R. G. (1997). "A Withering Commitment." Shelterforce XIX(4): 2.

Bratt, R. G. (2002). "Housing and Family Well-being." Housing Studies 17(1): 14.

Cox, K. R. (1982). "Housing Tenure and Neighborhood Activism." Urban Affairs Review 18(1): 107–129.

Dietz, R. D. and D. R. Haurin (2003). "The social and private micro-level consequences of homeownership." Journal of Urban Economics 54(3): 401–450.

DiPasquale, D. and E. L. Glaeser (1999). "Incentives and Social Capital: Are Homeowners Better Citizens?" Journal of Urban Economics 45(2): 354-384.

Engelhardt, G. V., M. D. Eriksen, et al. (2010). "What are the social benefits of homeownership? Experimental evidence for low-income households." Journal of Urban Economics 67(3): 249–258.

Friedrichs, J. and J. Blasius (2009). "Attitudes of Owners and Renters in a Deprived Neighbourhood." International Journal of Housing Policy 9(4): 435-455.

Gale, W. G., J. Gruber, et al. (2007). Encouraging Homeownership Through the Tax Code. Washington, DC, Brookings.

Galster, G. C. and S. P. Killen (1995). "The geography of metropolitan opportunity: A reconnaissance and conceptual framework." Housing Policy Debate **6**(1): 7–43.

Green, R. K. and M. J. White (1997). "Measuring the Benefits of Homeowning: Effects on Children." Journal of Urban Economics **41**(3): 441–461.

Haurin, D. R. and D. Brasington (1996). "School Quality and Real House Prices: Inter- and Intrametropolitan Effects." Journal of Housing Economics **5**(4): 351–368.

Hoff, K. and A. Sen (2005). "Homeownership, Community Interactions, and Segregation." The American Economic Review **95**(4): 1167–1189.

Kiviat, B. (2010). The Case Against Homeownership. Time Magazine.

Leventhal, T. and J. Brooks-Gunn (2000). "The neighborhoods they live in: The effects of neighborhood residence on child and adolescent outcomes." Psychological Bulletin **126**(2): 309–337.

Newman, S. J. (2008). "Does housing matter for poor families? A critical summary of research and issues still to be resolved." Journal of Policy Analysis and Management **27**(4): 895–925.

Reid, C. K. (2007). Locating the American dream. Chasing the American Dream, ed. William M Rohe and Harry L Watson. Ithaca, NY, Cornell University Press: 233–267.

Rohe, W. M. and M. A. Stegman (1994). "The impact of home ownership on the social and political involvement of low-income people." Urban Affairs Review **30**(1): 152.

Rohe, W. M., S. Van Zandt, et al. (2002). "Home Ownership and Access to Opportunity." Housing Studies **17**(1): 51.

Rohe, W. M., S. Van Zandt, et al. (2002). Social benefits and costs of homeownership. Low-income Homeownership: Examining the Unexamined Goal, The Brookings Institution Press: 381–406.

Rossi, P. H. and E. Weber (1996). "The social benefits of homeownership: Empirical evidence from national surveys." Housing Policy Debate **7**(1): 1–36.

Saunders, P. (1990). A Nation of Home Owners. London, Unwin Hyman.

Shlay, A. B. (2006). "Low-income homeownership: American dream or delusion?" Urban Studies **43**(3): 511–531.

Part III
System Dynamics Models

Chapter 9
Simulating the Multiple Impacts of Deferred Maintenance

Peter Lufkin, Rudy Hightower II, David Landsbergen, and Anand Desai

Abstract Deferring facilities maintenance is a policy option often with unknown outcomes. Tight budgets and the lack of immediate consequences make it tempting to delay necessary repairs without understanding the full implications of such delay. Facility managers often use a singular measure, the facility condition index (FCI) to summarize deferred maintenance. The FCI is a useful indicator of accumulated costs but fails to reflect the other possible consequences of deferral, such as increasing accidents, reduced occupancy, increasing energy demand, and increasing service calls. This chapter demonstrates a system dynamics simulation model that both recognizes the decision points in facility funding and makes explicit the multiple impacts of deferred maintenance. It proposes a structure for the evaluation of alternative funding scenarios and defines a new "best facility" indicator of condition. Development of the model is part of a broader collaborative effort among consultants, facilities managers at US National Laboratories, and academics to study funding decisions and the dynamic effects of deferred maintenance on costs and condition throughout the facility life cycle.

9.1 Introduction

Facility managers often have budgets insufficient to fully maintain their buildings and other real property. The United States government, for example, is one of the largest property owners in the world with over 400 thousand buildings either owned

P. Lufkin
Whitestone Research, 2050 Alameda Padre Serra, Santa Barbara, CA 93103, USA
e-mail: plufkin@whitestoneresearch.com

R. Hightower II (✉) • D. Landsbergen • A. Desai
John Glenn School of Public Affairs, The Ohio State University,
Page Hall, 1810 College Road, Columbus, OH 43210, USA
e-mail: hightower.23@buckeyemail.osu.edu; landsbergen.1@osu.edu; desai.1@osu.edu

A. Desai (ed.), *Simulation for Policy Inquiry*, DOI 10.1007/978-1-4614-1665-4_9,
© Springer Science+Business Media, LLC 2012

or leased (FRPC 2010). Due to historical underfunding, " … much of this vast and valuable asset portfolio presents significant management challenges … many assets are in an alarming state of deterioration; agencies have estimated restoration and repair needs to be in the tens of billions of dollars" (GAO 2003, p. 2). Concern regarding the proper management and upkeep of these assets is not a recent phenomenon, nor one limited to the public sector. One study (Lufkin 2010) estimated that in 2003, maintenance and repair expenditures for all US nonresidential buildings were 80% of the necessary amount.

Efforts at forecasting the costs of maintenance and repair have led to the development of a variety of tools. A simple rule of thumb in this context has been that the annual maintenance and repair (M&R) expenditures should be in the 2–4% range of the replacement value of the assets (NRC 1990). Surveys conducted by industry groups, such as the Building Owners Management Association and APPA (representing colleges and universities), have been used to collect data on actual M&R expenditures of their members. Optimization models to bring analytical rigor to these estimates have led to the creation of system replacement and life cycle models (Fuller 2010). Efforts to develop better measures of the condition of buildings and their operating costs got an added impetus in 2007 with the US Executive Order 13227, which called for, among other things, the development of performance measures to evaluate federal real property holdings.

But in spite of efforts to improve data collection, to develop optimal maintenance schedules, to estimate the life cycle costs of real property assets, and to develop better performance measures, we still know little about the short-term or long-term consequences of deferring necessary repairs. In this era of constrained budgets, the deferral of maintenance has often been a necessity. Yet, even in more favorable financial times, there has been a reticence to fully fund facility maintenance. Indeed, there is a sense among many managers that one is not capable of making the "hard decisions" if some appreciable portion of maintenance is not deferred, regardless of available funding.

The problem with such hard decisions is that their full impact is not recognized in any explicit way. Facility managers are at a disadvantage when determining funding levels and priorities, as they rely mainly on heuristics informed by their technical knowledge and experience. In evaluating alternative courses of action, they cannot employ cost–benefit comparisons or other analytical techniques without a comprehensive view of the consequences.

In this chapter, we describe a system dynamics (SD) simulation model that both recognizes the decision points in facility maintenance funding and makes explicit the multiple effects of deferred maintenance. It proposes a structure for the evaluation of alternative funding and is potentially a tool for facilities managers and non-facility professionals to explore the likely consequences of their decisions. This model is the product of collaboration among modelers, consultants, and facility managers.

9.2   Facility Funding as a Complex Problem

Facility managers are well aware of the complexity of their task, which involves making decisions under technical and budgetary uncertainty as they seek to ensure that their facilities support the overall mission of the organization. Adding to the uncertainty has been the lack of a systematic understanding of interactions and feedback among the various components of the facilities. The effects of the passage of time present a further complication, as the rates of change in deferral costs are unlikely to be constant, but instead, variable over time. The complexities of such interactions lead to consequences that are difficult to forecast. As Merton (1936) posited, the intended or unintended consequences of these interactions are often separated from the actions by time and space. For instance, deferring maintenance on a roof not only puts at risk the integrity of the roof but also increases the potential for water damage. The water damage could be as innocuous as a damaged carpet, or it could result in serious damage to the mechanical or electrical system jeopardizing the safety and productivity of the work environment.

Over their life cycle, facilities can serve multiple purposes with multiple goals that often change over time. This dynamic nature of the demands placed on a facility during its lifetime suggests that time should be modeled explicitly in any decision support tool. Additionally, facility condition, safety, productivity, and sustainability are not independent factors, but are, instead, interacting components of a system and must be treated as such. The interdependence of these nonlinear relationships results in emergent properties that cannot be predicted by aggregating or studying each activity separately. By developing a simple simulation model, we illustrate how one might begin to use currently available computational power and modeling tools to capture some of the dynamics and interactions inherent in facility-funding decisions.

9.3   Previous Research on Modeling Maintenance and Repair

The cost and timing of facility maintenance and repair have been the subject of studies from a variety of disciplines. A full review of this literature is beyond the scope of this chapter. However, we briefly mention the main lines of inquiry to provide a context for our model.

9.3.1   Prior Models

The Federal Real Property Council's guidance on how to create an inventory of real property (FRPC 2009, 2011) provides insight into the enormity of the task in just describing the current stock of assets. Over the years, a number of decision support tools have been developed that go beyond the rule of thumb that the annual maintenance budget should be somewhere between 2% and 4% of the replacement value of the assets. Ottoman et al. (1999) makes note of a large number of facility maintenance-budgeting models.

There is a long tradition of research in operations research and industrial engineering on the reliability and maintenance of industrial production systems (Ben-Daya et al. 2000). A number of optimization models have been developed that focus on the maintenance of industrial production infrastructure (Ben-Daya 1999), simultaneous optimization of production cycles and inspection schedules (Wordsworth 2001), maintenance optimization (Marquez and Herguedas 2002; Marquez et al. 2003), and just-in-time manufacturing (Abdul-Nour et al. 2002; Albino et al. 1992). Holistic efforts include Carrroll et al.'s (1998) model of the whole maintenance process involving costs, worker training, and effects of a reactive versus proactive approach to maintenance. Much of this research focuses on optimizing and scheduling maintenance, but there is little discussion of the consequences of not keeping to those schedules.

Simulation frameworks (Duffuaa et al. 2001) have been developed, and studies have been conducted to evaluate inspection and maintenance policies (Madachy 1996), organization and staffing, materials management, and shutdown policies. Yuan and Chaing (2000) model an optimal maintenance policy for systems subject to not only the effects of aging but also the effects of sporadic shocks. These studies continue the emphasis on modeling the optimal maintenance schedules, but do not address deferral and its consequences.

Empirical historical data-driven studies by organizations such as APPA (2001), the US Army Corps of Engineers (Bailey et al. 1989; Shahin 1992; Uzarski 1999), and the National Research Council of the National Academies of Science (Cable and Davis 2005) have focused on various aspects of the maintenance of infrastructure investments. Some of these approaches discuss the consequences of deferring maintenance, but their models often focus on single-component systems such as highways or roofs and do not capture the complexities inherent in facilities with multiple components (Federal Facility Council 2001).

9.3.2 *Measures of Facility Condition*

Much of the effort studying deferred maintenance (DM) is devoted to developing indices of facility condition (Cable and Davis 2005; Hegazy et al. 2010). The most commonly used measure of the consequences of DM is the facility condition index (FCI), which is a simple ratio of the cost of deferred maintenance to the replacement value. Introduced by Rush (1991), the FCI is an indicator of facility condition and considered a negative correlate with facility investment. Simplicity is the basic appeal of the FCI, but also the reason for broad criticism. As a ratio of costs, the FCI does not relate directly to the condition or productivity of a facility. For example, the cost of runway lights is a small fraction of the replacement costs of an airfield, yet nonoperating lights could threaten the entire productive ability of an airfield. With concerns regarding the effects of deferring maintenance, there is a growing recognition of the need for nuanced measures of its effects on factors such as mission dependency, safety, the work environment, job satisfaction, and energy usage (Cable and Davis 2005; Stallings 2008; Vanier 2001).

While other facility metrics exist, their link with funding is not explicit, and they are seldom incorporated into actual management (Scarf 1997). Some of these additional metrics include the mission dependency index (relative importance of a facility), a work environment index (employee satisfaction), a suitability index (match of facility to mission) (Federal Facility Council 2004), and a customer satisfaction index (APPA 2001). According to the Federal Real Property Council's (FRPC) (2009) *Real Property Inventory User Guidance*, all federal agencies must report a rate of utilization, an FCI-like condition index, mission dependency, and annual operating costs for every facility. A recent report by the National Research Council (2012) provides an extensive list of beneficial outcomes related to facility investment, but no mention is made of explicit quantitative relationships.

9.4   A Conceptual Model of M&R Funding

As noted earlier, the consequences of deferred maintenance are known only in an anecdotal and piecemeal fashion. A formal model of deferred maintenance would provide decision makers with a structured and more persuasive view of the effects of alternative funding scenarios.

A model simulating deferred maintenance and repair funding begins by identifying decision points in the funding process and the set of relationships that link funding to specific outcomes. Figure 9.1 is a conceptual rendering of an M&R-funding model.

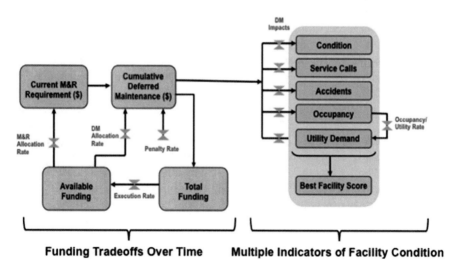

Fig. 9.1 A conceptual M&R-funding model

9.4.1 The M&R-Funding Process

A major value of the model is to simulate the impacts of varied M&R funding over time. Conceptually, we distinguish between two components of the model. With regard to funding trade-offs, management must decide how much of appropriated funds to withhold for contingencies and how much money to allocate to current M&R needs and to reduce deferred maintenance. The *funding trade-offs over time* component of the model is a representation of these decisions. As mentioned earlier, the FCI does not fully capture the full spectrum of consequences of deferring maintenance. The second part of the model addresses this problem. The *multiple indicators of facility condition* component of the model proposes other measures of funding impacts.

The detailed decision points and funding flows are shown in Fig. 9.1. The *funding trade-offs over time* process begins at the bottom, in the middle of the figure with *total funding*. Total funding is determined outside the model, the combination of perceived need and organizational budget priorities.

Moving to the left along the arrow from total funding is the *execution rate*, which is applied to total funding to determine the actual *available funding* for repairs. This rate is usually <1, as funding initially appropriated for M&R is usually less than the perceived need. Rather than some vaguely larcenous notion, the execution rate provides flexibility to the decision maker to adjust to changing priorities or unforeseen demands. The execution rate among US military services, for example, can vary from 60% to 110% (Whitestone Research 2011).

The two arrows emanating upward from available funding allow the available funds to be distributed to *current M&R requirements* or *cumulative deferred maintenance*, which is past M&R requirements that were not funded. *M&R allocation rate* and *DM allocation rate* capture the allocation of available funding for current and past maintenance, respectively. Often, a high level of DM becomes a lightning rod for criticism and an argument for earmarked expenditures.

An important aspect of this model is that *cumulative deferred maintenance* is not simply the sum of all previous deferred maintenance. Like compound interest on an investment, the deferred maintenance is assigned a fixed or variable penalty rate, which acts as a dynamic compounding factor that assigns a larger cost to old deferred maintenance versus new. The compounding effect is achieved through the *penalty rate*. This penalty forces managers to trade off funds for current maintenance and repair with funds to reduce the deferred maintenance growing increasingly more expensive.

The value of the penalty rate is largely unknown, though subject to much speculation. One study of historical maintenance records estimated an annual rate of slightly less than 1%, but the authors suggested that this rate was low because management intuitively gave high priority to those repairs, such as a roof leak, whose cost would quickly rise with neglect (Lufkin 2006). The uncertainty and speculation surrounding penalty rate makes it an important variable in the analyses of alternative scenarios. The decision to reduce deferred maintenance versus spending on current M&R requirements could depend upon what penalty rate is assigned. The penalty rate itself can be explicitly modeled not only as a function of the cost of money but also as a function of the probability associated with the failure of a

Table 9.1 Selected outcomes related to M&R funding

Outcome	Measure
Condition	Deferred maintenance, FCI
Production	Utilization rate of physical space
Safety	Number and type of incidents
Efficiency	Number and cost of service calls
Sustainability	Energy and water demand, emissions

component and the potential consequences of that failure. In sum, the cumulative deferred maintenance is the cost of current year repairs not funded along with past deferrals compounded with the delayed impact of the penalty factor.

9.4.2 The Multiple Impacts of Funding

The second component, on the right-hand side of the conceptual model (Fig. 9.1), is the potential for developing a set of proposed measures that go beyond the FCI to reflect a broader understanding of facility condition. Table 9.1 lists some measures that could be associated with M&R funding. Although not a definitive list of outcomes, it does reflect the major concerns of experienced facility managers, as expressed during discussions with US Department of Energy experts.

The generally accepted practice has been to define facility condition simply in terms of the amount deferred maintenance. However, one could also conceptualize facility condition in many other ways; a facility could be considered in poor condition if it had safety issues or it used excessive energy. Stallings (2008), for example, has demonstrated that facility condition affects job satisfaction and derivatively productivity in schools.

Expanding the notion of facility condition could provide additional information that might affect maintenance and repair priorities. While encouraging us to include other indicators of facility condition, our technical advisors also emphasized the need for a single condition measure. In this model, we have proposed the *best facility score*, a normalized and weighted combination of the other measures. The precise functional relationships and weights for these additional measures and the summary measure are largely unknown and should be the subject of additional research. Case studies and other data collection activities would provide initial values for experimentation and construction of such measures.

9.5 A System Dynamics Model of Facility Funding

System dynamics is a research method that incorporates feedback, illuminates counterintuitive behaviors due to dynamic interactions, and aids in policy analysis and design (Sterman 2000). As an analytical tool, SD has been extensively used to examine interdisciplinary complexity in social, ecological, business, and policy

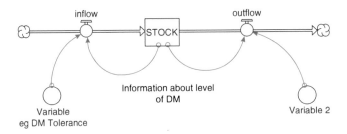

Fig. 9.2 Elements of a system dynamics model

systems (Meadows 2008; Richardson 1991; Sterman 2000) but, until recently, there have been few examples of its use as a facility cost simulation tool (Thompson and Bank 2010).

A virtue of SD is that it makes explicit assumptions and relationships otherwise left to the intuition of experienced managers. Facility managers have implicit expectations regarding the levels of deferred maintenance that they consider tolerable. The gap between this tolerable DM level and the actual amount of DM determines whether they will act to alter the amount of DM. The complexity in managing DM arises from the time delays and lags in the system between having the knowledge that leads to action and the response of the system to those actions (Richardson 1991).

9.5.1 Building Blocks of a System Dynamics Model

The basic components of a system dynamics model are stocks and flows. A system dynamics model (Fig. 9.2) defines relationships in terms of stocks, inflows and outflows, variables, and information flows. In this figure, the box in the middle represents a stock, such as DM, which expands and shrinks depending upon the rates of inflow from the left and the outflow on the right. The valves on either side regulate these rates of flow. The arrows from the stock to the valves depict information flows regarding the level of stock. For example, an alarmingly high level of DM may signal a decrease in the rate of inflow or increase in the outflow to catch up on DM. At the start of a simulation, the level of stock is predetermined, and its value is updated over the simulation time period. In the case of M&R-funding simulation, the variables can be decision points (e.g., tolerance for DM) or functions (e.g., the relationship between facility condition and funding levels that can influence the level of DM).

9.5.2 Implementing the Model

Our SD implementation follows the conceptual M&R-funding model discussed above. Figure 9.3 is a depiction of the model as implemented in the system dynamics software. Note that our preliminary equations underlying the model are presented in the Appendix. On the left is the model of the representation of how the stock of

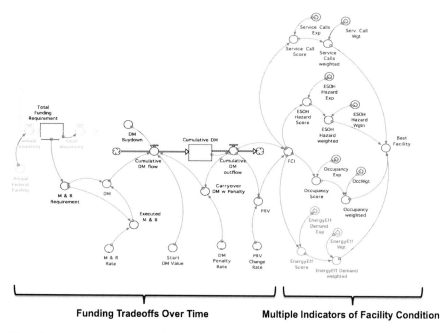

Fig. 9.3 A system dynamics model of M&R funding

DM is affected by the amount of available funds and the allocation decisions. The right-hand side of the figure illustrates how the multiple indicators of facility condition are a function of the level of deferred maintenance.

Table 9.2 lists the main elements of the SD simulation. The system dynamics model story begins with the *total funding requirement* to properly maintain a physical plant. This is located on the left-hand side of the model. Note that we have not explicitly modeled the determinants of this requirement, and therefore that section of the model on the top left-hand side is faded. Next, the *M&R requirement* determines the request for federal funds. In the first year, M&R requirement is the same as total funding requirement. The *M&R rate* is the percentage of the M&R amount requested that is available. Next, *executed M&R* is the total funding used for maintenance in the current year (M&R Rate times M&R Requirement). Facility managers often set aside some of the available funds for contingencies; hence, the executed M&R can be less than the available funds and that holdback would also be reflected in the M&R rate. The *deferred maintenance* (DM) is the difference between the M&R requirement and the executed M&R. *Cumulative deferred maintenance* is the sum of previous deferred maintenance, which is compounded because of the penalty, and any current deferred maintenance. *Carryover DM with penalty* is where the penalty is applied to the DM and is fed back into the cumulative deferred maintenance.

The model shows five performance indicators that capture the effect of deferring maintenance. They are measures of condition (FCI), safety (accidents), productivity

Table 9.2 Main elements in the SD model

Model component	Explanation
Total funding requirement	This requirement is the amount appropriated for current M&R and DM reduction of funds requested from the federal government to meet the infrastructure needs of the facility. This amount is simply shown in the model as a source of funds but is not explicitly modeled in the simulation
M&R requirement	This requirement represents the total need at the facility to fully fund M&R needs. For the purposes of this model, this is the amount of M&R funds requested at the start of each time period
M&R rate	Because of scarce resources, the available funds may not meet the need. This rate is the percentage of need met by the available funds
Executed M&R	These are the funds available for M&R
Deferred maintenance	The gap between current M&R needs and the available funds is the amount of M&R that has to be deferred; hence, it equals M&R requirement less the executed M&R
Cumulative DM	The box in the middle is the main stock that is the focus of this simulation. It represents the level of deferred maintenance over time. Input of new deferred maintenance flows in from the left, where the valve regulates the inflow. The cumulative DM outflow valve on the right controls the rate at which the DM stock is reduced
Feedback (information flow)	Information from the output valve on the right feeds back into the input flow valve via the variable "carryover DM with penalty" located below the cumulative DM stock
Plant replacement value (PRV)	The total value of the physical plant should it need to be completely replaced
Indicators of facility condition FCI, energy, occupancy, hazard, service calls	Information regarding the level of DM and the PRV flows into the FCI indicator on the right, which then informs the other scores that represent other aspects of facility condition
Best facility score	The best facility score is a composite-weighted combination of the indicators of facility condition

(occupancy), sustainability (energy demand), and efficiency (service calls). These measures respond to the cumulative amount of DM, including any level of current underfunding plus any past underfunding compounded by the penalty rate. Note the penalty rate applied to account for the potential additional damage that follows from the repeated deferral of necessary repairs.

All of the performance measures have been combined to create the new composite measure, the *best facility score*. This score will provide a single measure that will permit a quick summary evaluation of alternative funding scenarios. Ranging from 0 to 1, this score is the ratio of the actual calculated value to a benchmark value, where the benchmark is based on scores without DM and, by implication, full M&R funding.

The *FCI* is the traditional measure of facility condition. It is equal to one minus the DM divided by plant replacement value (*PRV*). *Service call score* indicates the additional service necessary due to DM and is an input to *best facility score*, composite

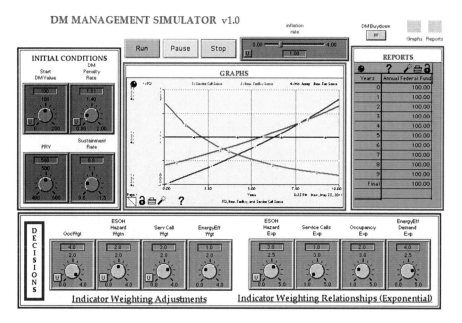

Fig. 9.4 DM simulation dashboard

indicator of facility condition. The other performance measures that constitute the best facility score are:

- *ESOH hazard score*—a measure of the degradation in environmental safety and other health safety considerations
- *Occupancy rate score*—a measure of reduced occupancy due to unavailability of space
- *Energy efficiency score*—an indicator of increased utility expenditures

As mentioned earlier, there is little information available about how to model these scores. So, although it is a composite score, the best facility score is modeled essentially as an inverse function of FCI.

9.5.3 Model Dashboard

Graphical user interfaces or dashboards that allow model users to directly manipulate the simulation have gained widespread use in business and public policy communities. Dashboards allow decision makers to learn by manipulating the model parameters to work through various alternative scenarios. Dashboards are designed to graphically illustrate information processed from variety of sources such as external inputs, data, documents, user knowledge, or outputs from other models. Figure 9.4 is a screen shot of the DM management simulation dashboard that allows the user to make incremental changes to model parameters and observe the results of each change. The simulation begins by setting the *INITIAL CONDITIONS* at their starting values. The *REPORTS* on the top right-hand side currently display the amount of federal funding available. For the purposes of illustration, it is set at a constant initial value of $100.

The *DECISIONS* at the bottom of Fig. 9.4 are a set of dials that decision makers can use to adjust the composition of the best facility score. The dials on the left can be used to set the weights assigned to the different indicators in the construction of the composite score. The dials on the right allow the user to adjust the equations that determine the values of the scores. There are four different variables shown in the *graphs*. As is customary in SD modeling, the horizontal axis represents time and the vertical axis varies depending upon which indicator is being tracked. The FCI is in blue and increases from left to right. Ideally, one would want the FCI to be above the black horizontal line, which indicates the user-defined minimum acceptable level for the FCI. The other two lines show two other measures of facility condition. The composite best facility score is the purple line that behaves inversely with respect to FCI and falls from left to right. The green line is the service calls score. As illustrated in the examples below, the graphic can be altered to show the behavior of different indicators over time.

9.6   Examples

In an early meeting for this project, facility managers from the National Laboratories described their biggest problem: how do you present the problem of deferred maintenance to senior managers in a succinct fashion that captures the complexity of its impact? The intuition that failure to maintain facilities has multiple impacts is not novel. But the translation from impressions and anecdotes into measurable relationships has largely been overlooked until now.

The power of simulation models, as illustrated in these examples, is in formalizing these impressions into a structure that allows the independent examination of the effect of different variables in the M&R model on the performance indicators.

To illustrate the functioning of this simulation model, we explore, in this artificial environment, a number of simple questions. For example, what is the behavior of FCI if both DM and the portfolio of facilities are varying over time? What is the nature of the lag between the change in the penalty associated with DM and facility condition?

It must be cautioned that modeling and simulation goals are not definitively predictive, but rather, illustrative for decision making. However, the ability to posit alternative scenarios allows decision makers to gain confidence in understanding possible outcomes of a variety of policy options. Through this approach, we can now begin to address the challenge posed by our management advisors as to how to present the complex problem of deferred maintenance to senior managers in a simple manner that still captures the complexity of the problem.

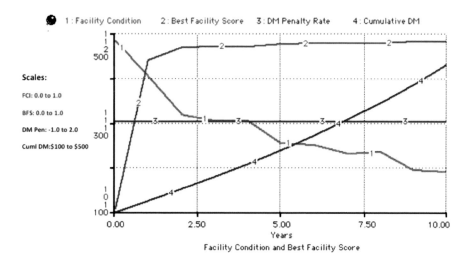

Fig. 9.5 Variation in PRV

The dashboard in Fig. 9.4 shows the dials that the simulation user can adjust to change the values of some of the model parameters. At the start of the simulation, the model builder sets the initial parameter values. After the initial run of the simulation, the model user can adjust the dials on the dashboard to explore how the model outputs would change due to changes in the initial conditions or other parameter values.

The three fictitious examples below illustrate how model outputs vary with user-defined changes. We make incremental changes in the simulation parameters to help the reader develop an intuitive feel for the behavior of the simulation outputs. In these simulations, we do not allow the FCI to fall below 0.8 on a scale where a score of 1 represents perfect condition. We have set the planning horizon at 10 years, so each simulation runs over a 10-year period.

9.6.1   Example 1: Changes in the Facility Portfolio Over Time

In all our examples, we begin with the assumption that, because of insufficient funds, DM increases as depicted by the brown line rising from left to right in Fig. 9.5. We keep all other parameters fixed so as to focus on how the FCI and the best facility score vary with respect changes in the facilities portfolio, which affects the value of PRV. Over the 10-year simulation period, we assume that new facilities will be acquired; some will be decommissioned while others may be refurbished to meet changing organizational needs. Hence, in this example, as a reflection of the changing facilities portfolio, we allow PRV to change during the 10-year simulation period. We do not show the changing PRV to reduce visual clutter. As one might expect, there are no surprises here as PRV varies, the orange FCI value in Fig. 9.5 declines, albeit haphazardly even though there is a smooth increase in DM.

The change in the best facility score (green line) tracks the changing FCI, but because it is composite score, it does not mirror the precise changes in FCI. The changes in PRV appear to influence the behavior of FCI, but the trend underlying FCI is a decline because the increasing level of DM dominates its behavior.

9.6.2   Example 2: Changing the Portfolio and the DM Penalty Rate

In our first example, we kept the penalty rate (blue line in Fig. 9.5) fixed at 1% over the 10-year period. One way of thinking about the DM penalty rate is that it is the cost of deferring maintenance. In reality therefore, we would not expect the rate to stay constant over long periods of time. The penalty rate would vary over time with changes in the economic inflation rate because of the heterogeneity in the type of maintenance that has been deferred and also potentially with the size of the DM. Hence, in this second example, we allow both the PRV and the DM penalty rate to vary simultaneously. This scenario begins to show how the interaction of changes in the penalty rate affects the rate at which DM increases. As it becomes "more expensive" to defer maintenance, its rate of increase is reduced (brown line at the bottom of the graph). The FCI (orange line) continues to decline as it did in the previous simulation, but the decline in the early years is not as steep as in Fig. 9.4.

The changes in PRV are the same in Examples 1 and 2; however, DM is now affected by the varying DM penalty rate. Note first that the decline in FCI in this example is not as fast during the first 2.5 years as it is in Example 1. Further, note that there is a lagged effect of the DM penalty rate change on FCI; although the penalty rate peaks around year 3.5, the decline in FCI remains rather flat during the time period between 2.5 and 5 years. Even though the penalty rate shows an increase after year 5, the DM begins a rapid rise due perhaps to insufficient M&R funding. Hence, in the latter part of the 10-year period, even though the behavior of the DM penalty rate is similar to that during the first 5 years, its effect on the rate of increase in DM is not as strong. The interaction between the changing PRV and available funding make it difficult to predict how FCI would behave as indicated by the slight improvement in FCI between years 7 and 8 even though DM is steadily increasing over that time period. Eventually, the fast increase in the accumulation of DM drags down the FCI.

By comparing the best facility score (green line) in Figs. 9.5 and 9.6, note that its behavior is not as sensitive to these changes as that of FCI, whose behavior in the two figures is markedly different.

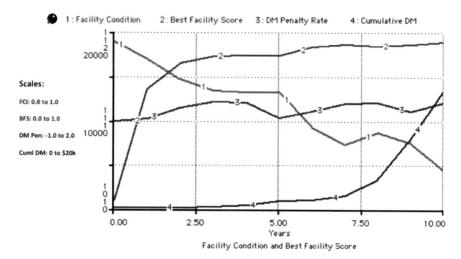

Fig. 9.6 Simultaneous variations in PRV and DM penalty rate

The lesson to be drawn here is that even though we are changing only one variable at a time, the behavior of FCI, which is normally perceived to track fairly closely the changes in DM, ceases to be closely linked to the behavior of DM. Interactions among PRV, DM penalty rate, and DM begin to have unpredictable effects on the behavior of FCI.

9.6.3 Example 3: Changing the Portfolio, the DM Penalty Rate, and M&R Funding

Although facility managers have some flexibility in determining how much funds to allocate to current M&R expenditures and how much to allocate to drawing down DM, the main indicator of how much maintenance will have to be deferred is the M&R rate, which is the proportion of the need that can be met by the available funds. In forecasting future M&R costs, it is not uncommon to assume a constant M&R rate or a fixed inflation factor for the foreseeable future. However, in reality, the actual funds received have a fixed component, which is closely related to the previous year's budget and a random component that, by its very nature, is difficult to predict.

In this scenario, in addition to the PRV and DM penalty rate, we also allow the M&R rate to vary over the 10-year period. To ensure ease of comparison, we show the same four variables in each of Figs. 9.5–9.7. Thus, although M&R rate is allowed to vary, in this example, we do not show it in Fig. 9.7.

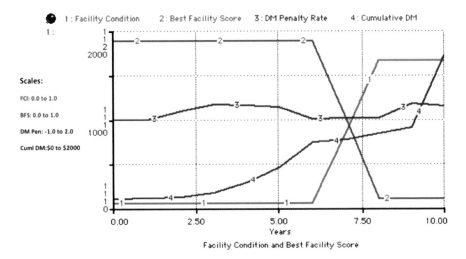

Fig. 9.7 Simultaneous variations in PRV, DM penalty rate, and funding

Again, the first and perhaps main thing to notice across Figs. 9.5–9.7 is that as more variables are allowed to vary simultaneously, even though the FCI is a simple function of PRV and DM, the FCI behavior quickly becomes unpredictable. Whereas in Fig. 9.5 the relationship between DM and FCI is fairly close, it begins to diverge in Fig. 9.6 and the two trends look different in Fig. 9.7.

The essential lesson to be learned here is the obvious one, which is that the facility manager's task is indeed complex. Even the simple cost-based measure of facility condition does not behave in a systematically predictable fashion as underlying factors vary in non-systematic ways over time. As our model becomes more realistic, by incrementally relaxing assumptions regarding the variability in different determinants of deferred maintenance, even a simple model with a single stock with feedback can behave in ways that are not obvious and often counterintuitive.

9.7 Closing Remarks

We built the M&R-funding model to serve three purposes: (1) to provide a formal structure to an otherwise as hoc process; (2) to propose alternative measures of facility condition that provide a richer view not captured by the ubiquitous FCI; and (3) to illustrate that even a simple model can help managers explore the impacts of different assumptions and the outcomes of different policies.

Although we have begun to ask questions regarding the effect of increasing DM on a broader set of facility condition measures, we have not yet answered the question often most pressing for facility managers: what inputs are necessary to attain a target condition? Using the model for such exploration could provide guidance on how to prioritize and strategically target M&R funding as well as expenditures to reduce deferred maintenance.

Acknowledgments We gratefully acknowledge financial support from Pacific Northwest National Laboratories. A preliminary version of this model was presented at the Whitestone Department of Energy Facility Cost Planning Workshop in San Francisco CA, May 23–25, 2011. We thank our technical experts, J. Edward Lee, Marvin E. Olson, and David Start, for sharing their practical knowledge of facility management and for their review of earlier versions of this work. Any remaining errors are the responsibility of the authors.

Appendix

Base Model Equations

The following equations represent the model implementation in **STELLA**

Cumulative_DM(t)=Cumulative_DM($t-dt$)+(Cumulative_DM_flow−Cumulative_ DM_outflow)$\times dt$

INIT Cumulative_DM = 100

INFLOWS:

Cumulative_DM_flow = (100 − Start_DM_Value) + Carryover_DM_w_ Penalty+DM-DM_Buydown

OUTFLOWS:

Cumulative_DM_outflow=Cumulative_DM

Total_Funding_Requirement(t) = Total_Funding_Requirement($t-dt$) + (annual__investing−total_dispersing)$\times dt$

INIT Total_Funding_Requirement=annual__investing

INFLOWS:

annual__investing=Annual_Federal_Funding

OUTFLOWS:

total_dispersing=Total_Funding_Requirement

Annual_Federal_Funding = 100

Best_Facility_Score = 1/(ESOH_Hazard_weighted + Occupancy_weighted + Service__Calls_weighted+EnergyEff_Demand_weighted)

Carryover_DM_w_Penalty=Cumulative_DM_outflow^DM_Penalty_Rate

DM = Sustainment_Requirement-Executed_Sustainment

DM_Buydown=0

DM_Penalty_Rate = 1.01

EnergyEff_Demand_weighted=EnergyEff_Score$\times$EnergyEff_Wgt

EnergyEff_Demand__Exp=4

EnergyEff_Score=FCI^EnergyEff_Demand__Exp

EnergyEff_Wgt = 1

ESOH_Hazard_Exp=3

ESOH_Hazard_Score=FCI^ESOH_Hazard_Exp
ESOH_Hazard_weighted=ESOH_Hazard_Score×ESOH_Hazard_Wgtn
ESOH_Hazard_Wgtn=4
Executed_Sustainment=Sustainment_Requirement×Sustainment_Rate
FCI=Cumulative_DM_outflow/PRV
Occupancy_Score=FCI^Occupancy__Exp
Occupancy_weighted=Occupancy_Score×OccWgt
Occupancy__Exp=2
OccWgt=3
PRV=500
Service_Calls__Exp=1
Service_Call_Score=FCI^Service_Calls__Exp
Service__Calls_weighted=Service_Call_Score×Serv_Call_Wgt
Serv_Call_Wgt=2
Start_DM_Value=100
Sustainment_Rate=0.8
Sustainment_Requirement=Total_Funding_Requirement
Min_Acceptable_Best_Fac_Score=GRAPH(TIME)
(0.00, 0.5), (1.00, 0.5), (2.00, 0.5), (3.00, 0.5), (4.00, 0.5), (5.00, 0.5), (6.00, 0.5),
(7.00, 0.5), (8.00, 0.5), (9.00, 0.5), (9.0, 0.5)

References

Abdul-Nour, G., M. Demers and R. Vaillancourt. 2002. Probabilistic safety assessment and reliability based maintenance policies: application to emergency diesel generators of a nuclear power plant. *Computers and Industrial Engineering,* Vol. 42, pp. 433–438.

Albino, V., G. Carella and O. Okogbaa. 1992. Maintenance policies in just-in-time manufacturing lines. *International Journal of Production Research.* Vol. 30, pp. 369–382.

APPA 2001. The *Strategic Assessment Model* www.appa.org/research/sam/index.cfm

Bailey, D.M., D.E. Brotherson, W. Tobiasson and A Knehans. 1989. *Roofer: an engineered management system for bituminous built-up roofs.* Technical Report Number M-90/04/ADA21852, US Army Construction Engineering Research Laboratory, Champaign, IL.

Ben-Daya, M. 1999. Integrated Production maintenance and quality model for imperfect processes, *IIE Transaction.* Vol. 31, No. 6, pp. 491–501.

Ben-Daya, M., S.O. Duffuaa and A. Raouf. 2000. *Maintenance, Modeling and Optimization,* Boston, MA: Kulwer Academic Publishers.

Cable, J.H. and J. S. Davis. 2005. *Key Performance Indicators for Federal Facilities Portfolios.* Federal Facilities Council Technical Report Number 147. Washington DC: National Academies Press.

Carrroll, J., J. Sterman and A. Marcus. 1998. Playing the maintenance game: How mental models drive organizational decisions, in R. Stern and J. Halpern (Eds), *Nonrational Elements of Organizational Decision Making.* IRL Press, New York: pp. 99–121.

Duffuaa, S.O., M. Ben-Daya, K.S. Al-Sultan and A.A. Andijani. 2001. A generic conceptual simulation model for maintenance systems. *Journal of Quality in Maintenance Engineering.* Vol. 7, No. 3, pp. 207–219.

Federal Facility Council. 2004. Key *Performance indicators for Federal Facilities Portfolios.* Washington, DC: National Academy Press.

Federal Facility Council. 2001. *Deferred maintenance reporting for federal facilities.* Federal Facilities Council Technical Report Number 141. Washington, DC: National Academy Press.

FRPC. 2009. *Real Property Inventory User Guidance.* Federal Real Property Council. Washington, DC: National Academy Press.

FRPC. 2010. FY 2009 Federal Real Property Report, Federal Real Property Council. September 2010. Accessed at http://www.gsa.gov/graphics/ogp/FY2009_FRPR.pdf.

FRPC. 2011. *Real Property Inventory User Guidance.* Federal Real Property Council. Washington, DC: National Academy Press.

Fuller, S. 2010. *Life-Cycle Cost Analysis.* Whole Building Design Guide http://www.wbdg.org/resources/lcca.php#ar.

GAO. 2003. *High Risk Series. Federal Real Property.* GAO-03-122. Washington, D.C.: General Accounting Office.

Hegazy T, Ahluwalia SS, Atalla M. 2010. Two condition indicators for building components based on reactive maintenance data. *Journal of Facilities Management,* Vol. 8, No. 1, pp. 64–74.

Lufkin, P. 2006. "Equipment Service Life Revisited" presented in collaboration with Lawrence Livermore National Laboratory at the CAIS User Group Meeting Las Vegas, Nevada.

Lufkin, P. 2010. "Life Cycle Cost Models for Federal Facilities," presentation to the Committee on Predicting Outcomes from Investments in the Maintenance and Repair of Federal Facilities; Board on Infrastructure and the Constructed Environment, National Research Council. Washington, DC.

Madachy, R.J. 1996. System dynamics modeling of an inspection-based process *Software Engineering: Proceedings of the 18th International Conference on Volume.* pp. 76–386.

Meadows, Donella H. 2008. *Thinking in Systems, a Primer.* Chelsea Green Publishing.

Merton, Robert K. 1936. The Unanticipated Consequences of Purposive Social Action. *American Sociological Review,* Vol. 1, No. 6, pp. 894–904.

Marquez, A.C. and S.A. Herguedas. 2002. Models for maintenance optimization: a study for repairable systems and finite time periods, *Reliability Engineering and System Safety,* Vol. 75 No. 3, pp. 367–77.

Marquez, C.A., J.N.D. Gupta and S.A. Herguedas. 2003. Maintenance policies for a production system with constrained production rate and buffer capacity. *International Journal of Production Research,* Vol. 41, No. 9, pp. 1909–1926.

National Research Council. 1990. *Committing to the Cost of Ownership: Maintenance and Repair of Public Buildings.* Washington, D.C.: National Academy Press.

National Research Council. 2012. *Predicting Outcomes of Investment in Maintenance and Repair of Federal Facilities.* Washington, DC.: National Academy Press.

Ottoman, G., W. Nixon and S. Lofgren. 1999. Budgeting for facility maintenance and repair, I: Methods and models. *Journal of Management in Engineering,* Vol. 15. No. 4, pp. 71–83.

Richardson, George P. 1991. *Feedback Thought in Social Science and Systems Theory.* Philadelphia, PA: University of Pennsylvania Press.

Rush, S. 1991. *Managing the facility portfolio.* Washington, DC: National Association of College and University Business Officers.

Scarf, P.A. 1997. On the application of mathematical models in maintenance. *European Journal of Operational Research.* Vol. 99, pp. 493–506.

Shahin, M.Y. 1992. 20 years experience in the PAVER pavement management system development and implementation in F.B. Holt and W.I. Gramling (eds), *Pavement Management Implementation.* Philadelphia: PA: ASTM.

Stallings, D.K. 2008. Public school facilities and teacher job satisfaction. East Carolina University.

Sterman, J.D. 2000. *Business Dynamics, Systems Thinking and Modeling for a Complex World.* Boston, MA. Irwin/McGraw-Hill.

Thompson B.P. and L.C. Bank. 2010. Use of System Dynamics as a Decision-Making Tool in Building Design and Operation. *Building and Environment.* Vol. 45, pp.1006–1015.

Uzarski, D.R. 1999. *Builder: Condition Survey Distress Manual for Assessing Building Condition.* US Army Construction Engineering Research Laboratory, Champaign, IL.

Vanier, D. J. 2001. Why industry needs asset management tools. *Journal of Computing in Civil Engineering*, Vol. 15, No. 1. pp. 35–43.

Whitestone Research. 2011. *FY10 Annual Operating Costs for Defense Facilities: Final Report*, Santa Barbara, CA.

Wordsworth, Paul. 2001. *Lee's Building Maintenance Management*. 4th Edition. New York: Wiley-Blackwell.

Yuan, J. and J. Chaing. 2000. "Optimal maintenance policy for a production system subject to aging and shocks", *Journal of Quality in Maintenance Engineering*, Vol. 6, No. 3, pp. 200–216.

Chapter 10
Pandemic Influenza Simulation with Public Avoidance Behavior

Wei Zhong, Tim Lant, Megan Jehn, and Yushim Kim

Abstract This chapter explores how classical mathematical models for epidemic simulation can be modified to properly incorporate relevant social and behavioral dimensions. Using the 2009 H1N1 influenza outbreak in Arizona as the research context, we modified a classical "Susceptible-Exposed-Infected-Removed" (SEIR) model and simulated it as a system dynamics model. The dynamics of influenza-related morbidity is examined, considering emergency risk communication and public avoidance behavior during the outbreak. Sensitivity analyses are performed to explore the impact of variability in uncertain parameters on epidemic dynamics in the community. We end this chapter with a discussion of the use of simulation models to inform efforts to prepare communities for pandemic influenza outbreaks.

W. Zhong (✉)
School of Public Affairs, Renmin University of China,
No. 59 Zhongguancun Street, Haidian District, Beijing 100872, China
e-mail: wzhong.ruc@gmail.com

T. Lant
Department of Health and Human Services, Biomedical Advanced Research and
Development Authority, 443 New York Avenue, NW #1203, Washington, DC 20001, USA
e-mail: tim.lant@gmail.com

M. Jehn
School of Human Evolution and Social Change, Arizona State University,
P.O. Box 872402, Tempe, AZ 85287, USA
e-mail: megan.jehn@asu.edu

Y. Kim
School of Public Affairs, Arizona State University, 411 N. Central Avenue,
Suite 400, Phoenix, AZ 85004, USA
e-mail: ykim@asu.edu

A. Desai (ed.), *Simulation for Policy Inquiry*, DOI 10.1007/978-1-4614-1665-4_10,
© Springer Science+Business Media, LLC 2012

10.1   Introduction

During this century, pandemic influenza outbreaks emerged as an imminent threat to society. The 2009 H1N1 influenza outbreak was the most recent example, following previous outbreaks in 1968, 1957, and the 1918 Spanish Flu. The Obama administration declared a public health emergency in response to the H1N1 outbreak in April 2009 and a national emergency in October 2009. In Arizona, the first case of H1N1 influenza was confirmed on April 29, 2009 (Shanks 2009), and by early October, a total of 2,243 people were infected and 30 people had died from the disease (ADHS 2009a). The second wave of 2009 H1N1 influenza in Arizona began in the fall of 2009 and continued through the 2009–2010 influenza season. Since the last major pandemic in 1968, technological advances such as the use of the Internet and other communication channels have helped inform the public about health risks. This increased access to health information may, in turn, reduce flu transmission through risk-avoiding behaviors. This chapter presents a system dynamics model of disease progression in Arizona during the 2009–2010 influenza season that incorporates risk perception and risk-avoidance behaviors as mitigating factors in human-to-human disease transmission.

Simulation has served as an important tool for enhancing the understanding of pandemic influenza dynamics and preparing for an emergency such as the H1N1 outbreak. The classical compartmental mathematical epidemiology models of Kermack and McKendrick (1927, 1932, 1933) have been used for decades to conceptualize and predict the spread of infectious diseases. Many additional approaches have been developed including agent-based models, multi-scale models, and network models that rely on computational advances and more sophisticated data structures. Figure 10.1, reprinted from Barrat et al. (2008), shows five distinct model types that have been designed to study epidemic spread processes. The first model type assumes a homogeneous random mixing of people. The second type embeds social structure, and people are classified according to demographic characteristics (e.g., age and sex). The third type includes specific contact networks that provide possible virus propagation paths, and the fourth type considers multi-scale factors (e.g., country or city) through different approximations of people's movement between subpopulations while still assuming homogeneous random mixing at a

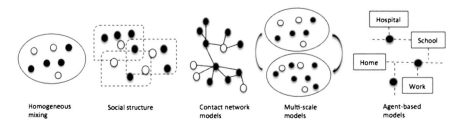

Fig. 10.1 Epidemic models. *Note*: The *open circles* represent individuals while the *filled circles* present the specific stage of a disease, as presented in Barrat et al. (2008), p. 181

lower scale. Finally, the agent-based model relies on the interactions and movement of single individuals on various scales.

The most widely debated and critical assumption in any epidemic simulation is the definition of a single "transmission event" which assumes that two individuals are within close enough proximity for an infected person to transmit the virus to a susceptible host. For instance, the classic S–I–R (susceptible, infected, and recovered) model of Kermack and McKendrick assumes random mixing—that the number of newly infected individuals is proportional to both the susceptible population and the infectious population, and that all individuals in the population mix randomly with all others. In the S–I–R model, the total population is divided into several subdivisions, called compartments, depending on disease status (e.g., susceptible, infected, and recovered). A system of coupled ordinary differential equations defines the transition rates of individuals moving from one compartment to the next, and the level of infectious disease in the population is then dynamically simulated as the solution of this dynamical system. This is the basic concept of compartment models such as S–I–R, and system dynamics models are often built to examine properties of epidemic process. The other influenza models make use of age-based, geography-based, or individual-based structures to specify contacts as more realistic interactions between population subgroups.

In reality, the "transmission event" can be quite varied. In the case of airborne pathogens such as influenza, viruses can be suspended in air, so infection can occur through either direct physical contact such as a handshake or close physical proximity in the case of sneezing or coughing, and it can also occur through other transmission mechanisms (such as touching doorknobs or handling money) that do not require that two individuals are in the same location at the same time. Therefore, while the compartment model has been frequently utilized to study influenza epidemics, it has also been criticized in that it is too simple to provide insightful information on pandemic influenza because it ignores human behavioral responses to the potential threat of such a disease.

This critique is fair, but not necessarily attributable to the compartmental structure of the model. Rather, understanding and modeling human responses to the risk of influenza requires more detailed information about the extent to which individuals can avoid transmission events. For example, classical compartment models assume "standard incidence," where individuals do not change their behavior during an epidemic but continue their regular activities as usual. However, empirical studies have reported that people do change their behavior, especially in pandemic situations (Ekberg et al. 2009; Lau et al. 2003, 2007). When confronted with the threat of pandemic influenza, people undertake actions to protect themselves from infection (Lau et al. 2003, 2007) and continue these protective coping behaviors until the epidemic ends (Leung et al. 2003; de Zwart et al. 2010).

The limitations of basic compartmental models have led to the introduction of the concept of *prevalence elastic behavior*, which refers to the adaptive actions people take in response to an epidemic (Philipson and Posner 1993; Philipson 2000). More recent studies on pandemic-related estimation incorporate this notion into epidemic models by substituting the classic standard incidence assumption along with the "mass action incidence" assumption (Larson and Nigmatulina 2009). People are assumed to reduce their overall social activities due to a pandemic, and the reduction is based on the propagation condition of the disease. A response such as foregoing contacts with other people is also called an "avoidance response" (Lau et al. 2010; Yoo et al. 2010). Instead of assuming a constant contact rate for each person (which is the same as that on normal days), Larson and Nigmatulina (2009) incorporate an avoidance parameter into their model, where the value is less than the normal contact rate and is simultaneously dependent upon the size of the remaining noninfected population in circulation.

The incorporation of public avoidance behavior has the potential to make these modified compartment models more accurate in anticipating the pandemic influenza spread dynamics (Epstein et al. 2008). However, these models still oversimplify human response, just as in the classic compartment model. While the basic model completely ignores the avoidance response, the modified model simply assumes that the total population reduces daily contact for self-protection, which the public risk communication literature has shown is far from reality. After receiving risk information, people tend to evaluate the information in the given social context and formulate varying levels of risk perception (Lindell and Perry 1983; Mileti and Darlington 1997; Nigg 1987). Responsive behaviors are the adaptive behavioral outcomes of risk perception, and people react to risk information in a variety of ways (Quarantelli 1983), with self-protective behavior being just one possible response.

While powerful and useful, therefore, classic mathematical models in epidemiology are often limited in properly incorporating social and behavioral dynamics during an epidemic period. Complexities in human behavior call for careful incorporation of relevant social dimensions in simulating a pandemic outbreak using the classic compartment model. This chapter illustrates how a classic "Susceptible–Exposed–Infected-Removed" (SEIR) model can be modified to incorporate public avoidance behaviors during a pandemic influenza outbreak in order to implement a system dynamics model. The 2009 H1N1 outbreak in Arizona is used as a case study. Sensitivity analyses are performed to explore the impact of variability in uncertain parameters on disease dynamics in the community. The chapter ends with a discussion on the use of simulation models in preparing for pandemic influenza outbreaks in communities.

10.2 Simulating Pandemic Influenza Dynamics

10.2.1 Classic SEIR Model

The first model used in our analysis is the standard four-compartment model, which is the SEIR model (Li et al. 1999; Rost and Wu 2008). SEIR is a refined version of the SIR model, which includes the latent period of an influenza virus. In the SEIR model, there are four health statuses relative to an epidemic (corresponding to the four compartments), and people can transit from one state to the next. Transition rates between compartments can be presented by the following equations:

$$\frac{dS}{dt} = -\alpha\beta S\frac{E+I}{N}$$

$$\frac{dE}{dt} = \alpha\beta S\frac{E+I}{N} - \sigma E$$

$$\frac{dI}{dt} = \sigma E - (\gamma + \mu)I$$

$$\frac{d\mathrm{Re}}{dt} = \gamma I$$

$$\frac{dD}{dt} = \mu I$$

The first compartment includes people who are susceptible to the disease (S); α is the infection rate depending upon the characteristics of the disease; and β is the contact (mixing) rate, which represents the average number of people each person is in contact with per day. Once a transmission event occurs between a susceptible and exposed or infected individual, the susceptible transits into the exposed status (E). Individuals in this state are asymptomatic—they are infectious, but do not show any disease symptoms. The symbol σ represents the progression rate from exposed (E) to infected (I). After the latent period (σ^{-1}) ends, the exposed become infected people (I) who are both infectious and symptomatic. The removed (R) compartment consists of people who either recover (Re) from the disease after the infection period (γ^{-1}) or die (D) while they are in the infected status. The γ is the recovery rate and μ is the mortality rate among infected people. N is the total number of people in the system, excluding those who died.

In this model, the recovered are assumed to acquire full immunity to subsequent infection so they never reenter the susceptible population. The standard incidence assumption is equivalent to assuming a constant contact rate, β. In this case, we can set the value for β equal to β_0, or the contact rate in normal or non-pandemic situations. However, this chapter presents additional analysis of the effect of relaxing this assumption to allow for adaptive behaviors due to public perceptions of risk. Figure 10.2a presents the classic SEIR model and its key parameters in a graphical format.

10.2.2   Modified SEIR Model

The second model extends the standard compartment model, incorporating people's avoidance response. In the modified model (Fig. 10.2b), the total population is divided into two subpopulations: the population of individuals who engage in avoidance behaviors and the population of individuals who do not engage in such behavior. Thus, the standard four-compartment model is modified into an eight-compartment model, including the susceptible who engage (S_a) and do not engage (S_{na}) in avoidance behavior, the exposed who engage (E_a) and do not engage (E_{na}) in avoidance behavior,

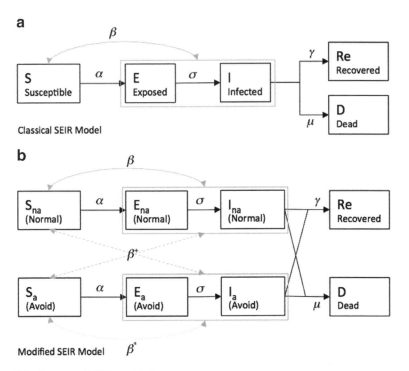

Fig. 10.2 Conceptual SEIR model diagrams

the infected who engage (I_a) and do not engage (I_{na}) in avoidance behavior, the recovered (Re), and the deceased (D).

Several assumptions are made here to divide the population into eight compartments. First, the division of the population is based on the proportion of the susceptible engaging in avoidance behavior during each simulation step. According to Drabek and Boggs (1968), people's avoidance behavior is dependent upon their risk perception. People who perceive high risk of a particular disease are more likely to engage in avoidance behavior, but not all high-risk perceivers will engage in such behavior (Quarantelli 1983, 1990). We assume that the proportion of the susceptible engaging in avoidance behavior is primarily determined by, but not equal to, the proportion of the susceptible that perceive a high risk of the disease. Furthermore, people engaging in such behavior will not change their behavior despite changes in their health status, as previously shown in the literature (Lau et al. 2007; Leung et al. 2003).

Second, we assume that public risk communication influences how those who are susceptible perceive the risk of getting such a disease during the epidemic. We also assume that the level of risk perception is determined by the type of communication channel used for risk information, and whether people believe that channel to be credible. Therefore, the proportion of people who perceive a high level of risk among the susceptible population will be dependent on the types of information transmission channels people use to receive information about pandemic flu (*the channel type*), how many people use each channel for risk information (*channel users*), and how many people believe that the channel they use is important in providing updates on the pandemic flu (*perceived credibility*).

A third assumption is that the spread dynamics of pandemic influenza is influenced by individual avoidance behavior through the contact rate (β). Avoidance behavior reduces the contact rate for people engaging in it, and the avoidance behavior effect (ϕ) is set to represent the reduction in the contact rate due to such behavior. Given the different contact rates resulting from individuals' choices regarding avoidance behavior, four influenza virus transmission mechanisms can be structured, as presented in the following matrix β:

$$\beta = \begin{pmatrix} \beta_{a,a} & \beta_{a,na} \\ \beta_{na,a} & \beta_{na,na} \end{pmatrix} = \begin{pmatrix} \varphi^2 \beta_0 & \varphi \beta_0 \\ \varphi \beta_0 & \beta_0 \end{pmatrix}$$

where $\beta_{a,a}$ represents influenza virus transmission from infectious individuals to susceptible, when both individuals are simultaneously engaging in avoidance behavior. Considering that people in both interaction compartments reduce their contact rate, the value is set to $\varphi^2 \beta_0$. $\beta_{a,na}$ and $\beta_{na,a}$ capture the interaction between susceptible people engaging in avoidance behavior and infectious people not engaging in such behavior, and the interaction between susceptible people not engaging in avoidance behavior and infectious people engaging in such behavior, respectively. Only one side engages in avoidance actions, so the contact rates are of the same value and assigned as $\varphi \beta_0$. Finally, $\beta_{na,na}$ represents influenza transmission from those who are infectious but not engaging in avoidance behavior to the susceptible who are also not engaging in avoidance behavior, where the value is equal to the contact rate in normal situations (β_0) because both interaction sides act as normal. Using this matrix, the transition rate from the susceptible to the exposed compartment within the two subpopulations can be specified as below. Other transition rates remain as in the standard SEIR model.

$$\frac{dS_a}{dt} = -\left(\alpha \beta_{a,a} S_a \frac{E_a + I_a}{N} + \alpha \beta_{a,na} S_a \frac{E_{na} + I_{na}}{N} \right)$$

$$\frac{dE_a}{dt} = \alpha \beta_{a,a} S_a \frac{E_a + I_a}{N} + \alpha \beta_{a,na} S_a \frac{E_{na} + I_{na}}{N} - \sigma E_a$$

$$\frac{dS_{na}}{dt} = -\left(\alpha \beta_{na,a} S_{na} \frac{E_a + I_a}{N} + \alpha \beta_{na,na} S_{na} \frac{E_{na} + I_{na}}{N} \right)$$

$$\frac{dE_{na}}{dt} = \alpha \beta_{na,a} S_{na} \frac{E_a + I_a}{N} + \alpha \beta_{na,na} S_{na} \frac{E_{na} + I_{na}}{N} - \sigma E_{na}$$

Finally, disease prevalence, which indicates the severity of the disease spread condition among the population, is another important component in the model. It is determined by the spread dynamics and simultaneously influences the number of

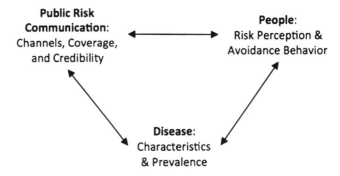

Fig. 10.3 Dynamics of disease, risk communication, and people's response

risk information followers. It is assumed that more people will follow risk information as the number of people who are infected or die increases (Aakko 2004). Adopting Larson and Nigmatulina's (2009) measurement, disease prevalence at time t can be captured as

$$\text{Disease prevalence } (t) = \frac{N_{\text{active}}(0)}{N_{\text{active}}(t)}$$

where N_{active} represents the population at a single time point, excluding those who have been infected or died. When the disease becomes more severe at time t, more people will follow the risk information, perceive a high risk of the disease, and engage in avoidance behaviors at time $(t+1)$. This change then reduces the size of the infected and dead population, which further reduces disease prevalence at time $(t+1)$, and decreases the percentage of people who engage in avoidance behaviors among the susceptible population at time $(t+2)$.

Figure 10.3 summarizes the dynamic relationship between disease, people's response, and risk communication as specified in the modified SEIR model.

10.3 Application to the Fall 2009 H1N1 Outbreak in Arizona

The two compartment models shown above are used to simulate the second wave of the 2009 H1N1 influenza outbreak in Arizona. First, we parameterize both models using available data. Second, each model is used to forecast the number of people infected during the 2009–2010 influenza season. Finally, sensitivity analyses are performed on key parameters. We use PowerSim as a tool to simulate the system dynamics model of pandemic influenza in Arizona.

Table 10.1 Model parameters and data sources

Key variables	Value	Data sources
Disease characteristics		
Infection rate (α)	1.4%	Coburn et al. (2009) and Yang et al. (2009)
Latent period (σ^{-1})	2 days	CDC (2009a)
Infectious period (γ^{-1})	5 days	Same as above
Period of exposed being infectious (ω)	1 day	Same as above
Mortality rate (μ)	0.3%	Donaldson et al. (2009) and Tuite et al. (2010)
Population characteristics		
Number of households	2,276,865	American Community Survey (2009)
Average household size	2.8	Same as above
Contact (mixing) rate (β)	21	Larson and Nigmatulina (2009)
Avoidance behavior effect (ϕ)	60%	Jefferson et al. (2008) and Larson and Nigmatulina (2009)
People engaging in avoidance behaviors among high-risk perceivers	92.6%	ASU risk communication survey (2009)
H1N1 news/information followers	73.1%	Same as above
Local TV coverage	95.6%	Same as above
Local TV is a credible source	95.7%	Same as above
National newspaper coverage	3.8%	Same as above
National newspaper is a credible source	73.7%	Same as above
Model initialization		
Initial no. of people exposed	328	Assumption (the same as the number infected)
Initial no. of people infected	328	ADHS (2009b)
Initial no. of people recovered	115,758	ACS (2009), ADHS (2009b) and CDC (2009b)
Initial no. of people died	30	ADHS (2009b)
% population with natural immunity	7%	Assumption

10.3.1 Data Sources

Table 10.1 summarizes the parameters used in the simulations, their (initial) values, and the sources of these values. Parameters related to the epidemic characteristics of 2009 H1N1 influenza were collected from CDC reports and earlier studies. According to the CDC, "the incubation period for influenza is estimated to range from 1 to 4 days with an average of 2 days" (CDC 2009a) and "influenza virus shedding (the time during which a person might be infectious to another person) begins the day before illness onset and can persist for 5–7 days" (CDC 2009a). In the simulation model, we assume a latent period of 2 days and an infection period of 5 days. Another implication from the CDC statement is that exposed individuals are not infectious at all times; they only begin to transmit the virus from the last day of their latent period (CDC 2009a).

The virus transmission rate can be estimated based on previous findings on the basic reproduction number (R_0), which is the number of secondary infections caused by a single infectious case introduced into the susceptible population. Considering the assumption that people can only die when they become infected, R_0 is equal to the product of the effective contact rate and the infectious period (Keeling and Rohani 2008). We use a value of 1.4, which is based on the medium value of the estimated basic reproduction number (Coburn et al. 2009; Yang et al. 2009). The mortality rate for H1N1 influenza is 0.3% (Donaldson et al. 2009; Tuite et al. 2010).

Two population characteristics were collected from the American Community Survey (ACS) in 2009. In Arizona, approximately 2.3 million households exist, with an average household size of 2.8 in 2009 (ACS 2009). Regarding the contact rate, studies on the number of interpersonal contacts have generally been based on convenience samples or data from European countries (Edmunds et al. 2006; Mossong et al. 2008), with few studies of the contact rate using the US population (DeStefano et al. 2010). We start the simulation using the assumption of Larson and Nigmatulina (2009) of an average daily contact rate in the USA of 21. Given previous research findings indicating that avoidance behavior could reduce people's contact rate by 30–90% (Jefferson et al. 2008; Larson and Nigmatulina 2009), we initialized avoidance behavior effect as 60%.

Population characteristics related to public risk communication and public avoidance behavior are from the 2009 ASU Risk Communication Survey (Jehn et al. 2011). This survey was conducted using a random-digit telephone survey of representative households in Arizona in October 2009, and included questions about risk perceptions, information search behavior, and protective behaviors in addition to other influenza-related questions.

While we assumed a relationship between risk perception and avoidance actions among the susceptible population, we do not know what proportion of the susceptible population who perceived a high risk of H1N1 flu engaged in avoidance behavior during the survey period; so we used information collected for the total population from the survey. As such, 92.6% of high-risk perceivers took at least one precautionary behavior among the six precautionary behavior measures examined in the survey (i.e., staying away from places where large groups of people gather; stopped shaking hands; stopped hugging or kissing; staying away from people with flu-like symptoms; stopped touching eyes, nose, or mouth; and washing hands more frequently). Therefore, we assumed that 92.6% of high-risk perceivers among the susceptible during the simulation step are the subpopulation engaging in avoidance behaviors at each simulation step.

Regarding risk communication components, items in the survey were related to channel type, its coverage, and perceived credibility. Survey respondents were asked to identify the *type* of channel through which they obtained H1N1 flu information during the month of the survey. The choices were local TV, national TV, local newspaper, national newspaper, Internet, radio, magazine, personal channel, and others. The personal channel included family members, friends, neighbors, colleges, schools, and doctors. Respondents could choose multiple channels and are defined as a *channel user* of each specific transmission channel they reported. Those who indicated that the channel they used to update information on the flu was "very important" or "somewhat important" were considered to perceive that type of channel as credible. In addition, approximately 73% of respondents reported that they closely or somewhat closely followed H1N1 news, and these people are referred to as H1N1 flu *information followers*.

The analysis of the survey data indicated that uses of two risk communication channels were statistically significantly related to whether the household respondent perceived a high risk of H1N1: local TV and national newspapers. In other words, whether recipients perceived a high risk of getting H1N1 flu was associated with whether they used either channel for pandemic information, and whether each channel's users perceived the channel as credible. In the simulation, the proportion of susceptible people perceiving a high risk of H1N1 flu at each point in time was based on the percent of channel users (defined as the product of the percent of people covered by each channel or *channel coverage*, and the percent of *information followers*) and the percent of people who believed the channel to be credible.

10.3.2   Simulation Setup

The simulation model is initialized with 328 exposed, 328 infected, 115,758 recovered, and 30 dead cases. The estimated initial number of infected people is based on the Arizona Department of Health Services weekly activity report (ADHS 2009b). No data are available for the estimation of exposed cases, so we assumed the number is at least the same as that of the infected cases at the beginning of the simulation. The recovered population initially consists of two groups of people: some portion of the elderly population who may have pre-existing immunity to the 2009 H1N1 influenza virus (CDC 2009b) and those who recovered from the disease by October 3, 2009 (1,915 cases; ADHS 2009b). Here we assume that 7% of the population has pre-existing immunity (14% of the population in Arizona is aged 65+, ACS 2009).

The first step of the simulation starts on October 4, 2009, and 1 day is used as one time step in the simulation. Experiments are run 364 time steps to cover the entire 2009–2010 influenza season. The simulation output is measured using two indicators: the number of people in the infected status per day (i.e., morbidity) and the number of people in the infected status each day since the beginning of the season (i.e., cumulative morbidity). Note that, in both models the unit of analysis is the household, so one "individual" actually represents one household. Previous research has indicated that determining self-protective actions is a family-level decision, and the whole household usually acts as one respondent (Ekberg et al. 2009; Vaughan and Tinker 2009). The simulation output is therefore calculated considering the average household size in Arizona.

Table 10.2 Simulation outputs

	Peak morbidity (step)	No morbidity (step)	Cumulative morbidity at season end
SEIR model	419,814 (92)	(275)	3,927,736
Modified SEIR model	51,407 (270)	–	1,650,945

Note: (Step) indicates time step in the simulation

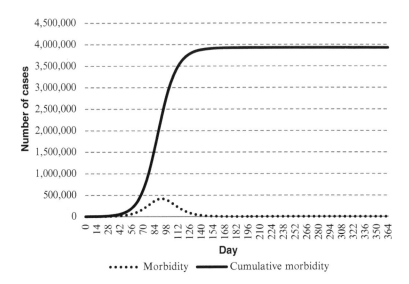

Fig. 10.4 Simulation output from classic SEIR model

10.3.3 Simulation Outputs

Table 10.2 presents the simulation results on morbidity and cumulative morbidity for both the classic and modified SEIR models. Figures 10.4 and 10.5 show how these two indicators change over time in each model.

Morbidity peaks on January 3, 2010 (92nd time step) in the classic SEIR model, which does not take into account public risk communication or people's avoidance behavior, and 419,814 people are in infected status on that day. Although the morbidity continues decreasing after that day, the disease continues to spread until July 5, 2010 (275th time step). By the end of the influenza season, the total number of people infected is 3,927,736, which is 61.6% of the total Arizona population.

When avoidance behavior is taken into consideration for the Arizona population, the impacts of the disease are mitigated and the peak number of infected cases is reduced to 51,407. The cumulative morbidity by the end of the influenza season is 1,650,945, which is a reduction of 58% as compared to the classic SEIR model output. The spread of the epidemic is also slowed. Morbidity reaches its peak on June 30, 2010 (270th time step), which is almost 6 months (178 time steps) after the

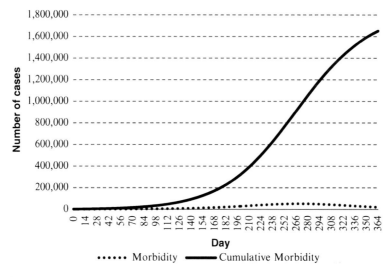

Fig. 10.5 Simulation output from modified SEIR model

peak morbidity day without considering avoidance behavior (92nd time step). One important difference found in this estimation as compared with the classical SEIR model is that the disease continues spreading during the entire season; the morbidity does not decrease to 0 at the last day of the season, which means that both the morbidity and cumulative morbidity will still be increasing, at least for some time, after the influenza season, unless other intervention approaches are taken.

10.3.4   Sensitivity Analyses

In the modified model, we make a number of assumptions regarding important model parameters whose values are uncertain, including the percent of the population with natural immunity, the effect of avoidance behavior, and the percent of the susceptible who engage in such behavior among the high-risk perceivers. All three parameters are known to be crucial elements in determining the outcome of epidemic modeling (Jenvald et al. 2007).Therefore, in this section, sensitivity analysis is performed on these parameters in order to better understand the impact of variability in key parameters on pandemic-related estimations of morbidity.

10.3.4.1   Sensitivity of the Percent of the Naturally Immune Population

In the modified SEIR model, 7% of the total Arizona population is assumed to have natural immunity against influenza. The elderly population (which may have higher levels of natural immunity based on exposure to previous epidemics) accounts for

Table 10.3 Peak morbidity from scenarios for variable proportion of the naturally immune population

% of natural immune population	0%	3.5%	7%	10.5%	14%
Peak morbidity (step)	124,870 (198)	84,502 (227)	51,407 (270)	26,078 (338)	–

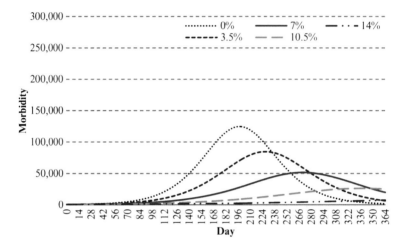

Fig. 10.6 Number of infected individuals per day of the epidemic assuming different proportions of naturally immune population

14% of the total population in Arizona; so sensitivity analysis is first conducted to explore whether, and how, changing the proportion of the natural immune population influences the pandemic spread dynamics.

With all other variables fixed at the values shown in Table 10.1, five values for the percent of naturally immune people among the total population were experimented with: 0%, 3.5%, 7%, 10.5%, and 14%. The experiment results are presented in Table 10.3 and Fig. 10.6.

When all of the population is susceptible to the influenza, the peak morbidity is 124,870, which occurs at step 198. As the percentage of naturally immune individuals increases in the population, the epi curves flatten out—i.e., the peak morbidity is decreased and the duration of the epidemic is increased. For example, increasing the proportion of the natural immune population from 0% to 3.5% can reduce the peak morbidity by 32.3%, and delay the peak morbidity by 29 steps. When the proportion of the naturally immune population in the total population is 10.5% or higher, the impacts of influenza on the community become limited. When this percentage reaches 14%, the morbidity increases slowly over time, and the peak morbidity does not even occur by the end of the influenza season.

Table 10.4 Peak morbidity from scenarios on avoidance behavior effect

Avoidance behavior effect	30%	45%	60%	75%	90%
Peak morbidity (step)	224,917 (151)	117,203 (199)	51,407 (270)	–	–

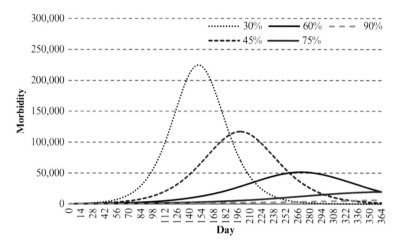

Fig. 10.7 Morbidity with different avoidance behavior effects

10.3.4.2   Sensitivity of the Avoidance Behavior Effect

In our initial model run, we assumed that avoidance behavior reduced the average individual contact rate by 60% (see Table 10.1). Here we examine the sensitivity of the experiment results to the change in the avoidance behavior effect. Previous research suggests that avoidance behavior could reduce people's contact rate by 30–90% (Jefferson et al. 2008; Larson and Nigmatulina 2009). Therefore, we conducted a sensitivity analysis by varying the potential reduction in contact rates as a result of avoidance behavior by 15% increments, from 30% to 90%. Experiments were run for each contact rate with the other parameters kept constant. The results are presented in Table 10.4 and Fig. 10.7.

The avoidance behavior effect plays an important role in determining the influenza dynamics. When the parameter is equal to or less than 60%, the peak morbidity is reduced by approximately 50% with an increase of 15 percentage points. The occurrence of peak morbidity is also greatly postponed. The extent of reduction in morbidity decreases when the parameter is higher than 60%, but the value still remains considerable. Furthermore, the influenza outbreak lasts for the entire season regardless of the scenario. The higher the avoidance effect is, the more the influenza outbreak is slowed. When the parameter is equal to or higher than 75%, the epi-curve does not show a peak by the end of the influenza season.

Table 10.5 Peak morbidity from scenarios on the proportion of people engaging in avoidance behavior among susceptible high-risk perceivers (% of people taking avoidance behavior among susceptible high-risk perceivers)

% of people taking avoidance behavior	30%	45%	60%	75%	90%
Peak morbidity (step)	299,632 (115)	236,793 (131)	173,956 (155)	113,579 (191)	59,675 (254)

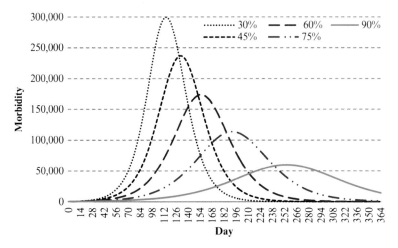

Fig. 10.8 Morbidity with different proportions of people engaging in avoidance behavior among susceptible high-risk perceivers

10.3.4.3 Sensitivity of the Percent of People Who Engage in Avoidance Behaviors Among Susceptible High-Risk Perceivers

Assumptions are also made in the modified SEIR model regarding the percent of people engaging in avoidance behavior among those who are susceptible and have a high risk perception. This proportion is assumed to be equal to the percent of people engaging in such behavior among all high-risk perceivers, which the empirical data indicates to be 92.6%. We conduct sensitivity analysis on this parameter, reducing its value to 30%, 45%, 60%, 75%, and 90%. The experiment results for each value are presented in Table 10.5 and Fig. 10.8.

As expected, when the parameter value is set at 90%, the simulation result is close to the results based on the original data. Under this scenario, the peak morbidity is 59,675, which occurs at step 254. Also, decreasing the proportion of people who engage in avoidance actions among high-risk perceivers increases the peak morbidity and accelerates the influenza spread. For example, the decrease in this parameter from 90% to 75% increases the peak morbidity by 47.5% (compare the purple curve with the black curve), and the occurrence of such a peak is brought forward 63 steps to step 191. The outbreak is the worst when the percentage engaging in avoidance actions is reduced to 30% (orange curve). The peak morbidity is increased to approximately 300,000 at step 115. In other words, more than 13% of the Arizona population becomes infected on a single day in this scenario.

10.4   Discussion

Public health officials had been warning the public that another pandemic was imminent, as the CDC director stated on April 2007 that "we know that a pandemic will eventually occur. We always say it's not a question of if; it's a question of when" (Ulene 2007). This recent pandemic outbreak re-emphasizes the consequences of another novel virus-caused influenza pandemic. Understanding spread dynamics in communities is crucial for health planning, preparedness, and intervention.

In order to minimize the impact of pandemic influenza, both CDC and HHS have made it a priority for public health officials at all levels to participate in pre-pandemic planning efforts (Das et al. 2008; Ferguson et al. 2005). One prerequisite for effective planning is to accurately forecast the spread dynamics of the epidemic as closely as possible. Current researchers have attempted to include public avoidance behavior in the classic compartment model, arguing that such individual behavioral adaptations play an important role in mitigating impacts of disease (Epstein et al. 2008; Yoo et al. 2010). Pandemic-related morbidity and mortality are most likely overestimated by classic compartmental models and can be better estimated using the existing modified compartment models. However, how this behavioral component is included in the modeling requires further examination in order to provide accurate estimates.

In this chapter, we experiment with social and human factors to understand their role in the dynamics of an epidemic. Epidemic simulation must not be considered as a straightforward engineering or medical problem, but rather a problem which requires consideration of complex human systems. Social and behavioral factors are important determinants of disease dynamics and need to be carefully considered as important components of simulation models. Our simulation illustrates this point by demonstrating how human responsive behavior can be included in epidemic modeling. Because the current model includes individual risk perceptions and responsive behaviors, which are commonly observed during an epidemic but are ignored by most epidemic models, this model provides a more realistic picture of the spread of a pandemic influenza.

The simulation model frames the public's avoidance behavior as part of public risk communication, so it provides decision makers with a lever for public intervention through communication. The simulation results suggest that effective public risk communication can slow the spread of a pandemic and therefore buy critical time to allow public health officials to introduce other public interventions, particularly the production and distribution of vaccines for the general public. Although public officials cannot rely solely on risk communication and people's avoidance responses to prevent adverse health outcomes, effective risk communication makes the impact less devastating. Furthermore, public managers can use the model to systematically evaluate and compare the effectiveness of different strategies related to public risk communication.

The alternative models presented are still constrained by crucial limitations inherent in the SEIR compartment models. One major concern is the homogeneous population assumption, as classic compartment models assume a group of identical people in terms of their contact patterns and the effect of an epidemic on them. In the modified SEIR model, we included some heterogeneity by splitting the population into eight compartments based on individual behaviors. However, such a change introduces only a limited degree of heterogeneity in people's contact patterns, and the biological characteristics of the disease are still the same for all individuals. One way to address this problem is to develop an individual-based model and include important types of heterogeneity for epidemic simulation (Mniszewski et al. 2008), which can also be resource intensive (Bobashev et al. 2007; Rahmandad and Sterman 2008).

Another limitation is that no public intervention effort, specifically vaccination, is considered in this model because we aim to develop a baseline model without large-scale public intervention. Different types of public interventions can be further included in this model to test the effectiveness of such an effort. In addition, exposed and infected individuals can be medically treated to shorten their latent and infected period, which is not taken into account in the present models. However, the influence of those medical treatments on the simulation results may be limited because we use the average length of the latent and infected period from the empirical data, which has already included the effect of medical treatments. Simulations can also be used to explore the consequences of reducing the likelihood of contact by implementing nonmedical strategies such as closing down schools, to reduce the transmission of infections and thereby compare the relative efficacy and potential costs of different policy options available to decision makers.

Simulation models are built for many purposes, such as planning, forecasting, and moderating stakeholders' competing values. Unlike statistical models, the estimation of the key variable parameters is not the primary purpose of using simulations. Simulation models like those presented in this chapter are most often used to help researchers understand the dynamics of a system, given various conditions in certain contexts or to experiment upon a suite of potential theoretical and practical ideas to better harness the system the decision makers are interested in. How to best utilize such a resource is largely up to the creativity of the researchers and decision makers, and the effect of this approach on decision making requires further examination.

Acknowledgments This study was funded by the Arizona Department of Health Services (ADHS) through a Health and Human Services (HHS) preparedness grant, Arizona State University College of Public Program's research seed grant, and the National Research Foundation of Korea Grant (NRF-2010-330-B00262). The authors thank Diane Reed and Andrew Lawless at ADHS, and Ken Anderson at Maricopa County Research & Reporting. We also thank Deborah Schumacher, Tanida Rojchanakasetchai, and Barrie Bradley, who helped conduct this research.

References

Aakko, E. (2004). Risk communication, risk perception and public health. *Wisconsin Medical Journal, 103*(1), 23–27.

American Community Survey. (2009) Retrieved February 3, 2011, from http://factfinder.census.gov/servlet/DatasetMainPageServlet?_program=ACS&_submenuId=datasets_2&_lang=en.

Arizona Department of Health Services. (2009a). *Arizona weekly influenza summary: MMWR Week 40*. Retrieved February 3, 2011, from http://www.azdhs.gov/phs/oids/epi/flu/pdf/h1n1_report_october14.pdf.

Arizona Department of Health Services. (2009b). *Arizona weekly influenza summary: MMWR Week 39*. Retrieved February 3, 2011, from http://www.azdhs.gov/phs/oids/epi/flu/pdf/h1n1_report_october7.pdf.

Barrat, A., Barthélemy, M., & Vespignani, A. (2008). *Dynamical processes on complex networks*. Cambridge, UK: Cambridge University Press.

Bobashev, G. V., Goedecke, D. M., Yu, F., & Epstein, J. (2007). A hybrid epidemic model: Combining the advantages of agent-based and equation-based approaches. In S. G. Henderson, M. H. Hsieh, J. Shortle, J. D. Tew & R. R. Barton (Eds.), *Proceedings of the 2007 Winter Simulation Conference* (pp. 1532–1537). Washington, D. C.: The Society for Computer Simulation International (SCS).

Centers for Disease Control and Prevention. (2009a). *2009 H1N1 early outbreak and disease characteristics*. Retrieved February 3, 2011, from http://www.cdc.gov/h1n1flu/surveillanceqa.htm.

Centers for Disease Control and Prevention. (2009b). *Updated interim recommendations for the use of antiviral medications in the treatment and prevention of influenza for the 2009-2010 season*. Retrieved February 3, 2011, from http://www.cdc.gov/h1n1flu/recommendations.htm.

Coburn, B. J., Wagner, B. G., & Blower, S. (2009). Modeling influenza epidemics and pandemics: Insights into the future of swine flu (H1N1). *BMC Medicine*. doi: 10.1186/1741-7015-7-30.

Das, T., Savachkin, A., & Zhu, Y. (2008). A large scale simulation model of pandemic influenza outbreaks for development of dynamic mitigation strategies. *IIE Transactions, 40*(9), 893–905.

de Zwart, O., Veldhuijzen, I. K., Richardus, J. H., & Brug, J. (2010). Monitoring of risk perceptions and correlates of precautionary behaviour related to human avian influenza during 2006 - 2007 in the Netherlands: Results of seven consecutive surveys. *BMC Infectious Diseases*. doi: 10.1186/1471-2334-10-114.

Destefano, F., Haber, M., Currivan, D., Farris, T., Burrus, B., Stone-Wiggins, B., et al. (2010). Factors associated with social contacts in four communities during the 2007-2008 influenza season. *Epidemiology and Infection*. doi: 10.1017/S095026881000230X.

Donaldson, L. J., Rutter, P. D., Ellis, B. M., Greaves, F. E. C., Mytton, O. T., Pebody, R. G., et al. (2009). Mortality from pandemic A/H1N1 2009 influenza in England: Public health surveillance study. *BMJ*. doi: 10.1136/bmj.b5213.

Drabek, T. E., & Boggs, K. S. (1968). Families in disaster: Reactions and relatives. *Journal of Marriage and Family, 30*(3), 443–451.

Edmunds, W. J., Kafatos, G., Wallinga, J., & Mossong, J. R. (2006). Mixing patterns and the spread of close-contact infectious diseases. *Emerging Themes in Epidemiology*. doi: 10.1186/1742-7622-3-10.

Ekberg, J., Eriksson, H., Morin, M., Holm, E., Strömgren, M., & Timpka, T. (2009). Impact of precautionary behaviors during outbreaks of pandemic influenza: Modeling of regional differences. *American Medical Informatics Association Annual Symposium Proceedings, 2009*, 163–167.

Epstein, J. M., Parker, J., Cummings, D., & Hammond, R. A. (2008). Coupled contagion dynamics of fear and disease: Mathematical and computational explorations. *PLoS One*. doi: 10.1371/journal.pone.0003955.

Ferguson, N. M., Cummings, D. A. T., Cauchemez, S., Fraser, C., Riley, S., Meeyai, A., et al. (2005). Strategies for containing an emerging influenza pandemic in Southeast Asia. *Nature, 437*(8), 209–214.

Jefferson, T., Foxlee, R., Mar, C. D., Dooley, L., Ferroni, E., Hewak, B., et al. (2008). Physical interventions to interrupt or reduce the spread of respiratory viruses: Systematic review. *BMJ*. doi: 10.1136/bmj.39393.510347.BE.

Jehn, M., Kim, Y., Bradley, B., & Lant, T. (2011). Community knowledge, risk perception and preparedness for the 2009 influenza A (H1N1) pandemic. *Journal of Public Health Management and Practice, 17*(5), 431–438.

Jenvald, J., Morin, M., Timpka, T., & Eriksson, H. (2007). Simulation as decision support in pandemic Influenza preparedness and response. In B. Van de Walle, P. Burghardt & C. Nieuwenhuis (Eds.), *Proceedings of the 4th International Conference on Information Systems for Crisis Response and Management* (pp. 295-304). Brussels, Belgium: Brussels University Press.

Keeling, M. J., & Rohani, P. (2008). *Modeling infectious disease in humans and animals*. Princeton, NJ: Princeton University Press.

Kermack, W. O., & McKendrick, A. G. (1927). A contribution to the mathematical theory of epidemics. *Proceeding of the Royal Society London, 115*(772), 700–721.

Kermack, W. O., & McKendrick, A. G. (1932). A contribution to the mathematical theory of epidemics: The problem of endemicity. *Proceeding of the Royal Society London, 138*(834), 55–83.

Kermack, W. O., & McKendrick, A. G. (1933). A contribution to the mathematical theory epidemics: Further studies of the problem of endemicity. *Proceeding of the Royal Society London, 141*(843), 94–122.

Larson, R. C., & Nigmatulina, K. R. (2009). Engineering responses to pandemics. *Information Knowledge Systems Management, 8*(1-4), 311–339.

Lau, J. T., Griffiths, S., Choi, K. C., & Tsui, H. Y. (2010). Avoidance behaviors and negative psychological responses in the general population in the initial stage of the H1N1 pandemic in Hong Kong. *BMC Infectious Diseases*. doi: 10.1186/1471-2334-10-139.

Lau, J. T., Kim, J. H., Tsui, H. Y., & Griffiths, S. (2007). Anticipated and current preventative behaviours in response to an anticipated human-to-human H5N1 epidemic in Hong Kong Chinese general population. *BMC Infectious Diseases*. doi: 10.1186/1471-2334-7-18.

Lau, J. T., Yang, X., Tsui, H. Y., & Kim, J. H. (2003). Monitoring community psychological responses to the SARS epidemic in Hong Kong: From day 10 to day 62. *Journal of Epidemiology and Community Health, 57*(11), 864–870.

Leung, G. M., Lam, T. H., Ho, L. M., Ho, S. Y., Chan, B. H. Y., Wong, I. O. L., et al. (2003). The impact of community psychological responses on outbreak control for severe acute respiratory syndrome in Hong Kong. *Journal of Epidemiology and Community Health, 57*(11), 857–863.

Li, M. Y., Graef, J. R., Wang, L., & Karsai, J. (1999). Global dynamics of a SEIR model with varying total population size. *Mathematical Biosciences, 160*(2), 191–213.

Lindell, M. K., & Perry, R. W. (1983). Nuclear power plant emergency warnings: How would the public respond? *Nuclear News*, Febrary, 49–53.

Mileti, D. S., & Darlington, J. D. (1997). Society for the study of social problems. *Social Problems, 44*(1), 89–103.

Mniszewski, S. M., Valle, S. Y. D., Stroud, P. D., Riese, J. M., & Sydoriak, S. J. (2008). Pandemic simulation of antivirals + school closures: Buying time until strain-specific vaccine is available. *Computational & Mathematical Organization Theory, 14*(3), 209–221.

Mossong, J., Hens, N., Jit, M., Beutels, P., Auranen, K., Mikolajczyk, R., et al. (2008). Social contacts and mixing patterns relevant to the spread of infectious diseases. *PLos Medicine, 5*, 381–198.

Nigg, J. M. (1987). Communication and behavior: Organizational and individual response to warnings. In R. R. Dynes, B. D. Marchi & C. Pelanda (Eds.), *Sociology of disasters: Contribution of sociology to disaster research* (pp. 103-117). Pelanda. Milan: Franco Angeli Libri.

Philipson, T. J. (2000). Economic epidemiology and infectious disease. In A. J. Cuyler & J. P. Newhouse (Eds.), *Handbook of Health Economics* (pp. 1761–1799). Amsterdam, the Netherlands: North Holland.

Philipson, T. J., & Posner, R. A. (1993). *Private choices and public health: The AIDS epidemic in an economic perspective.* Cambridge, MA: Harvard University Press.

Quarantelli, E. L. (1983). *People's reactions to emergency warnings.* Newark, DE: Disaster Research Center, University of Delaware.

Quarantelli, E. L. (1990). *The warning process and evacuation behavior: The research evidence.* Newark, DE: University of Delaware, Disaster Research Center.

Rahmandad, H., & Sterman, J. (2008). Heterogeneity and network structure in the dynamics of diffusion: Comparing agent-based and differential equation models. *Management Science, 54*(5), 998–1014.

Rost, G., & Wu, J. (2008). SEIR epidemiological model with varying infectivity and infinite delay. *Mathematical Biosciences and Engineering, 5*(2), 389–402.

Shanks, J. (2009). *Arizona swine flu: Maricopa County gets first case.* Retrieved February 3, 2011, from http://www.nationalledger.com/cgi-bin/artman/exec/view.cgi?archive=36&num=25842.

Tuite, A. R., Greer, A. L., Whelan, M., Winter, A. L., Lee, B., Yan, P., et al. (2010). Estimated epidemiologic parameters and morbidity associated with pandemic H1N1 influenza. *CMAJ, 182*(2), 131–136.

Ulene, V. (2007, November 15, 2010). *Bracing for a flu pandemic. Los Angeles Times,* Retrieved. June 4, 2007, from http://www.latimes.com/features/health/la-he-themd4jun04,1,3259716. column.

Vaughan, E., & Tinker, T. (2009). Effective health risk communication about pandemic influenza for vulnerable populations. *American Journal of Public Health 99*(s2), S324-S332.

Yang, Y., Sugimoto, J. D., Halloran, M. E., Basta, N. E., Chao, D. L., Matrajt, L., et al. (2009). The transmissibility and control of pandemic influenza A (H1N1) virus. *Science, 326*(5953), 729–733.

Yoo, B. K., Kasajima, M., & Bhattacharya, J. (2010). *Public avoidance and the epidemiology of novel H1N1 influenza A.* Cambridge, MA: National Bureau of Economic Research.

Chapter 11
Iterative Storytelling in Public Policy: A Systems Thinking Approach

Rudy Hightower II

Storytelling is the most powerful way to put ideas into the world today...
They [stories] are the currency of human contact—Robert McKee

Abstract This chapter claims that iterative storytelling is a critical function of public policymaking and can provide a systematic mechanism to better understand the how and why of public policies. Further, it is posited that if public policy scholars or practitioners can first tell a comprehensive story of their research, then they can build an appropriately bounded and useful model. Using system dynamics (SD), the essay argues that the "language and the thinking skills" of writing are analogous to the tools necessary to build models of complex public policy problems [Richmond, Barry (2004) *An Introduction to Systems Thinking.* 2011 STELLA Software Manual. ISEE Systems]. The essay also argues that the critical, sequential tasks for addressing complex public policy problems include (1) telling a comprehensive initial story, (2) building a model, (3) implementing the underlying model, and (4) continually updating the initial story as more information becomes available. The chapter presents public policy stories and demonstrates how to convert "policy modeling paragraphs" into SD causal loop diagrams and stock-and-flow models suitable for simulation and subsequent policy decision making using an international relations story and the Infinite Loop Phenomenology concept.

R. Hightower II (✉)
John Glenn School of Public Affairs, The Ohio State University,
Page Hall, 1810 College Road, Columbus, OH 43210, USA
e-mail: hightower.23@buckeyemail.osu.edu

A. Desai (ed.), *Simulation for Policy Inquiry*, DOI 10.1007/978-1-4614-1665-4_11,   203
© Springer Science+Business Media, LLC 2012

11.1   Introduction

Stories and storytelling are in the primary, earliest group of patches that comprise the quilt of humankind's social experiences. The act of storytelling is a "beginning of humankind" type activity where the earliest forms of the communication media were thought to have been primarily oral combined with gestures and expressions. In *The Art of Business Storytelling*, Kelsey Ruger posits, "Stories have been used since the beginning of time to share knowledge, human history, and ideas…Stories work where facts don't because humans don't always make rational decisions. We generally make decisions based on emotion, and then look for the facts that support those decisions" (Ruger 2010).

Respecting, but deviating from, the insightful work of Dvora Yanow on the stories that built spaces tell (Yanow 1995), this chapter focuses on public policy stories and thus it is the human who tells the story, humans who listen to and process the story, and humans who adapt to outputs of the story. Following this framework, the act of storytelling fits squarely into the constantly unfurling social science realm since the dissemination of story content, in terms of problems, policies, and models, feeds back to the storyteller, resulting in changes to subsequent presentations of the same tale. Further, Daphne A. Jameson's research on storytelling as an effective businesses communication method concluded that storytelling is an important way humans resolve conflicts, link a group to its past, and influence others within an organization (Jameson 2001).

But, argued herein is that public policy stories, like organizations, have neither the same structure nor lead to the same organizational behaviors. The structure of a traditional story follows the Aristolean *Poetics'* three-act model of Beginning–Middle–End and has a unifying nature. Lyle Wallis, president of modeling and simulation company Decisio Consulting, goes so far in valuing storytelling to argue that storytelling provides an analytic framework for research inquiry and that the analytical story, described by Aristotle (1954), has to describe events over time that are driven by cause and effect relationships. However, to make sense of the complexities of modern public policy problems and incorporate modeling and simulation techniques, this chapter argues that an alternative storytelling structure is needed. This alternative mimics traditional storytelling since "…there is a strong parallel between good writing and good modeling. They both require brevity and clarity" (Brauer 2011). Public policy students, scholars, and practitioners require a storytelling framework and an associated research method that illustrate unique behavior-over-time stories that have fuzzy beginnings and endings. These policy stories, like literary stories, can capture dynamic changes either immediately after they occur or after substantial time delays and can describe problem structure with an endogenous point of view.

Professional public administrators should be able to analyze the structure of public policies using a recursive, or step-by-step storytelling framework, and subsequently be able to convert these stories into models appropriate for repeated simulation, evaluation, and refinement. Over 40 years ago, Thomas Dye provided a still-relevant rationale for public policy modeling saying,

> The explanation of public policy can be aided by the construction of a model that portrays the relationships between policy outcomes and the forces that shape them. There seem to be many advantages, however, to developing an explanatory (vice predictive) model of policy outcomes at the outset of any research into this area (politics and public policy). Such a model can provide hypotheses about what policy outcomes should be under given circumstances. These hypotheses can then be tested against data derived from real political systems. If the hypotheses are proved correct, the model can be retained; if not, then the model can be modified or replaced by one that more closely corresponds to the real world of politics (Dye 1970).

And in keeping with the need for public policy modeling, the overall objective of this chapter is to show that this "iterative storytelling" framework, and its associated computer modeling and simulation techniques, are not restricted to intimidating ivory towers, highly classified laboratories, or advanced mathematics classrooms. These dynamic story-based research, analysis, and presentation methods are readily available, accessible, and useful tools for public policy students, emerging scholars, and practitioners.

11.2 Iterative Storytelling

A television news report is not new. It is history. A "live" news broadcast, on the other hand, represents real-time or near real-time storytelling that can both influence current decisions and behaviors and drive future actions. Similarly, a public policy story unfurls in real time. Therefore, any analysis of any component of the public policy process unfurls in this same behavioral pattern over time. Similar to Bayesian statistics where a model variable's probability distribution is constantly updated with new relevant data, iterative storytelling's constantly inputting, time-dependent nature serves as an alternative to traditional public policy research methods.

This chapter examines such an alternative facts-based storytelling method, "iterative storytelling." Iterative storytelling is defined as a story without a concrete beginning or end, and one in which the actualization of the story is in real time and results of actions and information constantly change the subsequent telling of the story. Iterative storytelling is a first cousin to a "living story," David M. Boje's concept of a here-and-now, never-ending, multi-relational storytelling paradigm that exists wedged between narrative (storytelling the past) and "antenarrative" (future predictive storytelling) (Boje 2011). The argument is that systemic examination of the continually changing, iterative nature of stories is critical for effectively analyzing the formulation, implementation, and evaluation of public policies. And, when this iterative storytelling process is used to describe modern public policies, a remarkable twist occurs: the story is not seen as predictably and sequentially structured from beginning to middle to end, but instead it constantly changes due to story inputs from top-down, bottom-up, and outside-in sources. The importance of this twist is that this constantly iterative storytelling process is common throughout the myriad of social science disciplines, and also found in all phases of public policymaking.

Modeling public policy problems requires continual interaction between researchers, analysts, and decision makers. While the type of interaction can be verbal or written, the key characteristic of effective model building is that the interaction process remains iterative. The public policy modeling process needs to receive constant "mid-course corrections" not unlike the jib-and-tack strategies of a sailboat captain or the guidance systems of ground-to-air missiles. As previously mentioned, contrasted with the screenwriter's adherence to the Aristotelian three-act, Beginning–Middle–End story structure, iterative storytelling of public policy problems is better described by a "Start-change-Middle-change-Stop-change-Start again" structure. Although the use of the words "start" and "stop" vs. "beginning" and "end" may seem trivial, it represents a vitally important distinction for public policy modeling and simulation. While a *Poetics*-based story may very well have a beginning and an end, since social sciences deal with the continuum of humankind's existence, virtually no public policy model can include either the time period or the number of variables necessary to address complex problems from beginning to end. Thus, modelers and policymakers frame their iterative storytelling models, the mental and the computer-generated versions, by starting at a point in time after the "beginning" and stopping at a point in time before the "end."

The process of iterative storytelling, like all research methods, has its drawbacks. In their seminal research on verbal reports as data, Nisbett and Wilson (1977) illustrated that the cognitive processes of someone telling a story is neither fully understood nor a reliable gauge for content validity. There exists in the mind an "epiphenomenon" which states that storytellers, or those who are concurrently or retrospectively accessing their short-term memory for guidance on how they acquired expertise or how they interpreted a problem, are beset with intransigence error. The cognitive epiphenomenon further states that story retelling is akin to having an external body observing the actions of an actor or agent and then interpolating their actions to build a model of specific cognitive processes. But, since an external entity can never have the "privileged information" of what is actually going on inside an actor's head, the resulting cognitive model is inherently flawed. Thus, caution should be taken when engaging in iterative storytelling of complex public policy problems (Nisbett and Wilson 1977).

Also critical to note is that iterative storytelling is not the same as the often-misused concept of "feedback." Whereas feedback is traditionally viewed as receiving opinions or information based on particular actions, in the systems thinking sense, feedback encompasses a much broader context, that of a constant, reciprocating cause and effect influence (Senge 1990). Feedback is continually on-going, not dependent on any final policy result or outcome. In *A Framework for Political Analysis,* David Easton (1965) described the policy process of *input, conversion, output, and feedback*, while Ira Sharkansky (1970) described the policy process with linkages from the Environment (inputs) to Public Policy, to Impact (feedback), and to Outputs. Interestingly, Sharkansky hypothesized but did not test the interdependent relationships that are consistent with the iterative storytelling concept posited in this chapter. Sharkansky further posited that,

> …linkages show that policy and the environment can each influence the outputs of service. Both the nature of the outputs and the elements in the environment can influence the impact (outcomes) which the service has the population. Systems theorists frequently talk of the process by which policies feed back into the environment to condition the subsequent in outs from that environment to the decision makers (Sharkansky 1970: 68).

Sharkansky's point precisely relates to how iterative storytelling embraces this never-ending, systemic view of the feedback concept. In iterative storytelling, inputs from internal system variables and from individual actors combine with external environment "shocks" to constantly influence organizational patterns of behavior. So, while traditional views of feedback are strictly focused on evaluating the results of actions or a process, iterative storytelling provides a richer descriptive framework since it does not require policy enactment or completion before valid and relevant influences are injected back into the model building process.

Although often confused with anecdotes, "those stories told to illustrate problems or discuss policies but not necessarily descriptive of how something works or fails" (Birkland 2005: 10), iterative storytelling is the process by which information and/or actions are constantly being injected and/or fed back into policy formulation and implementation phases, providing a systematic inquiry tool for improved understanding of the *how* and *why* of specific public policies. Though this chapter will focus on a systems thinking approach, it is important to note that iterative storytelling applies to all public policy research methods where the critical, sequential tasks for addressing complex public policy problems include (1) telling a comprehensive initial story, (2) building a rationally bounded model, (3) executing the underlying model's math, and (4) incorporating newly discovered data into the initial story.

11.2.1 Telling a Comprehensive Initial Story

The most significant initial challenges of modeling and simulation in public policy inquiry are (1) the selection of the primary topic under investigation, and (2) determining the associated "story" variables to serve as guides for future policymaking. However, once these topics are formulated, the challenge then shifts to "just getting started." Related to the "writer's block" that hinders one from beginning the first paragraph of a novel or screenplay, creating the "starting point" in iterative storytelling is often considered the most difficult task in the writing process. To eliminate the trepidation often found in starting a public policy story that is destined for modeling and simulation, one can adopt a standard "starting line" format. Employing the time-tested story beginning "Once upon a time…" is thought to be an effective kick start to story building because it allows the storyteller to gather his or her thoughts, so to speak, before laying out the detailed story parameters (McWilliams 1998). Thus, a public policy modeler can begin the iterative storytelling process with a simple, adaptable "policy modeling paragraph" that goes:

> *Once upon a time...*they wanted to know if, during the period, the rate, or rate of change of this was causing the level of that to behave like this for them.

This standard storytelling format can then be converted into unique public policy problems and then injected into most model building, simulation, and decision-making software programs. Simplified examples of this conversion process include:

> Example 1: *Once upon a time...*the Columbus, Ohio City Council **(they)** wanted to know if, for the next three years **(during the period)**, an annual 10% reduction (**rate of change**) of vacant houses **(this)** would cause what measure of crime reduction **(level of that),** while simultaneously causing property values **(this)** to increase **(behave)** how much **(level of that)** for central city residents **(them)**.

> Example 2: *Once upon a time...*the U.S. Department of Energy **(they)** wanted to know if, for the next 25 years **(during the period)**, the annual allocation of 10% **(rate, or rate of change)** of the maintenance budget **(level of that)** paid towards deferred maintenance needs **(change of this)** of buildings would cause what measurable change of overall facility condition **(level of that),** while simultaneously extending **(behave)** the life of buildings by what amount **(level of that)** for each U.S. National Nuclear Security Agency's laboratory facilities **(them)**.

> Example 3: *Once upon a time...* the Ukrainian Ministry of Health **(they)** wanted to know if, for the next 50 years **(during the period)**, a one-time or annual payment **(rate, or rate of change)** of how much **(level of that)** to families for each child born would cause a family income **(this)** increase **(rate of change)** resulting in what measurable change in national population **(level of that),** while simultaneously building **(behave)** the future working population tax base by what amount **(level of that)** for each of their 24 national administrative districts **(them)**.

The importance of developing this initial story "policy modeling paragraph" cannot be overstated. If public policy students, scholars, or practitioners can first design a summarizing initial paragraph of their research plan or policy issue, then they can adequately complete the subsequent components of the iterative storytelling process: building model boundaries, executing the model, and incorporating feedback.

11.2.2   Building a Rationally Bounded Model

A key objective of storytelling is to build and transmit "mental models" from the modeler to a client, policymaker, or an audience. Since it is impossible to include all the possible variables that impact any public policy issue, the mental model created includes boundaries that can limit the research items to a manageable number. For example, policy makers intent on crafting and implementing policies to stem negative population growth could build simulation models that include hundreds of influential variables present in either the inflow or outflow section of the model, e.g., fertility rates, mortality rates, immunization rates, car accident rates, smoking rates, and immigration and emigration flows. However, the modeler, in conjunction with the policymaker, selects which possible combination of variables (1) describes the complexity level of the policy issue, (2) has a good chance of providing relevant, measurable data, and (3) can, within the chosen model boundaries, provide the appropriate level of contextual validity (Forrester 1969). As Cameron Norman states:

> Those looking to take on systems problems tend to find two main questions (challenges) starting out: what are the boundaries of the system, and how does all the information within those boundaries fit together? With these elements one starts to provide the context and boundary conditions for imagining a system and thus, the foundations for a model of it (Norman 2011).

11.2.3   Executing a Model's Underlying Formal Structure

As previously stated, iterative storytelling employs feedback loops and time delays. Such a model structure is inherently nonlinear and thus provides detailed insights into complex problem relationships not captured by simpler, correlation-seeking, fit-data-to-a-line linear research methods. According to the late economist Kenneth Boulding, "In narrative abstraction, and linear plot lines, the phenomenon of complexity becomes less nuanced, more coherent, and sometimes that is a good thing. Other times, such over-simplification is an erasure of the very nuances (little 'wow' moments) that make comprehensive and intelligent sense of a situation. Storytelling then, from a cognitive theory of complexity, allows inquiry into how participants are sensemaking complexity" (Boulding 1956). Thus, iterative storytelling models can illuminate the temporal and causal dimensions of complex problems and thus can lead to better understanding of the relationships between the structure and behaviors of public organizations. Furthermore, executing nonlinear model structures via simulation can also identify possible leverage points to change public organization performance, often in near real time. The insight gained from executing such models leads to advancement in organizational frameworks, theories, and models. In Thompson's opinion, these advancements should all attempt to explain the part of human behavior that is determined by the social structures that create order within these social systems Thompson 1969). Graphically, the links between frameworks, theory, and models are illustrated in Fig. 11.1 (Schlager 2007).

11.2.4   Incorporating Newly Discovered Evidence into the Initial Story

Iterative storytelling provides vital information in the initial and subsequent phases of designing computer models. Additionally, the results from running a model simulation, especially when there is newly discovered evidence or instances of counterintuitive behavior, provides critical feedback that influences the performance of the model in sequential time periods. As Ludwig von Bertalanffy, founder of General

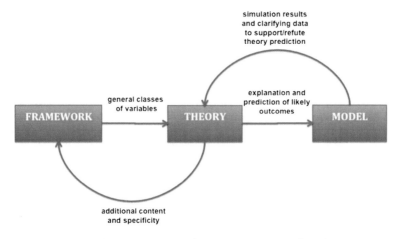

Fig. 11.1 Relationship of frameworks-to-theories-to-models (adapted from Schlager)

System Theory and author of the book of the same name argued, "feedback arrangements are widely used in modern technology for stabilization of certain action, as in thermostats or radio receivers; or for the direction of actions towards a goal where the aberration from that goal is fed back, as information, until the goal or target is reached" (Von Bertalanffy 1960). The combination of systemic feedback inputs turns iterative storytelling into such a stabilizing, reinforcing, or balancing function for public policy formulation, implementation, and evaluation. The iterative storytelling process thus becomes an important component of the systems thinking framework.

11.3   Systems Thinking and System Dynamics

A number of definitions exist for "systems" and "systems thinking." However, a useful definition of system thinking is that it is a philosophical and analytical method that focuses on the interrelationships of a system's parts and how these relationships affect behavior over time. The systems thinking approach looks at the system as a whole by systematically analyzing causal relationships and information flows between all model elements. This holistic, "10,000 m," operational view used in systems thinking contrasts sharply with other traditional analysis processes that seek insight into problem complexity by breaking systems down into their separate components (Richmond 2004). Yet, as Peter Senge states in his work on systems thinking, *The Fifth Discipline, the Art & Practice of the Learning Organization*:

> …the art of systems thinking lies in seeing through the detail complexity to the underlying structures generating change. Systems thinking does not mean ignoring detail complexity. Rather, it means organizing detail complexity into a coherent story that illuminates the causes of problems and how they can be remedied in enduring ways (Senge 1990: 124).

Other key system thinking principles include (1) looking at complexity as primarily a structural and behavioral problem, (2) adopting an endogenous point of view to problem complexity, and (3) characterizing most systems as "closed-looped," including feedback that influences inputs. Important to note, the literature places these feedback loops at the core of systems thinking, describing them as "the basic unit of systems" (Meadows 2008: 5) and as "the fundamental building block of system dynamics (SD) models…the basic unit of analysis and communication of system behavior" (Richardson 1999: 4).

In regards to its specific analytical techniques, systems thinkers employ computer modeling and simulation to illustrate, and predict system behavior. Included in the systems thinking toolkit are: behavior over time graphs (BOTG), which indicate the actions of one or more variables over a period of time; causal loop diagrams (CLD), which illustrate the relationships between system elements; stock (accumulation) and flow (rate of change) models, which like the CLD describe the interrelatedness of variables but also include feedback loops; and simulators, which simulate the interaction of system elements over time (Radzicki and Taylor 2011). This collection of system thinking tools combine to form the applied research method known as system dynamics.

11.3.1 System Dynamics

Originating from servo-mechanical engineering work in the 1950s, MIT Professor Jay Forrester created system dynamics, a unique research analysis, modeling, and simulation methodology that incorporates feedback loops and time delays into the investigation of complex problems. Forrester's SD spread rapidly from the engineering world into business management and later into the social sciences. Forrester's 1969 work, *Urban Dynamics,* controversial to this day, told a counterintuitive story of urban development and decay that public policy and community leaders either had great difficulty accepting or outright rejected (Forrester 1969). Nonetheless, as the insight gained from SD modeling and simulating of complexity grew, so too did the popularity and applicability of this particular research method.

SD is a nonlinear, behavior-over-time research method employed by the system thinking approach. SD uses ordinary differential equations and computer modeling and simulation to provide behavior prediction and foster informed decision making. Further, SD methods support iterative storytelling processes by allowing the modeler to set manageable research boundaries, analyze feedback loops, identify structural leverage points, and incorporate time delays. The importance of SD to public policy, as this article attempts to present, is that many public policy stories include accumulations (stocks) and rates of change (flows). Since policy problems can be converted into SD models and simulated, then this ability to "look into the future" can aid those engaged in current public policy decision making.

Converting these iterative public policy stories into SD models is made much easier with the use of the "language and the thinking skills" of writing (Richmond

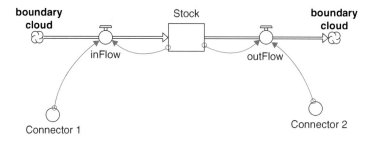

Fig. 11.2 The basic building blocks of system dynamics modeling

2004), whether it is a short story, screenplay, or novel. Richmond proposed that language arts tools are analogous to the computer-based modeling and simulation tools necessary to investigate complex public policy problems (Richmond 2004). After the initial story "characters" and "plot" are modeled into a "policy modeling paragraph," the storyteller then iteratively build layers of detail to accurately capture the variables, boundaries, time delays, feedback loops, and desired outcomes of a particular public policy problem. As system dynamicist and STELLA® software programmer Karim Chichakly emphasizes, "…a basic premise of SD is that structure and behavior are linked, one of the key ideas behind storytelling is to allow the behavioral story to grow as the structural story unfurls…" (Chichakly 2009).

In this iterative storytelling sense, the SD modeling and simulation icons are described below and graphically depicted in Fig. 11.2.

Stocks ("nouns"). An accumulation of something, of stuff, whether it be tangible as in water in a bathtub, population of a country, number of houses sold, cash in the bank, etc., or intangible such as amount of love for another, level of anger, self-esteem, etc. In SD modeling software, Stocks are typically represented as a rectangle.

Flows ("verbs"). A rate of change, either as an inflow or an outflow. Flows are represented graphically as valve or faucet icons.

Converters (conjunctions or adverbs). Variables selected by the modeler, in conjunction with the client or policymaker, which are assumed to be the determinants that affect the flow rate and stock accumulation behavior over time. Converters are either depicted as a circle or simply without any graphic, but instead as the textual title of the variable.

Connectors. Information or action directional links between stocks, flows, and converters. In most modeling software packages, connectors are shown as solid arrows to symbolize an action, and dashed arrows to indicate information passing between model icons.

Boundary Clouds (story start and stop markers). As previously mentioned, no social science topic starts at the point that the modeler selects. The starting point boundary (the "leftmost" boundary) from which any model begins is never actually the starting point of the issue under theoretical investigation. Likewise, any model's endpoint boundary (the "rightmost" boundary) is never the end of the policy issue. All public policy stories began long *before* the leftmost model boundary starts and, if left alone, will continue long after the rightmost model boundary ends. This concept, rather simple and seemingly heuristic, is nonetheless critical, and therefore should be internalized by all public policy modelers.

Feedback loops. Incorporation of "reinforcing" (compounding) or "balancing" (returning to a previous or goal-seeking level) loops that affect behavior over time. As core components of systems thinking, reinforcing, and balancing feedback loops create the nonlinear characteristic of the SD research method.

11.3.2   The Math

This chapter adds to literature that proposes that modelers use to develop "detailed precision and a non-ambiguity not inherent in literary descriptions" (Forrester 1969). Moreover, to counter the perception that storytelling resides solely in the qualitative narrative realm, this article also seeks to show that iterative stories can, and should, include formal dimensions that can be empirically testable. However, it is very important to note that public policy students, scholars, and practitioners do not necessarily need to possess differential equation skills in order to craft a comprehensive story, and then translate the components of the story into tools for creating "behavior over time" models and simulations. Fortunately, the mathematical "heavy lifting" in systems dynamics modeling and simulation runs behind the scenes of each particular SD software package. Thus, critical skills necessary for effective model building are those related to macro-level thinking, micro-level variable selection, iterative storytelling, and, probably, cognitive psychology. But, while this chapter is not intended to bog down the reader with advanced mathematical concepts and equations, it would be remiss not to at least briefly describe the mathematics that drives the systems thinking approach to iterative storytelling.

In mathematical terms, the basic structure of a formal SD computer simulation model is a system of coupled, nonlinear, first order differential equations,

$$\frac{\mathrm{d}x(t)}{\mathrm{d}t} = f(x, p)$$

where x is a vector of levels (stocks or state variables), p is a set of parameters, and f is a nonlinear, vector-valued function. Simulation of such systems is easily accomplished by partitioning simulated time into discrete intervals of length $\mathrm{d}t$ and stepping the system through time one $\mathrm{d}t$ at a time. Each state variable is computed from its previous value and its net rate of change $x(t)$: $x(t) = x(t - \Delta t) + \mathrm{d}t \cdot x(t - \Delta t)$. The computation interval $\mathrm{d}t$ is selected small enough to have no discernible effect on the patterns of dynamic behavior exhibited by the model.[1]

---

[1] Taken from the System Dynamics Society webpage, The Field of System Dynamics. http://www.systemdynamics.org/what_is_system_dynamics.html Accessed 22 April 2011.

Initial Story - Compounding Behavior (reinforcing feedback loop)

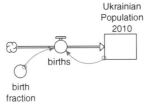

First Story Iteration-Draining Behavior (balancing feedback loop)

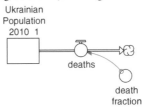

Continuing Story Iterations - Reinforcing and Balancing Behavior
(simulations reinforcing and balancing loops)

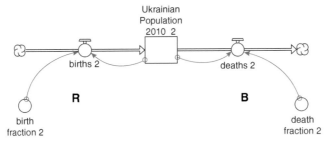

Fig. 11.3 Iterative story of a population stock and flow model

In the sample population model above the iterative story could be represented
graphically in a stock and flow diagram as in Fig. 11.3. However, the model's underlying variable values and differential equations, in the format population(t)=populat
ion($t-\Delta t$)+(births−deaths)×dt, are typically represented in modeling software as:

Ukrainian_Population_2010(t) = Ukrainian_Population_2010($t-\Delta t$) + (births −
    deaths)×Δt
INIT Ukrainian_Population_2010=45778500

INFLOWS:
births = Ukrainian_Population_2010×birth_fraction

OUTFLOWS:
deaths = Ukrainian_Population_2010×death_fraction
birth_fraction = 10.8/1000
death_fraction = 15.2/1000

11.3.3 Systems Thinking Archetypes[2]

Over the last 50+ years, system thinkers have developed a set of recurring model structures that explain common behaviors over time and illustrate both the intended and unintended consequences of organizational behavior. These systems thinking "templates," commonly known as archetypes, are used by modelers in the initial phase of storytelling and model building to define research boundaries, select variable determinants, and identify potential behavioral or structure change leverage points. Summarized from William Braun's (2002) The Systems Archetypes, the ten current systems thinking archetypes are:

Limits to growth—a reinforcing process of accelerating growth (or expansion) will encounter a balancing process as the limit of that system is approached; continuing efforts will produce diminishing returns as one approaches the limits.

Shifting the burden—a problem symptom can be resolved either by using a symptomatic solution or applying a fundamental solution; once a symptomatic solution is used, it alleviates the problem symptom and reduces pressure to implement a fundamental solution, a side effect that undermines fundamental solutions.

Eroding goals—similar to Shifting the Burden, this archetype states that a gap between a goal and an actual condition can be resolved in two ways: by taking corrective action to achieve the goal, or by lowering the goal; when there is a gap between a goal and a condition, the goal is lowered to close the gap. Over time, lowering the goal will deteriorate performance.

Escalation—when one party's actions are perceived by another party to be a threat, and the second party responds in a similar manner, further increasing the threat; the two balancing loops will create a reinforcing loop-to-loop figure-8 effect, resulting in threatening actions by both parties that grow exponentially over time.

Success to the successful—if one person or group (A) is given more resources than another equally capable group (B), A has a higher likelihood of succeeding; A's initial success justifies devoting more resources to A, further widening the performance gap between the two groups over time. Success to the Successful rewards the winner of competition with the means to win again; it may also penalize the losers, i.e., a university's athletic programs' national-level success and brand recognition makes their high school student recruiting efforts more successful, which in turn makes their athletic programs more successful.

Tragedy of the commons—identifies the causal connections between individual actions and the collective results (in a closed system); if the total usage of a common resource becomes too great for the system to support, the commons will become overloaded or depleted and everyone will experience diminished benefits.

---

[2] For a detailed discussion of system archetypes and their applicability to business situations, see William Braun. For system archetypes in general see Kim and Anderson.

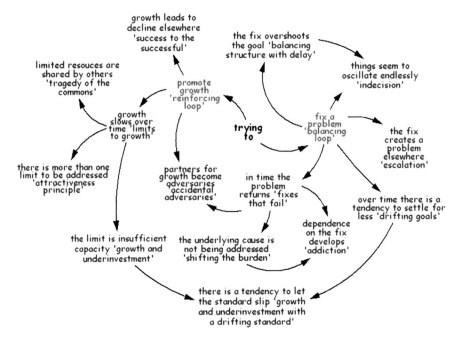

Fig. 11.4 The evolving nature of system archetypes (Bellinger 2009)

Fixes that fail—a quick-fix solution can have unintended consequences that exacerbate the problem; the problem symptom will diminish for a short while and then return to its previous level, or become even worse over time.

Growth and underinvestment—applies when growth approaches a limit that can be overcome if capacity investments are made. If a system is stretched beyond its limit, it will compensate by lowering performance standards, which reduces the perceived need for investment. It also leads to lower performance, which further justifies underinvestment over time.

Accidental adversaries—when teams or parties in a working relationship misinterpret the actions of each other because of misunderstandings, unrealistic expectations or performance problems, suspicion and mistrust erode the relationship. If mental models fueling the deteriorating relationship are not challenged, all parties may lose the benefits of their synergy.

Attractiveness principle—the result sought by a firm and which is the target of a growing action may be subject to multiple slowing actions, each of which represents an opportunity and an opportunity cost to managers. Insight into the interdependencies between the slowing actions is a critical insight into deciding how scarce resources should be utilized to reduce or remove the slowing actions.

Though one particular archetype may initially explain the link between organizational structure and behavior, often one finds that a particular archetype invariably leads to a totally different framework (Fig. 11.4).

Also extremely important to reemphasize, the system archetypes are just starting points to evaluate the structure of complex problems. The modeler and client/policymaker follow the archetype identification process with an engagement to variable selection and setting the model's boundaries. This sequential process builds detail, breadth, and depth in the investigation of complex issues. These initial iterative storytelling actions put the systems modeler/public policymaker team squarely on the path of more insightful decision making.

11.4 Infinite Loop Phenomenology in Iterative Storytelling

Iterative storytelling is a useful informational processing framework uniquely suited for public policy study. Processing and sharing information and ideas are necessary for organizational effectiveness and lead to changes in organizational behaviors. A key consideration of any vertical or lateral information processing model is the presence of constant feedback loops in the form of after action reports, analysts' evaluation, and high-level monitoring. Not only do feedback loops affect an organization's operational processes, they also can dictate organizational structuration decisions for public managers. Public sector managers, at a personal cognition level, internalize the idea that feedback is a constantly occurring phenomenon in policy formulation, implementation, and evaluation. This never-ending feedback flow, herein called "Infinite Loop Phenomenology" (ILP), thus becomes a pillar of iterative storytelling and thus also becomes a driver of continual organizational learning and change.

There is a substantial, multidisciplinary literature theorizing that learning comes from both acquiring knowledge and experiencing events. In the systems thinking literature, the late Barry Richmond posited that "learning depends on both the quality of the feedback provided- where quality includes both content and packaging- as well as the willingness and ability to hear the feedback" (Richmond 2004). To capitalize on the learning opportunities presented by iterative storytelling, public organization managers need to be cognizant of ILP principles, including:

- A public policy, once enacted, continues on indefinitely, unless there is a built-in termination mechanism, or unless acted upon by external forces that specifically seek to stop the policy (Bardach 1976).
- Individuals, groups, and organizations are constantly changing based on a constant flow of internal and external feedback influences and/or shocks, i.e., top-down directives, bottom-up after action reports, or outside-in technology advancements.
- Public sector leadership constantly manages reinforcing, and balancing feedback loops and determines future courses of action for their organization.

An analogy that illustrates the ILP concept can be found in the popular children's song made famous as the ending of 1990s Public Broadcasting System's television show, *Lamb Chops*. Norman Martin's "*The Song That Never Ends*" is a single verse, self-referential, and infinitely recursive song that naturally flows in a cyclical fashion, repeating the same verse over and over. The lyrics are:

This is the song that never ends,
It just goes on and on, my friends.

Some people started singing it not knowing what it was,
And now they can't stop singing it forever just because…(repeat at top)

Public policy students, scholars, and practitioners, who recognize that the entire public policy process is never-ending, also realize that ILP principles constantly frame their iterative storytelling efforts. As such, constant information processing and program evaluation lead to a feedback loop that never ends. Using the same melody of *The Song That Never Ends*, one could sing:

This is the public policy that never ends,
It just goes on and on, my friends.
Some people started employing it not knowing what it was,
And now they can't stop employing it forever just because…(repeat at top)

Thus, knowing that the ILP concept exists and influences organizational objectives and design choices, public policy leaders are responsible for establishing clear exit strategies or building in termination catalysts for a particular public policy. Furthermore, public managers remain responsible for establishing definitive metrics that signal to their organizations that their efforts, and their iterative story, may have reached predetermined objectives and/or the carrying capacity of the public service delivery target population. Therefore, while any iterative public policy story may never really end, it may, for political, budgetary, or organizational reasons, slow to an indefinite intermission.

To further illustrate this concept and its enduring nature, one can look to international relations complexity. Clearly, the feedback loops and inherent time delays that are the foundations of ILP are influential and possibly deterministic in international relations and foreign policy. As an example, a number of variables have been theorized to explain, or at least frame, the argument concerning the historical lack of development of Africa compared to that of Europe and North America. ILP's contribution to the argument applies the systems thinking archetype model "Success to the Successful" to explain the cavernous development gap between modern Africa and Europe/North America. Examining the structure of the "Success to the Successful" model, this SD archetype states that when two entities compete against each other for the same limited resources, the following occurs:

- The *Allocation to A instead of B* results in more *Resources to A*.

    ○ Subsequently, more *Resources to A* enhance the *Success of A*, which enhances the perception that there should be an *Allocation to A Instead of B*.

- With more Allocation to A instead of B, there are fewer Resources Allocated to B.

    ○ Fewer *Resources to B* impedes the *Success of B* which further reinforces the perception that resources should be allocated to *A Instead of B*.[3] Structurally, the "Success to the Successful" model consists of two reinforcing feedback loops which act together to create an ever-widening gap of "self-fulfilling prophecies" that continue indefinitely, or until a significant internal or external shock changes the structure of resource allocation (Fig. 11.5).

---

[3] http://www.systems-thinking.org/arch/arch.htm.

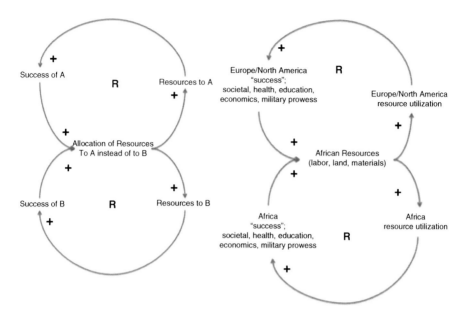

Fig. 11.5 The basic structure of the "Success to the Successful" model (*left*) and the same model adapted for a specific International Relations issue

Many economic and behavioral studies have looked at the Africa-to-Europe/North America developmental difference. Two focus areas for such evaluation are either (1) the starting point of the anomaly: explanations of what societal, environmental, and technological events led to the original tipping point where Europe and North America became more capable of exploiting African resources than could indigenous African communities, e.g., rise of the nation-state concept, African droughts and famines, Western warfighting prowess and weapons technology, or transportation innovations; or (2) the leverage points that keep the current disparate condition ever-widening: the world financial system, exploitation of energy resources, wars and epidemics, or African despots' endemic corruption.

Redrawing the basic "Success to the Successful" model using, say, the 500 year time period 1500–2000, the uber-macro iterative story of African development could be argued as:

- Two groups (or peoples), Europeans/North Americans vs. Africans, competed for the same limited labor, land, and material resources of the African continent.
- Prior to transportation developments that allowed Europeans/North Americans to deploy commercial and military missions deep into Africa, there was a point where Africans were more capable of exploiting their indigenous resources than were Europeans/North Americans. Eventually, Europeans/North Americans increased their capability to utilize African resources to a point where both groups were equally capable. At this point in time, the "*Success of A*" and the "*Success of B*" would also be the same (in SD parlance, the state of equilibrium).

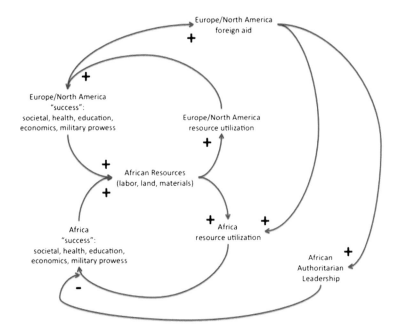

Fig. 11.6 Simplified view of the "Success to the Successful" model of African development transitioning to the "Shifting the Burden" archetype

- Over time, as Europeans/North Americans utilized more African resources, the more successful the Europeans/North Americans became. Subsequently, the more successful the Europeans/North Americans became, the more future African resources they could utilize.
- Since both groups competed for the same limited resources, the more resources utilized by Europeans/North Americans, the less resources were available for Africans to utilize.
- With fewer resources available, the success of Africans declined. And, since the Africans were less successful, the Europeans/North Americans could in turn utilize even more resources.

The resulting international development phenomenon represented a reinforcing feedback loop or vicious downward cycle that has increased exponentially over time, and thus prevented Africans from capitalizing on the overall resource utilization of their continent. One could posit that because of this exponential function, the increasing and widening gap between the success of Europeans/North Americans and the success of Africans will undoubtedly continue into the foreseeable future.

Of course, many, many other variables influenced African development over the past half millennium, and this essay is not an attempt at defining or explaining such international relations complexity. The objective herein is to illustrate the presence of ILP principles and show how causal loop diagramming tools aid in the iterative storytelling of such a complex topic. Fig. 11.6 takes the African development iterative storytelling example a step further and expands the "Success to the Successful" SD archetype. Specifically, the diagram shows the addition of the following feedback loops: (1) European/North American foreign aid to Africa, and (2) the impact of African authoritarian leaders. Interestingly, the model structure adapts to a "Shift the Burden" archetype with "Europe/North America foreign aid" mistakenly seen as a sufficient symptomatic vice foundational solution to improving African development. Of course, further data collection and variable specificity would be required to increase the validity and rigor of this simplified causal loop model. Nonetheless, the model is illustrative of the ILP principles and shows the possible leverage point identifying and insightfulness inducing of system thinking modeling tools.

Therefore, looking through the iterative storytelling lens of ILP, one could ask if any governmental or nongovernmental organizations engaged in nation building, development, or reconstruction and stabilization could act as leverage to affect measurable change in the model. This simplified example of SD modeling represents how to craft an iterative story base from which to conduct experiments and seek more informative, empirical social science evidence.

Regardless of how confusing or complex a systems dynamics model may appear, the model nonetheless grew from an iterative story beginning with a "policy modeling paragraph." For example, the model depicted in Fig. 11.6 may to some be daunting to comprehend at first glance, yet through the iterative storytelling process, both this model and its associated simulation capability is within the capabilities of students, scholars, and practitioners.

11.5   Conclusion

The perennial challenge for public policy students, scholars, and practitioners is to stay relevant and useful to policy decision makers. Employing a system thinking approach to complex problems, or providing any research method that addresses causality, represents an effective means to foster this relevancy and usefulness. Students, scholars, and practitioners can become adept at both iterative storytelling and in translating their stories into nonlinear, time-delayed, feedback-influenced models that capture the breadth and depth of complex public policy problems. Therefore, there is tremendous room for further research in iterative storytelling's role in public policy inquiry and systems thinking, modeling, and simulation. Armed with comprehensive storytelling skills and increased model building proficiency, public policy students, scholars, and practitioners will undoubtedly be able to develop new, dynamic frameworks, theories, and models for the public policy sciences.[4]

---

[4] Other chapters in this edited volume delve much deeper into (1) the process of converting a public policy problem into a model for simulation and decision making, (2) the complexity present in any research topic, and (3) the challenge of selecting, and omitting, variables to best define the boundaries of a problem.

Complexity model building acumen is not exclusively the domain of mathematicians, economists, or statisticians. In her article, *Why We Should be Suspect of Bullet Points and Laundry Lists,* SD educator Linda Booth Sweeney provides a pointed retort to an infamous New York Times article:

> Whether one is an educator, business leader, physician, urban planner, engineer, community organizer, or military general, it's time to be curious about how *this* is connected to *that. We all need to move beyond laundry list or bullet point thinking [referring to PowerPoint presentations] to seeing and thinking about patterns of interaction, networks and other lines of inquiry and problem solving that more closely matches the more interdependent, complex world we live in.*

As this chapter attempted to illustrate, embracing the concept of iterative storytelling, broadening system thinking skills, and acquiring basic-to-intermediate level SD modeling proficiency can go a long way forwards in increasing the investigative range and explanatory toolkit of public policy students, scholars, and practitioners. And, as Cameron Norman suggests, "The goal isn't to create the best model or the right model, for neither of those exist…what it is about is creating appropriate, useful models. All stories are fiction, but for systems thinkers, some stories are useful." (Norman 2011).

All of life on Earth is an iterative story told by physical systems (physics, geology, weather, etc.) and biological systems (humans, plants, animals, etc.). So, the important lesson for students, scholars, and practitioners is to tell and retell stories, to model and simulate them, and help inform decision making of complex public policy problems.

References

Aristotle (written 350 BCE). E.g. (1954) translation *Aristotle: Rhetoric and Poetics.* Intro by Friedrich Solmsen; Rhetoric translated by W. Rhys Roberts; Poetics translated by Ingram Bywater. NY: The Modern Library (Random House).

Bardach, Eugene, 1976. Policy Termination as a Political Process, in *Policy Sciences,* 7 (2), 1976: pp. 123–131.

Bellinger, Gene. 13 January 2009. System Archetypes. Website: http://www.systemdynamics.org/wiki/index.php/File:Sysarch01.jpg. Accessed 02 May 2011.

Bertalanffy, Ludwig Von, 1960. *Problems of Life.* Harper Torchbook. Pp 143.

Birkland, Thomas A. 2005. *An Introduction to the Policy Process: Theories, Concepts, and Models of Public Policy Making,* Second Edition. M.E. Sharpe.

Boje, David M. 2011. *Storytelling and the Future of Organizations: An Antenarrative Handbook.* Routledge, New York, NY.

Boulding, Kenneth. 1956. General Systems Theory as the skeleton of science. *Management Science,* Vol 2, No. 3. pp. 197–208.

Brauer, Ralph. 2011. Presentation given at the System Dynamics Society's 2011 International Conference. Washington, DC.

Braun, William 2002. *The System Archetypes.* Website: http://wwwu.uni-klu.ac.at/gossimit/pap/sd/wb_sysarch.pdf. Accessed 03 May 2011.

Chichakly, Karim. 21 May 2009. *Storytelling Simulations.* Website: http://blog.iseesystems.com/modeling-tips/storytelling-simulations/. Accessed 03 March 2011.

Dye, Thomas R., A Model for the Analysis of Policy Outcomes, in Ira Sharkansky (ed) *Policy Analysis in Political Science,* 1970. Markham Publishing.

Easton, David. 1965. *A Framework for Political Analysis*. Prentice-Hall.

Forrester, Jay W. 1969. *Urban Dynamics*, Pegasus Communications, Waltham, MA.

Jameson, Daphne A. (2001). Narrative Discourse and Management Action. *Journal of Business Communication*, 38 (4), p. 476–511.

McWilliams, Barry. 1998. *Effective Storytelling, A manual for beginners*. Website: http://www.eldrbarry.net/roos/eest.htm. Accessed 18 January 2011.

Meadows, Donella H., 2008. *Thinking in Systems, a Primer*. Diana Wright (Ed.). Sustainability Institute.

Nisbett, R. and T. Wilson. 1977. "Telling More than we can Know: Verbal reports on mental processes." *Psychological Review* 84(3): 231–259.

Norman, Cameron D., 2011. *Storytelling, Sense-making, and Systems Thinking*. web log: http://censemaking.wordpress.com/2011/01/15/storytelling-sense-making-and-systems-thinking/

Radzicki, Michael J. and Taylor, Robert A., *Introduction to System Dynamics, version 1.0*. On U.S. Department of Energy (DoE) webstite: http://www.systemdynamics.org/DL-IntroSysDyn/. Accessed 16 February 2011.

Richardson, George P. 1999. *Feedback Thought in Social Science and Systems Theory*. Pegasus Communications, Waltham, MA.

Richmond, Barry. 2004. *An Introduction to Systems Thinking*. 2011 STELLA software manual. isee systems.

Ruger, Kelsey, 01 March 2010. The Art of Business Storytelling. Web log: http://www.themoleskin.com/2010/03/the-art-of-business-storytelling/

Schlager, Edella. 2007. In Paul Sabatier (ed) *Theories of the Policy Process, 2nd Edition*. Westview Press.

Senge, Peter M., 1990. *The Fifth Discipline: The Art and Practice of the Learning Organization*. New York: Doubleday/Currency.

Sharkansky, Ira, Environment, Policy, Output, and Impact, in Ira Sharkansky (ed) *Policy Analysis in Political Science*, 1970. Markham Publishing.

Sweeney, Linda Booth. Web Log: http://lindaboothsweeney.net/blog/?p=172.

Thompson, Victor A., 1969. *Bureaucracy and Innovation*. University of Alabama Press.

Wallis, Lyle. 01 March 2011. *Big Data, Analytics, And Storytelling*. Web log: http://www.decisio.com/

Yanow, D. 1995. Built Space as Story. *Policy Studies Journal*, 23, pp. 407–422.

Index

Printed by Publishers' Graphics LLC
MO20120614